# SISTERS UNLIMITED

jessica
howie

# SISTERS UNLIMITED

## The guide to life, love, bodies and being YOU

### jessica howie

Vermilion
LONDON

1 3 5 7 9 10 8 6 4 2

First published 2002 by Vermilion,
an imprint of Ebury Press, Random House,
20 Vauxhall Bridge Road, London SW1V 2SA
www.randomhouse.co.uk

Random House Australia (Pty) Limited
20 Alfred Street, Milsons Point, Sydney,
New South Wales 2061, Australia

Random House New Zealand Limited
18 Poland Road, Glenfield, Auckland 10, New Zealand

Random House South Africa (Pty) Limited
Endulini, 5a Jubilee Road, Parktown 2193, South Africa

The Random House Group Limited Reg. No. 954009

Editor: Miren Lopategui
Design: the Senate

Papers used by Vermilion are natural, recyclable products made
from wood grown in sustainable forests.

Printed and bound by Tien Wah Press, Singapore

A CIP catalogue record for this book is available from the British Library.

ISBN 0 09 188416 0

# CONTENTS

Foreword 6

Thank You 8

Introduction 10

From Girl to Woman 18

Bod-Ease 38

Your Health 52

Let's Talk About Sex 70

Boyz 90

Da Sistahs! 110

Are All Families Mad? 130

I'm a Survivor 152

Doing It! 182

Sistah Support 206

Index 220

# Foreword

**Hi ladies!** You are going to love this book. It's a must-have for any girl. I've just finished it and wish I'd had it 20 years ago! (Oops...am I really that old?) It's got just the best tips in it and loads of ideas to help you navigate through what I found to be the most difficult time of my life.

From the age of 12 I just started feeling... a lot – I hope you know what I mean by that... that sort of raw sensitivity – and to make it worse all the big issues were cropping up: periods, boyfriends, friendship, family issues. As if that wasn't bad enough, a few years down the line I added sex, booze and drugs to my list of overwhelming things to worry about. During all this time, I think the thing I found toughest of all to deal with was how alone I felt. How no one really understood me or what I was going through. That's where *Sisters Unlimited* comes in.

I found the whole becoming a woman thing a nightmare. Half of me wanted to be 20 NOW and the other half was petrified. I started young too. I was 11 when I got my period, and I started growing boobs at about that time too. For some reason my family thought it would be fun to point this out at every given opportunity. I remember hearing my granny on the phone to my best friend's mother, telling her that I had become a woman, i.e. I had started my period. I NEARLY DIED!! I didn't want everyone to know!!!!!

It was about this time that I went into the tunnel. I didn't want to listen to anyone, I felt misunderstood and raw, and had been having real trouble understanding some of my mother's behaviour towards me. She was an alcoholic and consequently didn't remember half the horrid things she said to me. But I remembered them. I felt really isolated as none of my friends had an alcoholic parent. I didn't know what to do, so I stopped eating. It was definitely a cry for help; I wanted the pain I was feeling to show. Thank goodness my dad and step-mum sat me down before things got too out of hand. We talked honestly about everything for hours and afterwards it was like this incredible weight had been lifted from my shoulders. It also meant they were a lot more understanding about my issues around my real mum. Anyway, I'm not suggesting you all stop eating because that's a bit drastic, but do talk before things get out of hand — it really helps!

Sex is a subject that Jess covers brilliantly in this book. I always found talking about sex embarrassing and my human biology and sex-ed classes always made me giggle frantically. So here's a no-nonsense guide to everything you need to know about sex! Hoorah! (I've learnt a couple of things myself, so thanks, Jess!!!) I think one of the most important things is to love and respect yourself. If you love yourself (not in a cocky way but in a confident way) you are going to be mucho sexy to the opposite sex (or the same sex... whatever tickles your fancy!). And if you respect yourself, hopefully you'll never get into a situation that you wish you weren't in!

One last thing before I let you get on with this bible of womanhood: Drugs. It's a sad fact that many of you will come in contact with drugs at some point or another, and I can speak from experience when I say BE CAREFUL. It's like playing Russian roulette. Some people seem fine and can take or leave the odd spliff now and again, but for some (like me) this can lead onto much harder drugs pretty quickly and before you know it it's not fun any more. I don't want to lecture you, so I'll shut up there, but read the book. It will help you make informed decisions about all the things I've talked about and a whole lot more.

## Good luck!

## xoxoxoxo Davina

# Thank You

Thank you most of all to Jamie for having belief in me enough to help me have belief in myself. Thank you for your support in every aspect of my life, including the editing of this book, your invaluable business advice and your deep love and confidence in me and *Sisters Unlimited*. You have taught me who I want to be and how to love. I love you.

Thank you to my family for giving me the raw materials to grow as a person. Thank you Mum for showing me so much of the world and so many of its treasures. Thank you Dad for always letting me be myself (and make my own mistakes). Thank you Josh for making me laugh (and cry). Thank you Grandma for always being there and being the rock of the family (and for your home made roast dinners!) Thank you Auntie Sue for helping me heal. Thank you to all of my family, I love you all very dearly.

Thank you to India Rose for all our cuddles, games and annoying Daddy sessions. You're a beautiful soul who teaches me more than you know.

Thank you to all of my beautiful sistahs! You each inspire me with your love and wisdom and you constantly remind me of the real strength and beauty that is woman. Sophie, Caren, Lisa, Antonya, Daisy, Josie, Tammi, Georgia, Manushka, Emma, Kate, Alex, Monique and Avril. Thank you for letting me be me, your friendships make me whole.

Thank you Jae, Shaka, Blob, Servan and Gus for being great friends and showing me how intimate, supportive and fun men can be.

Thank you to Torin my godson for always making me smile.

Thank you to Lisa Darnell my agent for believing in the book (and for getting me to rewrite the whole thing!)

A huge thank you to the Random House team, especially: Kate Adams, Fiona MacIntyre, Sarah Bennie and Lesley McOwan for helping shape and contribute to the book and for holding the vision of *Sisters Unlimited* so clearly. You all helped make the book what it is.

Thank you to my fantastic copy editor Miren Lopategui, your input was invaluable.

Thank you to Marisa Sebastian and Elisabetta Minischetti for doing a brilliant job of designing and illustrating the book and making it look so great.

Thank you Gail Rebuck for seeing the potential in the book from the start.

Thank you to all the people who've helped make the website what it is and for having faith in *Sisters Unlimited* when it was just an ambitious idea in my head (especially those of you who haven't yet even been paid). Servan, Ross, Claire, Caren, Alex, Antonya, Gypsy, Jason and Andrew (don't worry Andrew I know I still owe you that money!)

Thank you to my spiritual and life teachers for opening my eyes to the unlimited amazingness that is each and every one of us. Denise Linn, Gabrielle Roth, all my teachers at the Psychosynthesis Institute and Sue Rhind.

Thank you to Davina McCall for giving your time and energy to *Sisters Unlimited*. You're a fantastic Sistah!

Thank you to all the contributors and advice givers, Ann Marie Woodall, Fiona Horne, Gael Lindenfield, Anita Roddick and Rachel Creeger.

Thank you to Oprah Winfrey for blowing my mind constantly with what you're doing for the world. You are a true role model.

Thank you to all of the people that replied to and passed on my probing circular emails.

I dedicate this book to all of the Sistahs! who are starting out on their journey to womanhood. Keep on daring to be yourselves.

# Introduction

☞

# Read This!

Hello, girlfriends, and **welcome!** We are entering a new phase, ladies, in our own lives and the world at large. We're all going to be playing a huge part in this world becoming a groovier and more harmonious place. But let's not get ahead of ourselves. This book is about you, and unleashing your unlimited potential. You might not realise it right now, but you've got it all in you already – and this book is going to help you find it!

What you're about to read is one woman's outlook on the world – mine. I didn't write *Sisters Unlimited* just so that other young women would take on my views, but to encourage you to start looking inward and realise that all the answers are already inside each and every one of you. My job is just to help you find those answers more quickly. This book has come to you for a reason; you're ready to become an even groovier, more empowered chick **RIGHT NOW!**

# THE NEXT PHASE

If you've picked up this book and decided to read it, you probably still consider yourself a 'girl', but at the same time no longer a child. I often get asked, 'How old are you when you become a woman?' and it's a hard one to answer. There is no set age. I don't believe that one day you turn 18 (the legal age of an adult) and suddenly become a woman. I've met 20-year-olds who are still very much girls and some 13-year-olds who are well on their way to becoming women. Also, you might have some days when you feel grown-up and ready to take on the world and others when you feel like a four-year-old, incapable of even tying your shoes, let alone taking on any real responsibilities.

If you have picked up this book, you are already well on the journey to womanhood.

# LIMBO LAND

As exciting and empowering as this time can be, it can also be lonely and confusing. You might find yourself in 'limbo-land', where new responsibilities are expected of you but you haven't yet been fully given the freedom that you'd like. You're starting to feel more independent for the first time and are moving away slightly (or a lot) from your family, yet you're still under the control of others, whether it's family, school or the law. It seems that wherever you turn there's someone there telling you the rules and boundaries of your 'freedom'. This is certainly the overriding feeling most of the time, but at other times you still want the security you get from your parents and school. It's tricky. You're right, you are changing and you are ready for more responsibility and control of your life, but you're not an adult yet and there are still people who think they know what's best for you (and sometimes they do), and they will try to enforce that on you. Throughout *Sisters Unlimited* we'll be looking at new ways of communicating, to help you and your parents form mutual relationships of respect, so that you can experience this important transition in your life without having constant blowouts.

As well as these feelings of 'lack of control', there is a lot of other stuff going on:

- Trying to figure out who you are and what you want from life.
- Discovering your sexuality with others for the first time.
- Dealing with pressure from your peers to be and act a certain way.
- A huge amount of exam pressure.
- Feeling there is no one who seems to really understand what you're going through.
- General feelings of sadness, loneliness and depression.
- Uncertainty about whether to get involved with drugs/drink/sex, etc.
- Not fitting in with your peers.
- Trying to figure out why the world is such a screwed-up place with so much hate and violence.
- Going out with boys for the first time and not really knowing what you want from a relationship.
- Worrying about pregnancy and STDs (sexually transmitted diseases).

For most of us there aren't many safe spaces to express these feelings and explore with others what we're going through. *Sisters Unlimited* aims to create a space where girls can come together and share their experiences, rather than always feeling alone during this challenging time.

My aim is to help you with these challenges. I had a pretty hard time during my teen years, too, so I've been through most of them myself. I was expelled from schools, went through my parents' divorce, got involved with drugs and had two abortions – and that's just for starters. During this time, I felt it was pretty unfair that I was up against so much but I know now that I wouldn't be me without these challenging experiences behind me. They've made me who I am. This book isn't about avoiding challenges but about learning how to deal with them. It's also about getting to know yourself better and liking what you find.

In fact, the most important teaching in this book is that denying your feelings and personal truths will end up hurting you. At the end of the day you've got no one to answer to but yourself, so if you aren't showing yourself love and respect, then you're missing out on really enjoying life. But ironically, liking ourselves for what we are is our biggest challenge. Don't try to be how you think others want you to be – be yourself. Doing that can take some work, and it can often be a long and difficult journey. But it's also the most rewarding journey you'll ever embark upon. Well done for getting this far, and remember at all times that you are beautiful just by being you.

*Sisters Unlimited* can be read any which way you want, but here are some tips and general explanations that may be helpful.

Introduction

# FIND A SUPPORT NETWORK

You may find it useful to read the book with a group of close girlfriends. This might just be you and your best friend, or a few of you – just make sure you choose people you're close to and who you can trust. Agree between you to start reading the book on the same day, and to read a chapter every one or two weeks (or whatever's best for you all). Then when you've read it, come together as a group to discuss it. You may find it helpful to appoint a group leader, or facilitator, to direct your group meetings. It will be her role to structure the time, lead the discussions and take care of the needs of the individual members of the group. If, say, she thinks someone is being particularly quiet and shy, she can encourage her to come into the circle by asking her a simple relevant question. She can also decide what you want the meeting to consist of – there are some exercises and rituals that are specifically designed to be done in groups. It's a good idea to delegate a different group leader for each meeting so you all get a turn.

## Directing group discussions:

- First, go around the circle and check in with how everyone is doing right now (spend about 2 minutes on each person).
- Divide each chapter you're discussing into sections and choose the key topics from each chapter you want to discuss – probably the ones with exercises.
- Run through each topic and open up the talk to the group. Get them to ask each other questions about anything they're unsure about, or feedback they may want from each other.
- Decide how long you want the discussion to be. If you feel that not everything was covered, maybe divide the chapter into two and have another meeting the following month.

## Remember:

- Don't all speak at once. Take it in turns to talk.
- Don't interrupt each other. If, however, the group leader thinks one person is taking up too much time, she should gently move them along. One of you might need more air time one week, though, so don't be too rigid about it.
- If concentration is starting to lag, take a break. Have a hot drink and a biscuit.
- You might want to take notes during the meeting, so take a separate note pad along just in case.
- If at the end you want to discuss something that wasn't raised, take it in turns to bring these up.
- You might want to bring someone new into the group, but choose wisely and don't do this more than once or twice as it can be disruptive. Make sure all of you agree to accept this new person.

Be respectful of each other. Agree that it's a closed circle and things will never be discussed with others outside it. All take a secrecy oath and NEVER use things against each other that you've said in the group.

## USE THE WEBSITE

I have set up a website, www.SistersUnlimited.com, which will give you a chance to have online discussions about the topics that have been covered in the book with experts and professionals. Through the website we'll also be arranging open regional groups for you to come together with other young women in your area to share your stories and experiences with one another. There will be experienced teachers and experts on different subjects to help facilitate and guide you through the sessions.

## FURTHER HELP

Some of the topics we'll be dealing with can be very raw so take it slow and be aware of your feelings. You may find this book doesn't affect you that much while you're reading it, but then you start feeling upset in a few months' time. If that happens, there is support available for you. At the end of the book we've provided contact numbers for helplines where you can talk directly to professionals. It's called Sistah Support (see p208).

With this book and www.SistersUnlimited.com I aim to achieve a support network for all of you.

## GENERALISATIONS

A big apology in advance for any generalisations I've made. I know that in the Boyz chapter (p92), I keep referring to 'boyfriends'. I'm not forgetting the readers that are gay or bisexual; it's just that I opted to go with the generalisation to make writing it easier. Likewise, in Are All Families Mad? (p131), I keep referring to parents, so to those of you who don't have parents or just have one, again, I'm sorry. Please don't think that because I've written a certain word I'm excluding anyone who doesn't fit under this category. I am aware of our different circumstances and am acknowledging them here. You can apply what I've written to all of you, whatever your circumstances.

# KEEP A DIARY

Writing a diary has helped me through most of my teenage years and still does to this day. It's a great vehicle for expressing frustrating emotions, lyrical insights, new love and tangled thoughts. We often hold onto emotions and experiences because we don't know how to express them. By getting into the habit of writing, we begin a new dialogue with our self and become more in touch with our inner voices. Creativity is vital in expressing who we are to the world. Writing regularly is a way of cultivating this form of creativity.

But most of all, writing a diary is a fun way of holding memories. You can read them later and see what was going on for you in the past and how you've changed and grown. But make sure you keep it well hidden, and don't make a big deal about it to family members or they will be tempted to have a look. Try buying one with a lock on it.

## Five good reasons to keep a diary:

❶ Letting out unexpressed feelings.
❷ Keeping all your thoughts in a place where you can go back to and read them later on in life.
❸ Getting to know yourself.
❹ Being able to show your kids when they're growing up that you were young once too.
❺ Developing your creativity – writing skills, poetry and story-telling.

I used to buy hardback pads of plain paper and cover them in photos and memorabilia that I was into that year. I've also bought page-a-day diaries so I'm encouraged to write every day. You could, perhaps, include in your diary a little bit about where you're at at the moment and who you are as a person.

When you see this symbol ●◆ , it means you might find it helpful to write your feelings down. Your diary may be a good place to start!

## THE EXERCISES

As you've probably gathered already, reading this book involves some input from you. Anyone can read a book and pick up a few new theories, but unless you actively participate while learning, you're not going to get very far – hence the exercises. Don't worry – they're nothing like the ones you do at school. You can decide whether to do them as you're reading or finish a chapter and come back to them later. Keep a notepad with you while reading so you can write things down.

Okay, enough of the preparation. It's time to get going. If by the end of reading this book you have learnt to like yourself a little bit more (hopefully, loads more), then my job has been done. I believe in you. You are the women of the future and there is much work to be done, so let's get started!

Oh yeah, and don't forget to come and join me on the website www.SistersUnlimited.com for more in-depth discussions and to air your own opinions.

# From Girl
## *to Woman*

Sorry about the long intro, but it's important that you get the most from reading the rest of the book. The good news is, you're still here. You must be someone who means business. This next part of the journey is really the groundwork for the rest of the book and your journey ahead, so strap in.

In this chapter you'll start to explore and discover what kind of a woman you want to be (and not be) and which of your childlike qualities are worth holding on to. You'll be gathering the essential tools for your journey ahead and having a go at a few fun exercises to help you let go of old clutter, whether it be in your bedroom or your brain.

# THE DIFFERENCES BETWEEN A GIRL AND A WOMAN

To help you have a clearer understanding of what being a girl and what being a woman means to you, I've designed the following simple questionnaire. Look at the questions below, then draw up a chart similar to the Girl or Woman? table below. Take time to think about your answers and write down everything that you think of. Don't think about your answers for too long and don't worry if you're right or not – there are no wrong answers.

- Do you consider yourself a girl or a woman? (Or a bit of both?)
- What do you dislike or think is hard about being a girl/woman?
- What do you like or think is easy about being a girl/woman?
- What qualities do you think girls/women have?
- What different roles can a girl/woman have?
- What visual images do the words girl/woman make you think of?
- What does being a girl/woman mean to you?

## GIRL OR WOMAN?

| Questions | Girl | Woman |
|---|---|---|
| Girl or woman? | A girl | |
| Dislike or hard | Not enough independence, going to school, restrictions on going out/drinking etc. | Responsibilities, pressure, people's expectations |
| Like or easy | Cooking and washing done for you, everything is paid for, no big responsibilities | Don't have to answer to anyone, freedom to do what ever you want |
| Qualities | Inquisitive, open, naive | Neurotic, bossy, strong |
| Roles | Schoolgirl, daughter, ballerina | Mother, wife, boss |
| Visual images | Skipping, whispering, laughing | Cooking, driving, getting married |
| Means to you | Safe, fun, experimental, curious | Scary, exciting, freedom, responsible |

## WHAT YOUR ANSWERS TELL YOU

Take a look at the words you've used to describe being a girl and the ones you've used for being a woman. Now ask yourself the following:

- Are there more positive words in one column than the other?
- Did you find the girl questions easy to answer but the woman ones hard?
- Do you get a sense that you feel more connected and in tune with being a girl or being a woman?
- Can you detect any negative preconceptions you have about being a woman?
- Do you feel excited or scared about what lies ahead?

This exercise will help you get a feel for how you perceive the experience of being a girl and a woman. When I did it a while ago, it showed me that I had some strong preconceptions about what being a woman meant. I was convinced it meant being neurotic, serious and a lot less playful than being a girl. I perceived women around me as taking life too seriously and always being worried about one thing or another. The idea of being like that scared the hell out of me and I kept promising myself to never lose my playful childish nature. Having these preconceptions made me resist moving into womanhood, as I thought I would become those negative things myself.

We all have mind-sets about things; we build ideas from our past experiences. Somewhere in your past a woman or a few women leave an imprint on you, and this can strongly affect your impression of womanhood. For most of us the biggest influence on our perceptions of women is our mothers. Take a look at your list. Are there any words in your Woman column that could describe your mother? Do you think they're justified and that they'll influence the way you'll be in the future?

Usually our preconceptions change as we have new experiences. My view on what being a woman means now is very different from what it was a couple of years ago. This is mainly due to the new relationships I've formed with a more diverse selection of older women. The biggest preconception I've been shown I was wrong about was that women aren't playful – how wrong I was!

# The Essential Qualities

As we grow up, it's very easy to get caught up in the stresses of everyday life – holding down a job, paying the bills, making a relationship work, having children, maybe, and taking care of domestic chores (and believe me the list does goes on). Soon all these responsibilities catch up with us and before we know it we've turned into stressed-out, neurotic, overworked women. So take some time now to think about what kind of woman you want to be. What qualities do you want to cultivate as you grow older? What qualities do you definitely not want to have? You might be very clear on how you don't want to be but not so sure of how you do want to be, and vice versa.

Below is a template that I've put together from a mixture of different girls answers to these two questions. We all value different qualities, though, so feel free to replace any of the below with your own answers, and add what you like. It's important that you know for yourself what kind of woman you want to be. No one can tell you that.

## THE ESSENTIAL QUALITIES OF WOMEN

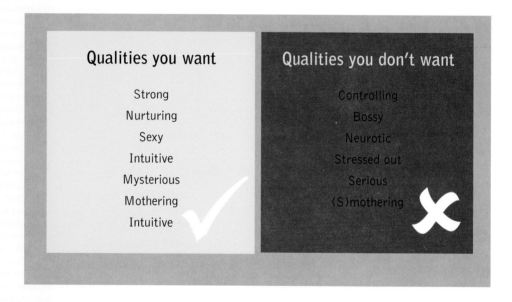

| Qualities you want | Qualities you don't want |
| --- | --- |
| Strong | Controlling |
| Nurturing | Bossy |
| Sexy | Neurotic |
| Intuitive | Stressed out |
| Mysterious | Serious |
| Mothering | (S)mothering |
| Intuitive | |

Start observing women you respect, whether they're famous or your Auntie. Recognise what you admire in them and also the things in other women that you want to avoid. Then draw up your own table for the qualities you do and don't want as a woman. Keep it somewhere safe so you can come back to it when you're older – that way you can check you haven't become the nagging nightmare or stressed-out mess you swore you'd never be.

# OUR INNER CHILD

As well as the 'essential woman' qualities opposite, there are also childlike qualities that are essential for being a happy adult. Too many people forget that. They focus on 'growing up' and end up taking life way too seriously.

Sadly, losing some of our childlike innocence is an inevitable part of growing up. When we're children we believe our parents are God-like – 'all powerful' beings who are in control of it all. We naturally trust them and believe everything they say, and this trust makes us feel secure. Then, at some point, most of us have this illusion shattered and we realise that our parents aren't actually perfect. From that point on, we lose some of our childhood innocence and start to look at things – and adults – differently.

It can be a painful awakening. But, although painful, this process can also empower us to be more in command of our lives. We can finally figure out who we are and make decisions for ourselves, rather than just echoing our parents' choices and identities.

The older we get and the more negative things we see and experience, the less trusting and innocent we become. But even though this chapter and book are geared towards making you wiser and become more of a woman, I also want to highlight the importance of keeping your childlike quality. To be able to see the world as a child does is a huge gift. Children don't always have a fixed idea of how things are going to be. They haven't had enough experience yet to assume or expect the worst. By keeping this innocence, we too can keep the ability to see things as if for the first time, free from pessimism. Spend some time watching children and see if you can recognise the following qualities in them – they're all worth holding onto.

- playfulness
- curiosity
- openness
- trust
- optimism
- being in the moment
- being able to forgive easily
- not being self-conscious
- adapting to new situations easily

As you can see, there are loads of benefits of keeping your childishness alive, even when you're an 80-year-old granny. Think of adults that you know that have a childish twinkle in their eyes – I bet they enjoy life more than most.

From Girl to Woman

# LETTING GO

Now you've got more of an idea of the kind of woman you want to be, you can start getting rid of some of your emotional and physical 'excess baggage' – things you no longer need. Letting go of the old is a great way to let in the new, because by creating physical and emotional space in our lives we leave room for change. And change is a fact of life. Think about it – now you change schools and boyfriends, and later on you'll be changing jobs and moving into a new home. The one thing we can be sure of in life is that change is inevitable and the better equipped we are to deal with it, the easier our lives become. To be prepared for change we need to learn how to let go of the things that no longer benefit us in our lives.

This can sometimes be easier said than done. Entering this new phase in your life is very exciting, but it can also be pretty scary, especially when it means letting go of the secure and familiar. Part of me used to be frightened of becoming a woman. What did it mean? Would I have to become fully responsible for myself? Who would be there for me? When I was a lot younger and I started growing pubic hair, which is one of the first signs of becoming a woman, I hated it so much I cut it all off. I didn't want to have a hairy vagina. Part of me was desperately clinging onto the little girl in me and many of us carry on doing this later on in life.

## SPRING CLEANING

Even though this might sound like a bit of a drag, it usually ends up being really fun. You get to spend ages sifting through all your old things, wallowing in sentiment about your past. You have to be disciplined, though; I know how easy it is to keep clutter. Include in your clearing out, clothes you no longer wear, albums you no longer listen to and books you'll never read. There are many people who could really benefit from your old stuff, so, rather than selling them, why not give them to a charity of your choice?

Now comes the really hard bit: throwing away sentimental things – love letters your first boyfriend wrote to you, ticket stubs of a special concert you went to, notes you wrote to your mates at school. I know I'm not alone in accumulating a huge amount of these types of things. For us females, reminiscing about the past is important; it can make us feel cosy and secure. Decide to throw out whatever feels right to you at the time. Be easy on yourself as this can be a particularly sensitive process. Ask yourself if you really need to hold onto these things. If the answer is yes, that's fine – you're not ready to let go of that particular thing yet. You can always come back to it at a later date. If you decide to throw anything away that is made out of paper, a great way to do this is by burning it. Fires are extremely potent instruments in any letting-go ritual. Otherwise, throw them out, making sure you stay in the moment. Feel what it's like for you to let go of these memory-jerkers and honour whatever feelings come up for you. You might want to write down how you feel.

Forgiving others – and, even more importantly, forgiving yourself – is another powerful way of wiping the slate clean and allowing yourself a fresh start. Forgiving yourself for everything you've done or said in the past. Yes, that's right ladies, everything. Forgiving yourself makes it easier for you to move on and acknowledge that you won't repeat the same mistakes in the future.

Time for another list. Write at the top of the page, 'I [your name] forgive myself for the following things I've done.' Next, write down everything you've done in the past that you feel bad about: telling someone a secret you promised you'd keep, screaming at your little brother because you were in a bad mood, ignoring a friend in order to look cool. Whatever it was, (even if it's a tiny thing you thought you'd forgotten), write it down. You might end up finding you've got a rather long list. Don't worry – at least you're being honest.

Once you've finished that list, get a new piece of paper and at the top write, 'I forgive the following people for the things they've done in the past.' This time write a list of all the people you need to forgive and a key word that relates to what they've done. Once again, you might find yourself surprised by how long the list is. But get it all down.

Take some time to sit with each list and, one by one, go through all the points you've written down. Take a thick pen and as you truly forgive yourself or another for a past action, strike a line through it. If there are still things uncrossed on your list, come back to them at a later point when you feel you are ready.

You'll probably feel a sense of elation from doing this exercise. Forgiving is a way of freeing ourselves from the past, again leaving more space in our lives for what the present has to offer. By the time you're done with this chapter you're going to have left a hefty amount of baggage behind. You'll start noticing new exciting things happening to you because you'll have freed yourself from past experiences that have been weighing you down.

 **BOTTOM LINE**

- Have a look at what being a girl and what being a woman means to you. How do you feel about both and which one are you now?
- Explore the kind of a woman you want to be, which qualities you want and don't want. Don't grow up to be someone you don't really like.
- Keep some of your childlike innocence and don't always assume something's going to be a certain way. Keep an open mind at all times.
- Start letting go of clutter in your life, whether it's in your bedroom or your brain. The more you let go, the more new exciting things will happen.
- Learn to forgive yourself for past acts, as well as forgiving others who have mistreated you. You don't have to do it all in one day but make a start – you'll have released yourself from a lot of old stale memories.

# THE JOURNEY TO WOMANHOOD

Okay, ladies, now that you're carrying a lighter load of emotional and physical baggage, you're ready to gather your essential tools for the journey ahead.

The time has come when you're ready to go out into the world as an independent woman. As you're about to set off on your journey you'll have with you a bag of tools (metaphorical ones, obviously!). Anyway, picture yourself standing there, with your bag open, and one by one place the following into your bag.

## THE ESSENTIAL TOOLS

❶ Knowing yourself and being able to hear your 'truth voice'.
❷ Loving yourself for who you are, not trying to be someone else.
❸ Focus and perseverance. Knowing your goals and going for them and having the ability to get back up when you've been knocked down.
❹ The ability to see the funny side of life. Not getting caught up with taking it all too seriously.
❺ Gratitude. Having the ability to see everything you've been given rather than adopting the 'glass is half empty' attitude.

## KNOWING YOURSELF AND HEARING YOUR 'TRUTH VOICE'

This one needs the longest explanation because it's something that most of us are very out of touch with. (It will also help you with all of the other tools on the list.) As you get older you will have to start making more decisions that are going to affect your whole life. What 'A' levels are you going to take? What university do you want to go to? Do you want to take a year out and travel the world? Are you going to take drugs? Are you going to sleep with someone without a condom? Any one of these decisions will shape your path and future to come. Knowing this, you can see that having a head start in knowing what you really want is a vital life skill. I'm not saying for a second that you can go through life totally avoiding messing up now and then; just that having an idea of what you really want and what's right for you, will help you in numerous ways.

● You'll get to know yourself better.
● Making the right decisions now will help you in the future.
● You won't live a life of regrets, because you'll be doing what you really want, now.
● When you are in touch with your truth everything in your life will flow more easily, i.e. the people you attract into your life will be more on your wavelength, your experiences will be more fulfilling.

Okay, now we know why we benefit from listening to our personal truths, the next step is to learn the best way to do just that. Listen close on this one, ladies, and I promise you it will make sense.

The first thing to do is to distinguish the part of you that natters all day long from the part of you where your personal truth resides.

The best way to do this is to find these two different voices in you now.

**The natterer** is easy to find. It's the voice inside your head that usually doesn't shut up. It's like having a running commentary on everything that goes on while you're awake. You'll hear it as soon as you wake up. 'What should I wear today? What should I have for breakfast? Did I do my homework? Blah Blah Blah...' It goes on all day – an endless flow until you've turned the light out once again and fallen asleep.

**The truth voice** (you can call it your higher self, inner wisdom, whatever you want) is easier to hear when you're quiet and calm, but you have to turn off the natterer first. Breathing deeply into your belly also helps you locate it. This part of yourself always feels calm and focused. There is no nattering with this voice, just clarity. You might not always like what it says, but you know it's the truth.

> Once you've located the two different voices, the next step is to develop an internal dialogue with your truth voice.

The best way to find the answers that already reside in you is to know what questions to ask. These could be questions about which friend to take to a party, or which guy to go out with, or even which subjects you should choose to take at school. Or maybe they're bigger, like 'Is he the right boy to sleep with my first time?' Or 'Should I try this drug?' However big or small the question is, make sure you have it clearly in your head. Ask yourself the question directly and see if an answer appears. Back up your initial question with other ones such as:

> Will this make me happy?
> How will this affect others?
> Is this what I really want or am I doing it for the wrong reasons?
> What are my motivations? (i.e. to make another happy, to fit in, because I'm scared etc.)
> How might this affect me long-term?

From Girl to Woman

Once you think you've got an answer, see how it makes you feel. Do you feel comfortable in your body or does it not sit quite right with you? You don't have to be in a rush to then put this new decision into action. You can sit with it for a while until you feel you're sure.

## So...

- Be silent and try closing your eyes to help you hear your truth voice more clearly.
- If there's a voice that is nattering and unfocused then that is probably not your 'truth' voice. Quieten it down and listen out for a calmer, more focused voice. (Don't worry, you're not schizophrenic – we all have different voices in our heads.)
- The more calm and focused you are, the easier it will be to find the answer.
- You might need to ask your question a couple of times before you get the answer. If you don't seem to be getting anywhere, be patient and come back to it later.
- When you have the answer, make sure you feel comfortable with it.
- Listen to your heart more than your head.
- Don't be in a rush to act on your answer. Sit with it until you feel ready.

The more we start listening to this voice, the more we start making the right decisions in all areas of our lives. Sometimes we already know the answer, but it just takes a little time to clear our heads from the internal chatter to hear it. The more we can do this, the easier and quicker it gets.

There are many things in life that can make us lose sight of how great we are. We start out as babies and young children feeling confident and free of judgement towards ourselves. But even by nursery school age some of us have started to lose faith in ourselves and lack a sense of love for who we are. It can start in the playground, by being left out of groups, not being chosen for a team, being teased, being told off insensitively by a teacher, the list goes on, and by the time we're young women we might have had most of our love and confidence in ourselves knocked out of us.

For most of us, and especially for us young women, this essential tool is really our biggest challenge. The main theme of this whole book is learning to love yourself and, hopefully, as you read through it you will start to do just that. Feel happy with who you are and love yourself for just being you. If we can't start to feel love for ourselves we will never be truly happy people (see Doing It!, p186).

**Don't expect to feel great about yourself overnight. It can take a lifetime – and even then you'll have your good and bad days.**

## So...

- It's all about self-acceptance. Learn to have compassion for yourself and don't be hard on yourself about everything.
- Know that we are all equal. It doesn't matter what we look like, how much money we have or how good our grades are, we all have something special to offer and give.
- Remember, you're stuck with yourself until you die, so you might as well learn to love yourself NOW.
- No one is perfect. Learn to love those imperfections in yourself.
- You can change in a second. You can decide right now to love yourself. So go on, what are you waiting for?

From Girl to Woman

## FOCUS AND PERSEVERANCE

Another essential tool to have is focus, knowing what your goals are, even if it's only one day at a time. For most of us life doesn't just drop the perfect exam grades and careers into our laps. We have to work hard at it and dedicate time to achieve what we want. I'm not saying you should map out your whole life, or know exactly what you want to be doing 10 years down the line. Just that you have some idea of what you want for your immediate future. Keep your spontaneity, but if you want to become good at something or get high grades then (unless you're one of the lucky few) you'll need to work at it. Set goals for yourself, and figure out ways of reaching them.

> There are two types of people – those who sit around talking about that amazing thing they're going to do and those who get off their bums and get on with doing it.

Most of us receive quite a few hard knocks along the way. It's how you deal with those knocks that's important. Do they make you give up and get despondent, or do you get back up and give it another go? You have to keep going. All the great success stories took focus and commitment.

## So...

- Stop talking about what you're going to do 'tomorrow' and do it today.
- Be a learner. Look out for the lessons in every experience you have.
- Be flexible. Don't get over attached to things so that when they don't work out exactly as you want you freak out.
- Be strong and get back up when you've been knocked down.
- Put in some time and effort if you want to get results. Perfect lives and careers don't just drop out of the sky.

## THE ABILITY TO SEE THE FUNNY SIDE OF LIFE

As pressures on us increase with exams and relationships, it really helps to be able to see the funny side of life. It can easily all get too serious, too quickly. Some of us actually thrive on the drama of it all. I know I do. Dramas are a great distraction from the mundane and can make us feel important. But at some point, though, we need to separate ourselves from them and stop taking it all so seriously. Even more importantly, stop taking ourselves so seriously. I promise you that you can find something to laugh about, no matter what's going on in your life. Humour will keep you young and healthy.

So...

- Don't get caught up in the drama of it all. Remember, life isn't a soap opera.
- Humour and light-heartedness will make you a more attractive person to be around.
- Laughing is great for you. People who've laughed a lot stay looking younger for a lot longer. (Knew that would get you, ladies!)

## GRATITUDE AND OPTIMISM

If you live in a Western society, are educated and are having three meals a day, already that puts you in the top 2 per cent of the world as far as luck goes. It's too easy to get caught up in moping about all the things you don't have – not getting enough pocket money, not being allowed out late enough or not having enough clothes. If you do this, you might not be appreciating a whole lot of more important things that you do have. If you have any of the following, then show and feel gratitude for them: a family that loves you, your health, food on the table, education, good friendships. The more gratitude you show to those around you and to the world, the more bounty and gifts you'll receive. **Fact.**

Some of you may have had a rough time, and maybe aren't lucky enough to have all of the above. If that's how things are for you, I'm not saying you should always fake it and pretend everything is fine and dandy – just that the time will come when you will be ready to focus on things you do have and you can start to put your life together again.

So...

- Be grateful and appreciate your life. It will help you acknowledge everything that you are blessed with.
- Stop concentrating on what you don't have and concentrate on what you do have.
- If you're really not happy, take charge of your life and start creating what will make you happy.
- Always be a 'glass half-full' person.

From Girl to Woman

# THE RUSH

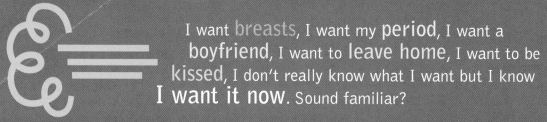

I want breasts, I want my period, I want a boyfriend, I want to leave home, I want to be kissed, I don't really know what I want but I know **I want it now**. Sound familiar?

If you're someone who is always in a rush to get that next hit from life, you probably started way back when you were a little girl. What kind of games did you play when you were younger? Did they mainly consist of pretending you were a lot older? Were you always the Mum, the Boss or the University student? Are you someone who loved pretending to be the adult? We often carry this with us all through our teens. And what about now? Are you always the first to try new things, like clubbing, taking drugs or having sex? Do you ever have people say things to you like, 'You're 14 going on 20', 'You'll be bored by the time you're 20 if you continue at this rate,' 'You're growing up too fast.'?

Anything new can be a tempting and exciting prospect – especially for those of us with curious minds. It's a natural process: we're all learners and are constantly soaking up new knowledge through new experiences. I believe most of us do the things we want to, whether we are told to or not. Think about all the times in your life you've looked back and thought, 'When so and so gave me that advice and I really wasn't interested, maybe they actually had a point.' The fact is we've all got to learn from our own mistakes. It's just the same with this book. I'm not dictating to you at what age you should do this or that. I don't know that answer. We all go at our own pace, and we have our own reasons for when and how we do this. My reason for rushing was that I wanted independence as early as possible, to be my own person and maybe to prove something to the world and myself. So instead of telling you at what age you should lose your virginity or take drugs or leave home, I want you to instead ask yourself if you can momentarily slow down and listen to what it is you really want to do next. (There's that truth voice again!) If we're always rushing, this voice often gets ignored.

This is where what you've learnt from the essential tools comes in handy. Check in with them next time you're about to rush into something head first and you might just find yourself taking a better route. The more you start using them, the more you'll know what you really want to do next. Not just what you think will look cool or impress your mates.

Even though the rush may be on, remember to enjoy being 'a young lass'. It's a brilliant place to be and you can never go back. You've got your whole life ahead of you to experiment and try new things. These decisions you make now will have an effect on the rest of your life. Don't end up living a life of regrets.

## ONE STEP AT A TIME
Just as much as there are some of us who love rushing towards adulthood, others of us are frightened of growing up and becoming women. Those of us who come under this category tend to hold off becoming women by not rushing into sexual relationships and not being obsessed by fashion, boys and body image.

If you feel scared of becoming a woman and it's something you'd like to change, then understand that it's up to you to decide when you're ready. Be honest with yourself about your fears and maybe even take some time to write them down. Once you've got them on paper, you'll see many of them are things you don't actually need to be scared of because you're the one in the driving seat – with your feet on the accelerator and brake. Push down on that brake if things seem to be going to fast. Be honest with yourself about which fears you think you might be able to let go of, and start letting go of them today.

## THE BOTTOM LINE

- As you set out on your journey to womanhood, fill your bag with these five essential tools: hearing your truth voice, loving yourself, focus and perseverance, seeing the funny side of life and being grateful for what you have.
- Don't always rush into everything that you do. The urge to grow up quickly might seem tempting but don't lose out on your childhood, because you won't get it back.
- If you want to take things slowly, then do. You dictate what pace you want to try new things.
- If you're scared, remember that you're in the driving seat, and you can go into womanhood as fast or as slow as you like.

From Girl to Woman

# GIVE IT TO ME STRAIGHT!

*I get teased at school by the other girls because I'm not into the same things as them, like boys, clothes and how big my breasts are. Instead I really enjoy sports and making up plays. I'm 14, but most of my friends are younger than me. I don't feel in a rush to grow up and be like them, but the bullying is getting to me and I'm fed up with not fitting in. Do you think there is something wrong with me? (Sarah, 14)*

There is absolutely nothing wrong with you. Being mature isn't just about the things you do or the things that you are into; it's also about being comfortable with being yourself, even if it means being slightly different from your class mates. We all grow up and get into different things at different times and the people who are bullying you are obviously not wise or cool enough to realise that. Being mature hasn't got anything to do with how many people you've got off with or how big your breasts are; it's to do with your attitude and knowing who you are, and not changing that for anyone. People that bully are the ones that need to grow up. Don't compromise yourself and change because some idiots are calling you names. Carry on doing what feels right to you.

*I find life pretty dull most of the time so I keep trying new things (however dangerous) to make life more exciting. More often than not, though, I get myself into trouble of one kind or another. My mum keeps telling me to slow down and stop being in such a rush to be an adult (my boyfriend's 28), but I'm scared that if I stop, my life will get boring again. What do you think I should do? (Sonia, 16)*

What you have to remember is that being bored is a choice — you don't have to get into trouble or be wild to have a fun time. If you keep looking for that next buzz from life, then you will trick yourself into thinking that you need to do more and more dangerous things to have a good time. There are plenty of interesting things going on without having to put yourself in dangerous situations. Spend some time thinking about some stuff you can do where your age is irrelevant and you won't get into trouble. For a start, you could try reading this book with a group of mates and do the exercises and rituals together. As I've said before, we all grow up at different speeds and in different ways. Just don't forget to enjoy your adolescence.

*Sometimes, when life is really getting me down, the last thing I can do is be grateful for everything I have. Everything seems so awful that being positive feels impossible. I wish I could be more positive but I don't know how. Help! (Rachel, 16)*

Rachel, I don't know your situation, so I don't know in what way your life is so awful, but I can understand that looking on the positive side can sometimes be an extremely difficult thing to do. But it's worth having a go anyway. What I want you to do is write a list. At the top of the page write 'I'm grateful for...' and then start your list. You might have to start with really simple small things, like being able to breathe, being able to get out of bed, having a friend, having your sanity, etc. We all have at least some of these things. Remember, life does change and it often gets better. It's the belief that it's going to stay like this forever that can really get us down. Try treating yourself every day, whether it's something simple like watching your favourite thing on telly or making yourself your favourite meal. Be good to yourself and make an effort to do things you enjoy.

> " The older I get the more I think that life is crap. I used to have a really positive outlook but now I think people like that are idealistic and naïve. How do I stay positive and open-minded even when life keeps showing me that it's full of so much hard, painful things like death and war? (Fiona, 15) "

Life can definitely be full of loads of painful, tragic things. But for every negative thing there is, there is also something beautiful and exciting going on, like babies being born and love between people. You choose which side of life you want to concentrate on. Also, don't be lazy about it. Be proactive in making the world a place you do want to live in. Find out what you can do to help your community, the environment, or even children that are worse off than you. If you contribute to this world being a better place you'll feel more positive and probably meet a lot of other cool like-minded people along the way.

> " All the women I know are moody, stressed out and overworked. My mum is a great example of this. She's always telling me how easy my life is now, and to enjoy it because when I get older I'll have so many responsibilities and worries. Is this true and how can I make sure I avoid becoming like her when I grow up? (Susie, 15) "

Life's pressures can definitely make us stressed out and usually the older we get, the more pressure and responsibilities we have. So we might see older women as being stressed out and neurotic, but that doesn't mean they're all like that or that we have to be like that. You have to learn how to balance your workload and prioritise what's most important to you. Remember the fourth essential tool, seeing the funny side of life, and it will help you not take it all too seriously. Why don't you offer to help your mum out with a few things or cook her a delicious dinner, and also help her realise that life is actually something to be enjoyed. After all, you only get one!

From Girl to Woman

# RITES OF PASSAGE RITUAL

Well done, ladies, you've made it to the end of the chapter, and the beginning of the rest of your life. Let's celebrate with a 'rites of passage' ritual. I love rituals and often do them on my own or with friends. Apart from anything else, they're good fun and a great excuse to get a group of your mates together. This 'rites of passage' ritual is for you to celebrate the start of a new phase in your life and also to honour the part of yourself that you are letting go of. It's great to do at the time of the Full Moon.

**ALL YOU'LL NEED IS THE FOLLOWING:**
- Girlfriends – a group of about four to six is a good size.
- An open space. Either inside or outside is fine, but make sure the space is calming, clear of hectic scattered energy and somewhere you won't be interrupted.
- Incense and white candles.
- A pen and paper.
- An open attitude by all.

Choose one of you as the group leader. Whoever takes on this role will instruct the others what to do and make sure that the energy in the group stays focused (i.e. that you all stay on track and stop people talking about other things). If you're someone who doesn't usually feel comfortable taking the lead, why not have a go at it now? The habit of always being led can be one of the things you decide to let go of in the ritual.

- Sit in a circle and place a lighted white candle in the middle. All of you imagine a circle of white light around you – this is your protection shield.

- Write a list of everything you want to let go of as a 'girl' – say having petty fights with friends, being shy and quiet, putting all your focus into boys fancying you. Then write a list of everything that being a woman means to you and what you want more of in your life – being strong, patient and self-confident, having more money, a better relationship with family and a boyfriend. (Now is not the time to be bashful about what to ask for. There are no limits to what you can have.)

- Go around the circle and repeat in turn, 'I [your name] choose to let go of the following things as I enter this new phase of my life.' Then repeat your list. If there are things on it that you don't want to say out loud just say them in your head. Next go around the circle and say, 'I [your name] choose to have the following things in my life.' Name the things on your list.

- Now close your eyes and envisage yourself as the woman that you're becoming, say 10 years in the future. See her happy and strong in her power, then go to her and ask her if she has a gift or a message for you. If she does, accept whatever it is from her. Allow yourself to lose yourself slightly in your imagination. Don't think too much about what's happening, just trust that whatever you imagine is right. (Remember, there is no such thing as a wrong answer.) When you've received the gift or message, remember it and take it with you into your life. Know that you can access the words or gift whenever you need extra support or comfort through your journey into womanhood.

- I always include a round of gratitude, thanking the universe for its constant support. Let people thank whatever or whoever they personally believe supports them through their life, e.g. God, their parents, friends, etc.

- Again, close your eyes and close the circle by going around anti-clockwise and one by one choosing a word or image of how you feel right now in the moment (just say the first thing that comes into your mind). When you've all had a turn, open your eyes, lean forward together and blow out the candle, sending your love and gratitude to the goddesses that have been looking over you. Imagine the light spreading out and touching the whole of humanity with a sprinkle of love as it goes out.

- Find somewhere you can bury or burn your pieces of paper, sending out your affirmations to the energy of the moon and mother earth.

I hope you enjoyed what was perhaps your first ritual. In our culture we have lost so much of our sacred selves, our rituals, our initiations and our sense of tribe/community. These are things that, consciously or unconsciously, a lot of us yearn for and they're very much a part of being a woman. Joining together to dance or talk or share our desires and creativity. As women it's vital we keep our spirits alive. Rituals give us a direct link to this part of ourselves.

Well, ladies, you've made it to the end of chapter 1. I hope you have a clearer picture of the kind of woman you want to be and have reminded yourself to stay clear of becoming that scary headmistress or that neurotic Auntie you swore you'd never become. The woman you do become will be a product of all the choices you make along the way, so start embodying your vision of a gorgeous funky chick NOW!

But it's not all about hard work and no play. Having fun is the **Number One** priority – check out little kids because they know all about that. And don't forget to start using your bag of tools. I promise you they'll come in handy!

From Girl to Woman

# BOD-EASE

My guess is that 90 per cent or more of you reading this are unhappy with your bodies in one way or another. Whether it's wide hips or big bums, most of us have hang-ups about our body shape. As I write this, I have just heard on the radio that only 1 per cent of women in the UK are happy with their bodies. Which percentage are you in? Are you someone who constantly finds yourself staring at other girls' thighs? Do you ever look a girl up and down, sizing her up as she passes you in the street, wishing that your stomach were as flat as hers? After looking through a beauty magazine, do you feel depressed that you haven't got the same figure as the models inside? I know I've been guilty of all these things.

# OBJECTS OF DESIRE

Women have been objects of beauty and desire since the beginning of time, so scoring points in the looks department is nothing new – elaborate fashions and make-up, over-the-top hairdos and constraining pieces of apparatus to make us suck in our stomachs are just a few of the outlandish devices women have used to achieve ideals of 'beauty'. Luckily, unlike our ancestral sisters, we no longer have to squeeze ourselves into tight corsets, but if we look around we can still see that the way we look is distressingly important.

Every day, we're subjected to any number of images of beautiful women, but how often are women represented by the norm – whatever that might be? We at least know that not every woman is six-foot, skinny and big-breasted. According to the 1998 Bread For Life Campaign, 61 per cent of women feel inadequate to the image represented by the media and 89 per cent would like to see more average-sized women in the media.

A marketing campaign by The Body Shop was a great expression of how ridiculous this representation was. In 1998 Anita Roddick, founder of The Body Shop, developed Ruby, a curvaceous Barbie-type doll alongside which were the words 'There are 3 billion women who don't look like supermodels and only 8 who do.'

Anita spoke to me about her views on the beauty industry and her ideas behind the campaign.

> "There is an enormous difference between a role model and a stereotype. A role model tends to be active, inspiring you to take positive action. A stereotype is passive. Right away, that is negative to me. And a stereotype tends to trade in clichés and ideals. If you are bombarded with idealised stereotypes and end up hating yourself because you don't meet the ideal, then that too is negative.
>
> What I object to is the terrorism of the 'or', the attitude which says something can only be this way or that way. Instead, let's celebrate the genius of the 'and', the attitude which embraces the diversity of humankind. That was how we came to create Ruby. Ruby is a standard size 14. This shape is the average in the UK. We think that highlights just how extreme stereotyping for women is. So Ruby speaks for all those women who are tired of the pressure on their appearance.
>
> Ruby is saying, 'I may not be Miss World, but I'm me! And I think I'm great'. And women love her. They see themselves in Ruby and applaud her cheek and confidence. Ruby is all about a sense of self-esteem. She is encouraging women to challenge the culture of the beauty world, and to have the confidence to be who they want to be."

The Body Shop's marketing is unique in its message. For the most part, the media's message is, 'Skinny equals good, fat equals bad', making having a positive body image all the more difficult. In this chapter I'll be encouraging you to take another look. I'll be challenging you to change negative perceptions and to learn to celebrate the joys and pleasures our bodies can bring.

# ALL SHAPES AND SIZES

We all start developing at different times and in different ways. This is when the comparing starts, monitoring our own changes through our friends. Who's got the bigger breasts, the smallest thighs and the flattest stomach? The list goes on. We size ourselves up against other girls to see how we're doing. A male friend once said to me, 'Do you ever get pissed off with boys checking girls out so much and commenting on their figures?' I replied, 'Sometimes, but it's nothing compared to the amount other girls size each other up.' Think about it. How much time do you spend looking at other girls? I sometimes find myself staring really hard at other girls' bums (and I don't mean sexually, either!).

Often, our bodies develop at a different speed to our mental and emotional state. Some girls love the change and the new status it gives them, of becoming a woman, while others feel uncomfortable with their new body parts and the attention they may bring. Have a think about your own physical changes and how you're dealing or how you've dealt with them. Have there been some things you've embraced and other things that you've found awkward?

Here are some of your questions on the subject.

What I can't stand is that my bum and thighs keep getting larger but my upper body is still quite skinny. Will this balance out?' (Louisa, 16)

A common term for this body shape is 'pear shaped', meaning we are proportionally smaller on our upper body and more curvaceous and voluptuous on our lower half. This is actually an extremely attractive shape, but it can be hard to get used to if you've been used to going straight up and down, without any curves in between. So many women and girls often want a body shape that's more similar to a young boy's than one of a sexy grown woman. So stop worrying about whether it will balance out – you're perfectly in proportion already. Enjoy your hips and your larger bum. It's a very natural, sexy shape for a woman. If you look at any paintings from the past, all have women who were depicted with this classic body shape. We've just forgotten how beautiful and sensual it really is.

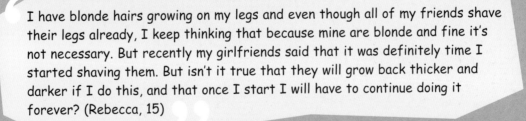
I have blonde hairs growing on my legs and even though all of my friends shave their legs already, I keep thinking that because mine are blonde and fine it's not necessary. But recently my girlfriends said that it was definitely time I started shaving them. But isn't it true that they will grow back thicker and darker if I do this, and that once I start I will have to continue doing it forever? (Rebecca, 15)

If you feel comfortable with having hair on your legs, then I don't see why you should shave them. Western culture is obsessed with women being as hairless as possible and young women in particular often feel obliged to follow this trend. The advice I'd give to you is not to become one of those girls that are obsessed

Bod-ease

with eliminating all their body hair and instead be flexible with it (you sound as if you're like that already). Sometimes you might want to shave and be hair-free, and at others you might be comfortable with having a bit of stubble and unshaved hair around the edges. If you do want to get rid of hair you can always wax it and then it won't grow back so thick. You can do it at home with the Body Shop home waxing (sugaring) kit. You use a cloth that you can wash and use again, which is great for the environment.

 I know this might sound weird, but I hate the fact that however much I eat I don't put on weight. I'm really, really skinny and I get teased for it all the time at school. I'm fed up with it and want to know if that means I will always be skinny or if there's anything I can do to put on weight. (Bianca, 14)

I guess that most girls would be jealous about this but I can understand how it's difficult, especially as you're getting teased. You probably feel less developed than the other girls and your curves haven't started forming yet. You must have a really high metabolic rate, which is why it doesn't matter how much you eat. Metabolism is something that slows down for most of us the older we get. When it does, we suddenly find ourselves getting bigger even though we're eating the same as we always have. You might stay skinny throughout your adult life, but I've known lots of girls who were skinny teenagers and then filled out in their late teens and early twenties.

 I am by far the tallest girl in my year, and even taller than most of the boys as well.  I really hate being this tall and I never get asked out by any of the boys. (Tanya, 16)

When you're young, being tall can feel like a burden, but when you get older it's often a blessing. All the gorgeous fashion models are tall, and so are most of our most glamorous, beautiful female celebs. Again, it's difficult standing out when you're young, but being tall should be something you learn to love. People will probably think you're older than you are, which can bring many advantages (I won't state them here as I could get into trouble!) One thing you must remember is not to stoop or hunch your shoulders because you feel embarrassed about being tall. Firstly, it's really bad for your back and secondly it looks really unattractive when someone is obviously uncomfortable in their body.

# BREASTS

Melons, jugs, pancakes, cupcakes, pert, bouncy, tits, boobies, juicy, pendulums, yum yum, come to mama... The world is obsessed, fascinated and in total awe of bosoms. Men and women alike find themselves staring, investigating and judging the flesh that hangs from a woman's chest. We just can't get enough of them.

Many of our famous supposed role models today decide to go for the 'op'. These are meant to be the empowered women of the 21st century. They have money and worldwide success, yet they're still not happy enough to avoid the surgeon's knife. It's not as though they're not gorgeous, with or without big boobs.

So why is it that having the breasts we want can make us so much happier? Most of the media images of women we see show women with a large cleavage, and show it at every given opportunity. Breasts are sexy and sex sells.

A television documentary, Perfect Breasts once explored how a growing number of young women in the UK are getting breast enlargements. Girls as young as 17 are opting for the op. The documentary annoyed me; it didn't explore the question, 'Why are more and more girls becoming obsessed and so unhappy with their bodies that they went to go through with a life changing operation?' But instead came across more like an advert, encouraging young girls to take that step. Girls as young as 12 were unhappy with their breasts because boys dissed them if they were flat. They were in genuine turmoil over wanting to have large firm breasts, to the extent that they didn't want to be physically intimate as they were scared of being teased.

So the debate remains, Why are we breast obsessed? Are we all in a state of arrested development and secretly want to be close to Mummy? What do breasts promise us? Who knows, perhaps small breasts will be back in fashion soon (hopefully, anyway!).

Here are a few commonly asked questions about boobs.

### One of my breasts is bigger than the other. Is this normal?
This is completely normal, especially while you are still developing. Most of us will have a slight difference, even when we have stopped.

### What can I do to prevent my breasts sagging in the future?
Wearing a bra is a good idea, even if your breasts are quite small. One day, however, the inevitable will happen, and no fancy creams can stop it.

### Is hair growing around the nipple common and is there anything I can do to get rid of it?
Yes, some women do grow hair around the nipple. You can remove it by plucking, though this may cause ingrown hairs. New treatments are becoming available every year, but they can be quite expensive.

### BRAS
You've probably started wearing a bra by now, and have been through that first slightly nervous, yet exciting, visit to the lingerie shop with your mum or best mate. It's up to you whether you want to wear a bra or not – I wear one probably about half the time. You might feel more comfortable in a bra when you're at school or out with friends because it will make your breasts feel less exposed, and the nipple isn't as likely to peek through when hardened. Some say a bra prevents the breasts from sagging when you get older but my jury's still out on this. I think childbirth, losing and putting on weight, and gravity pretty much decide this for us regardless of whether we've worn a bra or not. The most important thing is to find a bra that fits properly and is comfortable – there's nothing worse than bra straps digging into you all day.

Nowadays, we have so much choice in bras that it can be a minefield. Make sure that when you go to buy one you ask an assistant to help you out – some department stores provide special bra-fitting services. Get measured properly and check with the shop assistant that you've got the right size.

If you want to experiment with the way your boobs look with clothes, new modern bra designs can now help you create pretty much any shape you want.

- If you want a lift, there's the good old push up bra. They now design them so you can adjust the amount of cleavage you want to show.
- If you're getting sporty, buy a full support sports bra or even a crop top made with lycra.
- If you want your breasts to look larger all over you can try a padded bra, like the Ultima bra worn by Julia Roberts in Erin Brockovich. (I've tried one on and believe me, they make even my tiny breasts look pretty enormous.)
- If you want to make them look smaller you can try a 'Minimiser' bra (not something I've ever had to look into myself).

At the end of the day, ladies, try and enjoy your breasts and don't assume that they have to look like Pamela Anderson's to be appreciated. If you ask, most boys actually prefer real small ones to fake huge ones. (Not that we're doing it just for the boys!)

# TAKING ANOTHER LOOK

What is your relationship like with your body? Do you feel happy with it? Are you constantly trying to change it or do you ignore it?

## Body exercise ✏

Here is a very simple yet powerful exercise to connect you to your feelings towards your body. It can be done with your clothes on or off, depending which you feel most comfortable with. Choose a time when you know you're not going to be interrupted by nosy siblings or distracting phone calls. Then go to a room in the house where there is a full-length or large mirror. Stand in front of the mirror and just look at yourself for a while. Start to notice where it is you're looking at most. It might be the part of your body you like the least, or the part you like the most. Turn around and see yourself from different angles. Notice how you feel about looking at your body. Which bits, if any, are you thinking you'd like to change? Are you thinking of other women and how you wish you looked more like them, or are you happy with what you see? There could be a whole range of feelings coming up in you. Slowly, start to get a sense of your relationship with your body. You may find it quite effective to write down some key words or images that come to you.

# HOW WAS IT FOR YOU?

Some of you might have found the previous exercise relatively easy and maybe even enjoyable. That's fine — you are allowed to love your body as much as others might hate theirs. If you felt relatively at ease with the exercise, it's a sign you have a positive relationship with your body.

Be aware, though, if you had feelings such as, 'I like my body because I have been eating hardly anything for the last few months and I'm starting to achieve my goal of being skinny.' To help you have a clear understanding of where your feelings are coming from, I have listed below reasons for being happy with the exercise, and whether these are positive or not.

'I'm starting to look like one of those skinny models in magazines.' **NEGATIVE**

'That exercise is starting to pay off. I look a lot healthier now.' **POSITIVE**

'My friends are so envious of my new slimness.' **NEGATIVE**

'My bones look so beautiful, I can now see all of my ribs.' **NEGATIVE**

'I do like what I see but I would like my body more if my bottom half was slimmer as well.' **POSITIVE**

Can you see why they have different labels? The **NEGATIVE** reasons are usually those that come about because you are comparing yourself to others, or have become completely disgusted by fat and obsessed with bones. **POSITIVE** ones have a mixture of acceptance and wanting change. Go back to your own thoughts, which ones do you think are healthy and which ones aren't.

If you found the exercise hard, well done for having a go. This is the first step towards accepting your body. Have a look at why you found it hard. Was it because you think you are unattractive? Or are you disappointed with your weight? There could be several reasons why and it's important you get a clear sense of them.

If you couldn't make it to the mirror, try reading to the end of the chapter and returning to the exercise when you feel more ready. Respect the speed you want to take.

There aren't any exact guidelines for a healthy weight. What is healthy for one of us might be unhealthy for another. For example, being skinny is not a bad thing and, in fact, being thin can be healthy for some of us. The importance lies in our mind-sets around being skinny. Are you obsessive about it to the point you beat yourself up if you break your diet? Do you get depressed if you put on a couple of pounds? Do you weigh yourself religiously? All these things could show that your relationship with your body is unhealthy and you may even have an eating disorder (see I'm A Survivor, p170). Think about the amount of time you're spending thinking about your weight and the way you look. Do you really think it deserves that much attention?

Bod-ease

# YOU'RE NOT ON YOUR OWN

If we are lucky, most of us start to accept things about ourselves as we get older. This book is about learning to love and accept ourselves **NOW** so our paths ahead are easier. I've found listening to other women's stories the easiest way to do this. I once saw a television documentary in which celebrity women were interviewed about their bodies. It made me realise that even the most beautiful women have hang-ups about the way they look. It also surprised me that so many 'skinny' women seemed to feel like they were fat and had, or in the past had had, an eating disorder. One good thing about hearing all these women talk about their negative views about their bodies was that it hit home that young women aren't alone. It seems that no matter how beautiful and thin women are, they feel insecure about their bodies. Not that this is a good thing really, in fact it's pretty sad. But at least we know that women of all shapes and sizes have these insecurities and that the actual problem is in the mind, not the body.

## WHAT IS BEAUTIFUL?

When I was travelling across five continents, I talked to women from different countries about how they felt about their bodies.

> In my country a girl is naturally thin when she is young. She then has a family and becomes old and her figure changes and becomes larger. She does not think about this, it is just what happens. She does not fill her head with such vanities when she witnesses so much starving and suffering. (Nadia, 15, Bombay)

> You have no bottom or hips. To men in my country they would not go near you because they think you are ill with sickness. (Jenni, 32, Ghana)

> In my village you can see the women look very different from you. You look like a plank of wood, but I hear men like this where you are from. (Chuckle) (Amadey, 17, Uganda)

As you can see, what is considered beautiful in one culture might be considered ugly in another. As individuals we all have different tastes; there isn't one type of person that is good looking. Even though the media has tried to sell us a certain look, hopefully most of us don't buy into it and we can see the unique beauty in everyone.

# WHAT THE BOYS SAY

We might look and stare at our cellulite and be paranoid about the wobble in our bottom as we walk but are boys looking at us in the same way? I think boys find the whole body and beauty obsession with girls weirder than we think. When I've asked male friends and boyfriends what kind of figure they prefer on a girl, they don't seem to have that much of a preference and say that it's how comfortable and sexy they feel that really comes across.

Most boys can't understand this constant drive girls have to obtain the same body shape. They think there are great-looking petite skinny girls just as much as there are great-looking tall curvaceous girls. I think they're right.

> My girlfriend's always going on about how fat she is and it baffles me. She is completely skinny. I tell her to stop worrying about it and that she's beautiful just the way she is. (John, 16)

> I've been out with girls that have small breasts and girls that have huge breasts. Girls always assume that all boys love big breasts but it's just not true. I find small pert breasts far more attractive. (Mark, 15)

> Girls are always going on about their bums and tits but what I think is important is the face. The rest of it can be pretty much whatever, but they have to have a pretty face and a nice smile. (Dom, 17)

> I hate the way my girlfriend hates me seeing her naked - she'll always ask to turn the light off or try and keep her top on. She doesn't realise that I don't care about her being perfect model size. It's not as though I'm some Chippendale hunk! (Sam, 18)

I know for a fact that boys don't just stare at one part of our anatomy. They may want to look at our breasts but they don't scrutinise us in the way we do with ourselves and each other. Boys look at the whole package, as we do with them. We never fancy someone just because they've got huge muscles or a cute bum. We need to find the whole of them attractive. Boys are definitely prone to tease us about our bodies and the way we look, but that's more in front of each other so they can look cool.

FACT: Boys are a lot more easily pleased than you think!

Bod-ease

# HOLDING OURSELVES HIGH

No one type of woman is considered beautiful throughout the world. Even in the West, fashions and preferred body types have been constantly changing throughout the years. It is our choice whether we buy into the trends or not. For me, life is better when I see beauty in more than one thing. Feeling beautiful, whether this means applying make-up, feeling confident or being healthy, is the key to looking good. There are lots of ways of feeling and therefore looking beautiful.

Our body language is a good indication of how we feel about ourselves. Sitting up straight and maintaining direct eye contact indicates someone who is confident. If you put two equally good-looking people next to each other, the one with the better posture will be the more attractive of the two. The way we hold ourselves is key to looking and feeling good.

## So why not try it now, with this exercise?

Sit up straight, feel your inner grace and smile. Those of you who've done ballet or dance have an advantage here. Think of the times you've done ballet and walked with your toes pointing and your neck long. The word 'grace' comes to mind – not stiff and pointy but long and graceful. You might feel a bit awkward sitting up straight at first, but over time it will begin to feel natural. Observe yourself the next time you're out and about and talking to people. Remind yourself of your beauty and put grace into your movement.

**Things to remember:**
Don't always put your hands in front of, or touching, YOUR FACE – this is a sign of insecurity and trying to hide yourself. It can also spread spots.

**BREATHE DEEPLY AND SLOWLY** – this will help you have a sense of inner calmness and wellbeing and will be reflected in the way you hold yourself.

Have **EYE CONTACT** with people – it shows them that you are confident and immediately makes them feel closer to you.

**SMILE** – it's obvious but so often we forget to smile. This immediately makes a person glow and their inner beauty shine through.

 # THE BOTTOM LINE

- Don't get sucked into the narrow-minded stereotypical image of a woman's body that is fed to us by the media. Very few REAL women look anything like these six-foot skinny big-breasted supermodels. Nowadays, most of their photos are airbrushed and manipulated anyway.

- We come in all shapes and sizes, and our bodies change at many different times. Don't feel worried if you're developing at a different rate from everyone else. In the end it all pretty much evens out.

- Start coming to terms with how you feel about your body. Be honest with yourself about whether you're coming from a healthy or unhealthy place.

- If you do have hang-ups about your body you're in the majority. Even beautiful, skinny women want to change things about their bodies.

- Who says what's beautiful anyway? Beauty is in the eye of the beholder, so don't assume you have to be busty and blonde to be considered attractive.

- Boys aren't nearly as fussy as we think. They actually think our obsession with our bodies is weird and over the top. (And they're probably right!)

- Body language and how you hold yourself is key to looking and feeling good. Hold yourselves high and hold eye contact with people.

# GIVE IT TO ME STRAIGHT

> **"** My mum keeps telling me to watch what I eat. Every time I go near food she says, 'Are you sure you want to eat that?' I know she really cares about her own figure but I wish she wouldn't keep putting that on me. I'm happy with my body and I don't want to be model skinny. I wish she would get off my back. (Lisa, 16) **"**

**Well done for being so clear** about knowing that you can be happy without being model skinny. It sounds like you're pretty level-headed about your mum's unhealthy attitude, but it must be upsetting to have her on your back the whole time. Many other girls whose mothers go on at them to be careful about what they eat, start to have very unhealthy relationships with food. It sounds like you need to be really clear with your mum and tell her that you're happy with the way you look, and maybe even suggest that she has a look at her own relationship with food and how healthy or unhealthy it is. Tell her you are more than comfortable with your body shape and that you don't want her to be involved in your food intake. It sounds like your mum could learn a thing or two from you.

> **"** I have developed more quickly than any of the other girls in my year. All the boys constantly tease me and even try and grab my breasts when I walk past. Even though my breasts are big I don't feel very grown up yet and I'd actually prefer it if I didn't have them. When I'm older I think I'm going to apply for a breast reduction. Meanwhile, how do I put up with the teasing? (Debbie, 14) **"**

**It's never nice being teased**, especially about something that is out of your control and that you already feel uncomfortable with. It's completely out of order for boys to touch you and invade your personal space. Be very clear with them that you're not going to put up with it or you'll tell a teacher. Even though you might feel uncomfortable with your new body shape now, remember that it is new for you and the more you get used to it the more you will come to enjoy it. Also, when other girls catch up with you and you're no longer singled out, you might begin to love your breasts more. Ignore the teasing as much as you can and before you know it people will have caught up with you and you'll no longer be in an awkward spotlight.

> **"** They call me fatty at school. However much I try, I can't stop eating. My mum took me to the doctor and he told me I was three stone overweight and put me on some healthy eating plan. I really want to be thin like the other girls, but I can't stop eating. What can I do? (Elizabeth, 15) **"**

**Don't beat yourself up** about not being able to lose weight – usually when we're unhappy we eat to make ourselves feel better. Every time you think you're going to eat something, ask yourself if you're really hungry or if you just want escape any uncomfortable feelings. But you shouldn't feel like you need to lose weight just because these kids are bullying you. Do it for yourself. Losing a lot of weight takes real dedication and commitment, don't keep half-trying. When you're ready (and that might not be today) decide to put 100 per cent into it.

Hopefully, in this chapter you've started to gain some insight into how you feel about the body you have. Noticing unhealthy attitudes to your body is the first step towards changing things. Noticing is also one of the biggest and hardest steps, so well done for having the courage to do that.

Don't feel rushed to fix or change everything overnight. It doesn't happen like that. Be gentle on yourself and go at your own pace. You'll know when you're ready to make that leap. Sometimes, it can seem like jumping into the unknown, which can be a scary thing. Many of us have had these hang-ups about our bodies for a long time and we have forgotten what it's like to live without them.

Another way you can enhance change is by putting together your own support team as I mentioned in the Introduction. Bring together a few of your friends every month and discuss how you feel about your body and other topics. Choose someone to take on the role of group leader to guide the group.

I hope you've finished this chapter with more love and respect for your body than when you started, even if that means just being aware that it is there. Women and girls put an immense pressure on themselves to acquire the perfect body shape. Let's change that. If we learn to love our bodies as they are, we'll pave the way for our younger sisters to do the same.

# YOUR HEALTH

This chapter has some good general tips and advice on how to look after that precious body of yours. Something that most of us aren't really taught. It's not about being rigid and obsessive with your body but about having the information to help you decide how you want to look after it. We only get this one body and even though we don't often think about getting old when we're young, I'm here to tell you, it's going to happen! Prepare yourself now and enjoy your body, and hopefully you'll be one of those super-grannies who at the age of 80 rides a bike to their Bridge games, goes swimming in the sea, even in winter, and climbs Mount Snowdon in an hour. Okay, maybe I'm exaggerating a wee bit, but at least you won't be someone who nearly dies while running for the bus before you're even 20!

# DIETING VERSUS DIET AWARENESS

Diets have never got me anywhere. They are something I have tried regularly, and at times may have even lost a little weight, only to put on a lot more the next week. The only time my weight has changed and I've felt good in my body is when I have had diet awareness.

Diet awareness means that, instead of focusing on achieving an ideal weight and having a figure like Posh Spice, you concentrate on what you put into your body. Which foods make you feel good? Which ones make you feel tired and lethargic? Our bodies are extremely intelligent machines. They know what they need to be healthy and survive.

Until recently, I hardly ever drank water. I used to suffer from extreme dizzy spells and would often fall over when standing up suddenly. I started drinking the recommended amount of water, which is six to eight large glasses a day, and almost immediately my dizzy spells stopped. My body had been trying to tell me something was wrong.

Our bodies are very clever at letting us know how they feel. We just have to check in with them now and then and have a listen. My advice is to start while you're ahead, while you're young. The long-term consequences of eating badly and not exercising can be dire. Many of us have picked up bad habits from our parents and schools, but we can be more health-conscious for future generations by changing these now.

## HEALTH-CONSCIOUS TIPS

- It's a myth that omitting all fat from your diet is healthy. Some fat is essential. Fat is a vital part of every living cell. It is also the body's back-up fuel system. Fats carry the fat-soluble vitamins A, D, E and K into your blood. Without fats, your body could not use these vitamins. We could not be optimally healthy without fat in our diets. Problems occur when too much fat, or the wrong sort of fat, is consumed. For good health, fats should supply no more than 20–25 per cent of your daily calorie intake, and should consist of monounsaturated fats (olive oil and avocados) rather than saturated fats (butter, margariine and processed foods).

- Drink six to eight glasses of water a day, preferably filtered or mineral. Water makes up about 60–70 per cent of the body. It is essential to life and is one of the body's most important nutrients. Without it, the body wouldn't be able to function properly. Water lets you swallow and digest food, absorb nutrients and eliminate waste. When you sweat, it helps your body lose internal heat and cool you down.

- Eat three to five servings of vegetables and fruit a day. A serving is a medium-sized piece of fruit, a dessert bowlful of salad, two tablespoonfuls of vegetables or a glass of fruit juice. These foods provide vitamins, minerals and fibre, and can protect against some kinds of cancer. Aim to eat fresh or frozen produce whenever you can.

- Try not to eat processed foods and know your 'E' numbers (denoting food additives). Some additives can be relatively harmless, but others can cause severe reactions. Manufacturers can choose to quote either the E number of the additive or its chemical name or both in the ingredients list, which can be confusing for shoppers. With more and more people wanting to avoid foods with unnecessary additives, some manufacturers obviously hope that if they leave off the E number we'll think the food is more 'natural'. As a rule, if the ingredients list contains a long list of unfamiliar-sounding chemical names for ingredients that you wouldn't add to your own cooking, then you can be pretty sure it contains several additives. A long list of additives usually means the food is highly processed and has fewer 'real' ingredients.

- Eat less sugar. Sugar gives you calories but no other nutrients: no vitamins, minerals or fibre. Eating too much of it not only makes it difficult to maintain a healthy weight, but can also promote tooth decay. Try to cut down on sweets, soft drinks, biscuits and cakes and don't add sugar to drinks and food.

## YOU ARE WHAT YOU EAT

Now comes the tough bit – taking a look at your own diet. Make a list of your typical daily food intake. Does one type of food feature more than others? Do you eat too little? Do you eat too much? Take a look at why you think that is. Do you not have time to eat? Are you constantly on a diet? Do you not care about your body? Are you always hungry? Think about what you put into your body. If you are fine about what you eat and how your body feels, then great. You must be doing something right. If, on the other hand, you don't feel completely satisfied, make a change. The trick is to start straight away.

If you are living with your parents and you rely mostly on them for the foods you eat, have a chat with them about it. They might not have the same ideas as you about health, so try explaining some nutritional facts to them. Share your growing knowledge with your parents. It might seem daunting to them – they've been happy eating their own way for years and they don't want to suddenly change everything. It can seem like a big deal. They might think it's just a fad, like being a vegetarian for a couple of weeks. If this is the case, suggest that you make your own food. Tempt them with your delicious recipes and they might even end up having a taste. Another thing you could do is to say that you'll do the food shopping for a week and cook the dinners and they can decide at the end of the week if they are happy with the new meals. At the end of the chapter I've listed some good, easy-to-follow recipe books that are full of healthy and delicious ideas.

## MANIC ORGANIC

Nowadays most supermarkets offer an organic selection of foods. People seem to be put off by the fact that it's more expensive than non-organic food, but prices are gradually coming down, and now organic foods don't just cover fruit and vegetables, but also include a wide range of other foods such as chocolate, bread, crisps and cereal.

### Organic standards are to:
prohibit the use of artificial pesticides and fertilisers.
prohibit genetically modified foods and ingredients.
promote wildlife conservation and natural enhancement of soil fertility.

Your Health

## DON'T BE TOO STRICT

I don't want you to think for a second that I'm suggesting you eliminate all junk food and sweet naughty things. Far from it. I still eat lots of yummy chocolate and desserts – we've all got to have treats. I just don't eat them every day like I used to. The great thing is, if you're eating lots of vegetables and fruit and exercising, eating sugary fatty foods doesn't have such a bad effect on you. So allow yourself treats and don't feel guilty for them. If you are going to eat naughty foods the worst thing you can do afterwards is beat yourself up for it. It's all about balance. Another handy thing to remember is that when you are eating healthily you can eat huge amounts of food and never go hungry. Healthy food is easily digested, especially vegetables and fruit, as they have a high water content and go straight through you. Junk food and sweets take a long time to digest and contain unhealthy fats that cling to your vulnerable areas.

### Eat healthily, do some exercise and eat chocolate.

# GETTING INTO OUR SKINS

The word that some of you may hate and some of you may love – exercise. All of us have probably given it a go at some stage and if you are still at school, it's probably compulsory. Exercise can seem daunting if you haven't done it for a while, and even like the last thing you want to do with your time. I've been there.

It goes in waves for me. I can get almost obsessive about doing exercise to the point I burn myself out and don't do it again for a while. Then I go through stages where I don't so much as move a muscle for weeks. I've finally found a happy medium, exercising about three times a week.

Why do it? This might seem like an obvious question and you're right, it is, but then why do so many of us forget? If you're someone who hasn't exercised in a long time I urge you to do something, however small, today. You can find yourself saying 'tomorrow' until you suddenly find yourself aged 50, with several health problems. As soon as you've done even a little exercise, you can feel a huge difference in your body. The feel of muscles long forgotten, your energy levels picking up, the benefits of exercise are immense.

### Why exercise is good
- It releases endorphins to your brain that make you feel good and happy.
- It's great for all your vital organs, keeping them strong and working well.
- You will benefit from it later on in life, when you still look great and your body hasn't got as many aches and pains as it might do.
- It improves the quality of your skin, hair and nails.
- Your body becomes stronger and fitter – you won't even need to run for a bus because you can walk to where you're going without getting tired.

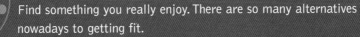

## Some fun motivators:

- Find something you really enjoy. There are so many alternatives nowadays to getting fit.
- Work out with someone else – it's easier when you can encourage each other.
- Splash out on some new exercise gear. Get yourself those latest trainers you wanted.
- Don't overdo it. Let your muscles rest so you don't get too worn out.
- Martial arts are a great way to get fit and at the same time you'll be learning an amazing skill in self-defence. Schools are cropping up everywhere for a wide range of martial arts, including Tai Chi, Wing Chun, Kickboxing and Capoeira.

There are many websites filled with information on getting fit for young people. See Sistah Support at the end of the book.

## THE BOTTOM LINE

- Rather than dieting, focus on the type of food you're eating. Diets are temporary and never really work.
- You are what you eat. Look at what it is you're eating, and if you know it's unhealthy, change it. If your parents don't want to change their diets too, be more in control by doing your own cooking and shopping.
- Never be too strict – you'll take all the enjoyment out of eating, and it is, after all, one of the most pleasurable things ever.
- Learn to find a balance. Eat healthily, do exercise and eat chocolate.
- Start to exercise and get stronger and fitter. Once you start, you'll actually learn to love it and you'll feel awful if you don't.

# PERIODS

Everything in our world is cyclical and that includes our bodies. Girls are very sensitive to their own unique cycle. The length of time it takes a moon to become full (i.e. 28 days) is the same length as the average menstrual cycle. Women are said to be very in touch with the moon and its energies and often refer to their periods as 'lunar cycles'.

Take a moment to think of your own cycle and the differences you feel at different times of the month. Just as your physical body is changing, so, too, your emotions are also affected by differences that can range from the subtle to the downright blatant. The more in touch we are with our bodies, the more aware of these changes we are. The most distinct thing you might notice is PMS (Pre-Menstrual Syndrome). The symptoms of PMS can be anything from feeling extremely sensitive emotionally, to physical changes such as swollen breasts, a bloated stomach and spots. Aaaaargh! The joys of being a woman. The positive side, though, is the reminder every month of being able to give birth, and the chance to be overly sensitive and have a good cry. Our cycles are a reminder of the power of women, our connection to mother earth and the nurturing soft qualities we are born with.

I still find it amazing just how much my periods affect my emotional state. I go through one or two days of being highly irritable and then a couple of days where I cry over the smallest thing. And this all happens before my period's even started! If you start to feel these overwhelming emotions suddenly coming out of nowhere, check where you are in your cycle. You may find, more often than not, that your period is due in a few days. You could start a period chart and have different colours for when you feel sad or when you feel angry, or when you feel like everyone is an annoying, irritating little twerp! Even though this emotional roller-coaster can seem a bit full on, I've always been quite happy that I get to feel all these strong emotions (and have a good shout at my boyfriend), knowing at the end of the day it's not because I'm insane or a bad person, but because my hormones are playing havoc.

## For immediate relief, try the following:

- Have a long hot bath with lavender oil and candles.
- Get a friend or boyfriend to rub your lower back.
- Take Evening Primrose Oil capsules to soothe the cramps.
- If you've got cramps, rub marjoram, lavender or camomile essential oils into your belly before going to sleep.
- Eat some of your favourite chocolate.
- Allow yourself a good cry and rent out a weepy movie.

# SEXUAL HEALTH

As soon as you become sexually active there are things you have to consider health-wise. An important test to have a year after the first time you have intercourse is a smear test – this is a straightforward test that detects any signs of cervical cancer. A swab is taken from inside the vagina and is sent off to a laboratory for testing – the results are usually back within six weeks. You can have this done at your GP's surgery or local family planning clinic, or you can go to a gynaecologist. We are currently advised to have a smear test once a year. I have one and also have a thorough test for all STDs (sexually transmitted diseases).

If you know you have had unprotected sex it is also important that you get tested for HIV. It is a simple blood test that, if done on the NHS, can take up to six weeks to get your results. The virus can take up to six months to be detected in the blood so it's advised two take two tests six months apart.

If you know you have had unsafe sex and are still having unprotected intercourse, it is only fair on the rest of the world that you get tested. You should consider your safety and others as soon as you become sexually active.

Even though STDs other than AIDS won't usually kill you, some of them if left untreated and undetected can cause infertility.

Over the page are some of the most common STDs, and their symptoms and treatment.

59

| STDs | Hepatitis B | Syphilis | Chlamydia |
|---|---|---|---|
| **What it is** | A virus resulting in liver damage | A bacterial disease that gets into the bloodstream causing sores and rashes | Bacterial infection in the genitals |
| **How you get it** | Any sexual activity and contact with all bodily fluids including saliva | All forms of sexual activity and possibly kissing as sores can appear on the mouth | Primarily through anal or vaginal sex, and possibly through oral sex |
| **How you prevent it** | A series of injections and use of protection during sex. Avoid intimate contact with someone who carries the virus | Barrier methods such as condoms but intimate contact should be avoided with an infected party | Condoms and spermicide while having sexual contact |
| **Symptoms** | Whilst some people experience no symptoms, the most common are rashes, nausea, vomiting, fatigue, body aches | If a sore appears it can become oozy and if untreated will develop into a rash | Itchy genitals, change in discharge, burning sensatino when urinating and possibly pain in the abdomen |
| **Treatment** | Hep B has its own vaccine but after contracting the virus, injections to help strengthen the immune system can also be administered | Antibiotics | Once diagnosed, infection is treated with antibiotics. However regular screenings for chlamydia can detect the infection early |
| **Long-term effects** | Untreated Hep B can lead to liver damage and death | Untreated syphilis leads to the breakdown of vital organs, brain damage and death | If untreated, it can damage urinary tract and reproductive organs leading to pelvic inflammatory disease (PID) and possible sterility |

| Genital Herpes | Genital Warts | Crabs | Gonorrhoea |
|---|---|---|---|
| Virus, producing blister-like itchy sores in the genitals | A common STD that can cause warts on the genitals and/or other areas of the body | Lice that feed off blood in the pubic area and also in hair and armpits | Bacterial infection of the genitals |
| Primarily mouth and genital sexual contact with someone with an active herpes sore | Any sexual activity or skin contact, most commonly through sexual intercourse | Skin-to-skin contact or sharing clothes with someone who has it | Any form of sexual penetration; oral, vaginal or anal |
| Always use condoms even when sores aren't visible | Barrier methods will help but are not 100% preventative as skin contact can still cause transmission | Avoid any close contact with an infected party | All sexual contact until infection is eradicated |
| Blister-like sores that can ooze and itch but generally clear within 7-14 days. Flu-like symptoms and difficulty urinating often precede an outbreak | Itchy warts appear in the genitals internally and externally. They can have different appearances such as hard, white or brown (external) lumps or soft and pink (internal) | Itching and specks of blood from bites. Crabs are visible on close inspection | Men suffer worse symptoms than women – pain when urinating and discharge from the penis. Women can get the same symptoms and swollen labia |
| Ointments, anaesthetic creams, baths and anti-viral medications can reduce the discomfort of an outbreak. Must sleep and eat well | The body's immune system can cure the virus. Otherwise topical medications can be used; alternatively, the warts can be burned, lasered or cut off | Shampoo treatment and washing | Antibiotics |
| A herpes sufferer will always have the disease, so controlling outbreaks is essential by washing regularly after treating infected area so virus is not spread to rest of body | Untreated warts can keep growing, possibly breaking and bleeding. There are links with cancer and a pap smear is the most reliable source of detection | If treated there are no long-term effects | Untreated it can result in pelvic inflammatory disease (PID) and sterility |

# WARNING CHLAMYDIA ALERT!

One STD that I want to highlight is Chlamydia. It is mentioned with the others in the chart but it has the highest rise of 140 per cent for young women aged 16-19 since 1995.

## HIV AND AIDS

Most STDs, if detected and treated properly, will not end up killing you. The exception to this is the human immuno-deficiency virus (HIV) and the disease it causes, AIDS (Acquired Immuno-deficiency Syndrome).

With the rise of HIV, we now all have a responsibility to protect ourselves and others when we are having sex. Condoms are the only way you can protect yourself from passing on or contracting HIV, and the condom needs to be worn properly. It's very easy when you are young and female to assume that you're not in a high-risk bracket for contracting the virus, but it's not true. You can get it from anyone at any time. When you make love you could be risking your life and those of others. I can't really emphasise enough how important it is to use condoms. Start now when you're young so you can get used to them.

One thing you can do if you've had unprotected sex is have a blood test that detects HIV antibodies. You should know, though, that the antibodies can be in your blood for up to six months without being detectable, so you should have another test six months after you had unprotected sex. If you have a long-term partner and you really don't want to carry on using condoms, you can both go and get tested for the virus. The risk you take here is that if your partner is unfaithful to you, and he doesn't use protection, you are again putting yourself at risk.

The virus can be passed on by blood, semen, vaginal fluid, bodily fluids and breast milk. It can't be passed on from casual contact, mucus, sweat, tears, vomit or saliva.

## PROTECTION

Also give sensible thought to preventing the risk of getting pregnant (if you don't want to be). Condoms are the only method to prevent both HIV and pregnancy. Make it a habit rather than an ongoing debate. Boys are very skilled at finding excuses against using them. I've heard everything from 'I don't feel anything, so I would just be doing it for you,' to 'They are so tight over my penis that I come immediately.' Don't believe a word of it. It is your RIGHT to use condoms, so stay with that and use them. Respect your body and choose not to let others make important choices for you. As young women, it is too common for us to not have enough faith in our own choices. Saying yes when we really want to say no, being bullied into doing things we don't want to do. Several of these broken promises to ourselves can lead to disappointment and unnecessary regrets that we have to live with (or die with!). Don't be bullied.

For sexual health and pregnancy issues, call The Family Planning Association who will put you in touch with your local family planning or sexual health clinics. These clinics can see anyone over 16 – and under 16s who are deemed competent to make their own choices – without informing their parents. The FPA's numbers and website are at the end of the book in the Sistah Support section. For abortion see also I'm A Survivor, p154.

Over the page are the most common forms of contraception, how they work and their advantages and disadvantages.

Your Health

| CONTRACEPTION METHOD | MALE CONDOM | FEMALE CONDOM | DIAPHRAGM | SPERMICIDE |
|---|---|---|---|---|
| **Effectiveness** | 88% | 90% | 90% if used with spermicide | 80% when used on its own. 88-90% when used with one of the barrier methods left. |
| **How it works** | A thin latex covering that the male wears. | A polyurethane sleeve that has rings on both ends. The female places it inside her vagina before sex. It blocks sperm, viruses and skin contact. | A soft rubber disk which you insert in your vagina before sex to fit over the cervix. It blocks sperm from entering the cervical opening. | A cream, jelly, foam or suppository that is squirted or inserted into the vagina. |
| **Advantages** | Provided free from some clinics and are easy to buy. Unlike other methods they protect from STDs. | It protects against STDs even better than the male condom. You can insert it before sex so it doesn't have to be interrupted. | You can put it in several hours before intercourse so it doesn't interrupt the mood. | Can give some protection against STDs, but a lot better if used with a condom. |
| **Disadvantages** | They can break or slip. Less effective than other methods if used on their own. Some guys complain that they can't feel as much. Can interrupt sex to put them on. | Can be quite difficult to use and has been known to squeak. | Can take a while before you get good at using it. It needs to be checked for holes and you have to leave it in for 8 hours after intercourse. Minimal effectiveness against STDs. | It can be really messy and it doesn't taste very nice. |

| BIRTH CONTROL PILL | DEPO-PROVERA | EMERGENCY CONTRACEPTION PILL OR 'MORNING AFTER' PILL |
|---|---|---|
| 97-100% when taken properly every day. | 99% | It is taken if you think you are pregnant and you don't want to be. Reduces the chance of pregnancy by about 75%. |
| A pill containing hormones that you take daily. The pill fools the body into thinking it is already pregnant. There are two forms and they all range in dosage. One form stops ovulation so that no egg is released. The other (which is slightly less effective) thickens the cervical mucus, making it hard for the sperm to swim into the Fallopian tubes to meet the egg. | An injection administered every 3 months. It disrupts the production of an egg and the menstrual cycle. | It must be taken no longer than 72 hours after unprotected sex. You take two pills 12 hours apart. |
| Extremely effective birth control. Can help regulate and make periods lighter and less painful. May reduce chances of ovarian cancer. | Highly effective against pregnancies and less of a hassle than taking the pill every day. | It is easy to use and is now available in some pharmacies, family planning clinics, sexual health clinics and some GPs. |
| You have to take it every day or it becomes less effective. Can cause side effects like nausea and mid-cycle bleeding (first 3 months), headaches, weight gain, bloating, breast tenderness, depression and reduced sexual desire. Doesn't prevent risks against STDs. Some pills may increase chances of breast cancer. | You have to have an injection every 3 months. Can take up to 18 months to resume normal ovulation. It is relatively new so there are no long-term studies on extended use. It doesn't protect against STDs. | It can make you feel very sick. Not reliable as contraception, the long-term effects of use unknown. Doesn't protect you from STDs. |

## THE BOTTOM LINE

- Periods can be a real downer. Experiment with different ways to ease your pain.
- Don't feel guilty for feeling a little bit grumpy or oversensitive once a month. Look at ways that can make your life easier, because you're going to be having them for a while yet.
- HIV can be avoided, but you need to protect yourself. Get used to using condoms now so they don't become a hassle further down the line.
- Take complete responsibility for protecting yourself because you're the one that's going to have to live with your decision.

# STRESS

It is now generally accepted – even by sceptical scientists – that stress and emotional strain do, in fact, affect our physical wellbeing. It's also been said that young people today worry more than ever before, and especially girls. Do you ever find yourself getting stressed out? Do you worry about different aspects of your life? Do the quick test below and see how much of a worry-wart you really are.

## WORRY

Below is a list of all the things you might worry about. Next to each one, write a number between 0 and 5, 0 meaning you don't worry about it at all and 5 being that you worry chronically about it. When you have finished, count up the numbers and give yourself a total score.

## The Stress Test

| | | | |
|---|---|---|---|
| Money | Peer pressure | Body issues | STDs |
| Weight | Pregnancy | Racism | Your mental health |
| The future | Friendships | Bullying | Your physical health |
| Family | Relationships | Drugs/drink/smoking | |
| Exam pressure | Trouble at school | Sex | |

## A score of 1-25 – 'Hey, man, I'm totally chilled.'

You seem to have a very laid-back attitude to life, which is great. Either challenges don't seem to rattle you very much or life hasn't dealt you a particularly difficult hand. Either way you are probably great to have around, bringing optimism and calmness to a situation. I hope you carry on riding that smooth wave of life.

## A score of 26-55 – 'It's starting to get a bit stressful around here.'

You're in middle ground here and, more often than not, you probably have a lot on your plate. Things can sometimes be hard for you to balance and prioritise as there is so much going on. Remember to go easy on yourself and slow down sometimes – life isn't worth all that worry and stress.

## A score of 56 and above – 'Aaaaaaaargh, I can't handle it.'

Oh, oh! life is definitely getting on top of you. You need to take some of the pressure off and learn how to not let everything get to you so much. You need to spend some time prioritising. Don't try and be too much of a superwoman – sometimes we just can't do it all. Figure out the main things that are making you worry and see if you can deal with them one at a time to try to ease the situation. Check out the guidelines opposite.

Go through your list again and look each point that you've got a 3 or above for. Think about why that particular thing is stressing you out so much. Is it just a feeling, or are there logical reasons for your worry. Write down all the reasons. Although we are often powerless about the situation itself, more often than not

## Take a look at the examples below:

### Getting pregnant:

My parents would kill me, I'm not ready, I can't decide whether to take the pill or not. (Claire, 14)

Here, instead of being worried, Claire could simply make sure she never has unprotected sex. She can decide to choose an effective birth control method from the chart on page 64, take control of her body and therefore lower the risk of getting pregnant.

### Friendships: ④

I'm starting a new school. I'm worried my old friends will forget me and that no one will like me. (Gaby, 13)

Gaby can make sure she makes an effort to stay in touch with her old friends. She can think back to when she made the friends she has now and remember how easy that was. She can understand that she can't control what might or might not happen in the future, so she could get on with enjoying the present moment.

I don't mean to miss the fact that some things are worrying – just that we also need to look at how we deal with situations, because, to some extent worrying and getting stressed out is a choice. Learn to breathe deeply, stay in the moment and come to terms with the fact that you can't control everything.

**WORK – STRESS BUSTERS!**

## Balance your time – realistically!
There are two ways of doing this. One way is to simply write a list of everything you have to do and cross off each thing as you do it. That way you can really see how much needs to be done – and there's nothing better than the feeling of crossing things off a list (or am I just a weirdo?).

The other way is to design a day-by-day diary chart, and to write under each day what you need to get done that day, then cross each thing off as you do it. If you don't manage to do something, move it down on to the next day.

## Prioritise – be honest about what's important
Sometimes we do all the easy, more enjoyable things first and keep putting off what really needs to be done. I can sit for hours in the morning going through all my emails (half of which are personal) and make phone calls when I really need to be getting on with work. Decide for yourself what needs to be done most urgently and then you can treat yourself later, doing something you enjoy more.

## Take breaks – don't burn yourself out.
I don't know about you, but I've got the concentration span of a goldfish. The best work you can do is when you completely focus for your limit and then take a well-deserved break. Have a hot bath, watch some telly, have a nice dinner. Then go back to it when you're fresh.

# GIVE IT TO ME STRAIGHT

 *How can I find out which types of food aren't good for me? I've heard that wheat isn't good for you. Is that true? (Michelle, 15)*

**We all have different body types** and food will affect us all differently. There are reliable ways to find this out, but they are usually very expensive. The best way is to listen to your body. Different foods will make you feel a different way. If you eat chocolate and you get a headache afterwards, that's a clear sign that it's not very good for your body type. Similarly, eating bread might leave you feeling bloated and lethargic. If you really want to discover which foods aren't good for you, you can do an elimination where you cut out, wheat, dairy, sugar and meat. When you start including them in your diet again you'll have a clearer indication of how they make you feel.

 *If I want to lose weight what is the best sort of exercise I can do? (Sarah, 17)*

**The best way to lose weight is to do cardiovascular exercises,** or exercise that get your heart pumping – anything like cycling, running, rowing or swimming will do. The best thing of all is to mix cardiovascular and muscle-toning and flexibility exercise, such as weights and sit-ups, with stretching exercises such as yoga and Pilates. Don't forget to do exercise that you enjoy or it will be a lot harder to keep it up.

*I've heard that yoga is really good for you, but there seem to be so many different types. Which type would you recommend? (Kelly, 18)*

**You're right, there are lots of types of yoga.** The best thing to do is try out a few. The main differences are that some are gentle and calming, and others are more high energy and challenging. It depends what you want from it. What you might want to do is to ask the teacher a little about the yoga they teach beforehand and sit in on couple of lessons. Often it's a case of finding the right teacher who can teach in a way that suits you. And remember, yoga isn't just about the body. It's also about calming the mind, your breathing and your general wellbeing.

 *I haven't had my period yet and I'm 17. Is this normal? (Diana, 17)*

**I wouldn't say that it's normal,** but it's not completely unheard of. The average age to start your periods is between 11 and 14, but some girls get them younger and some older. If you want to, see your GP about it and she can find out if you're eating correctly or enough, or if there is any extra stress going on in your life.

> " I find it really hard telling boys that I won't have sex with them unless they use a condom. I feel really pressurised when they give me all of their excuses about why they can't use them, and I always end up giving in. (Susannah, 17) "

Boys, boys, boys... They really are pros at getting out of using condoms, aren't they? I've heard every excuse you can imagine and I know how hard it can be sometimes to not be persuaded to let them have their own way. It really comes down to how much love and respect you have for yourself. It's your body and it's great that you are aware of wanting to use condoms in the first place. All the excuses the boys give you are rubbish, I can assure you of that. If you told them you weren't going to have sex unless they used one, I can guarantee they would still want to have sex with you. Please don't give in any more because the more you do the harder it will be to get into the habit of using them. And you must use them for protection.

> " I really hate having smear tests and the last time I went to get one, the nurse couldn't do it because I was too tense. He ended up putting this cold metal thing inside me to try and open me up and it just made me more tense. I know it's really important to have them regularly but how can I stop this happening again? (Gemma, 17) "

I think it's a case of finding the right nurse. Ask your friends if they have been to one that they feel comfortable with. If your nurse was male, try a female instead. Also, there are different sizes of instrument, so go ahead and ask for a smaller one. Well done for going to have one, though, because it is important that you have them regularly.

I hope this chapter has helped encourage you to have an even healthier relationship with your precious body. Look after it, respect it and take control of it. We often don't realise how great it feels to be healthy until we get unhealthy. Remember what it feels like even when you've got a cold – not very nice! So make sure you feel healthy all of the time. Don't take your health for granted just because you're young. Be good to your body now and you'll reap the rewards now and when you get older.

Your Health

# LET'S TALK ABOUT SEX

This chapter is about more than just sex. It also explores your relationship with your own sexuality. Sexuality affects everything in life – how you express yourself, your creativity and the way you communicate with people. It's invisible but you can't miss it. Women's sexuality is one of the most powerful forces in the world. Just look around you. It's everywhere – in the adverts and films we see and the music we listen to. Even though it's only recently that television has become so raunchy and pop videos have bordered on soft porn, female sexuality has been a force to be reckoned with for hundreds of years. Unfortunately, with any powerful force comes extreme fear and the need for some people to want to control it, manipulate it and abuse it. This chapter explores the power and beauty of our sexuality, what we want from lovers and how to avoid using our sexuality as a secret weapon.

# OUTSIDE INFLUENCES

Let's start by looking at some of the ways your sexuality and how you view sex has been influenced by the outside world.

## Once upon a time...

Most of us start exploring our bodies and sexuality from a very young age. There are lots of different ways of doing this – playing with your vagina and enjoying the feeling, playing kiss chase at school, playing games such as doctors and nurses with friends. Most girls I've talked to remember one or more of these instances. Don't feel weird about being curious as a child – most of us have explored our bodies at that age.

When we are children and developing our sexual awareness, we can be very impressionable to outside influences. (Sorry, parents, but I'm afraid you're involved in this!) One of your earliest influences is your parents. How they are with their sexuality will very much influence the way you feel about your own. If you were shown disapproval around your sexuality when you were a young child, you may well have grown up carrying these beliefs of guilt and shame into your adult life. The disapproval might have taken any form, from telling you off for playing with your genitals to looking embarrassed and awkward when you asked about sex and how you were born. There are some who feel open and positive about sex, answer all of their child's questions honestly from a young age and never tell them off for exploring or touching themselves, but not too many.

Here are some girls' views of how their sexual feelings were influenced by their parents.

> 66 I remember my mum always being really overprotective towards me. She was always going on about not trusting strangers, and she'd make me wear a full swimming costume on the beach when I was a toddler. She also told me not to trust boys because they're only after one thing. I'm definitely paranoid that boys are always only thinking about sex and getting me into bed. (Catherine, 15) 99

> 66 My mum once caught a [boy] friend and me when I was about eight, touching each other's private parts. She went mad and banned me inviting him over to the house ever again. I really thought I'd done something awful, and as she never talked to me about it, I thought touching someone else was a really bad thing. Obviously, I know now, that it's not, but when I'm getting off with someone, I still feel like I'm doing something a bit naughty! (Jessica, 16) 99

Do either of these stories ring any bells with you? Have they triggered off any thoughts about how your parents' attitudes to sex have influenced you? You might want to write something down here. ✒

## THE OLD VERSUS THE NEW

Another big influence on the way we feel about sex is society, which is torn between old-school and new beliefs.

Most old-school beliefs are deeply rooted in religion. You don't have to be a religious person or be brought up by religious parents to be influenced by this. The fact is that religion plays a huge part in shaping most people's attitudes to all aspects of life, especially sex and sexuality.

Unfortunately, many ancient religious texts have been distorted by human egos and fear (mostly male!), which have replaced common sense with teachings that our instinct for sex is something to be ashamed of, not talked about and only to be performed with a husband or wife. Religion has tried to put a lid on sex to the point of covering women in black cloth to help men avoid the temptation of lust. All this control and suppression has caused a huge backlash, which is at its most obvious in the pornography industry. Pornography and prostitution are two of the largest industries in the world. You only have to log on to the internet to see that.

Today, we live in a society that as well as having these 'old-school' beliefs of sex being naughty and sinful, has a new attitude born out of the media and entertainment business, in which images of sex are becoming more and more common and extreme. You can't avoid turning on the television without seeing sex-related programmes. I think for the most part, it's pretty healthy. Society is showing us that we're ready to be more open about sex, and I have no complaints about that. It's a fact that countries like Norway, Germany and Holland, which have a much more relaxed and open attitude towards sex, have lower teenage pregnancy rates and lower rape statistics. In fact, Britain has the highest teenage pregnancy rates in Western Europe.

We all know that 'sex sells', but where I believe the media's influence gets unhealthy and out of balance is when girls and women feel pressured into being sexy in order to sell themselves in their everyday lives. We already live in a world where appearance is everything. And this doesn't just apply to people – animals have to attract to survive. But, as we saw in Bod-ease (p38-51) these images of sexiness we're bombarded with are so much to do with a 'type'. A type of woman that most of us will never be able to be. We aren't shown that sexiness is about the individual, that it's something we all have. Instead, we're told that we have to be tall, skinny and big-breasted and that we should all aspire to fit in with the media's absurdly limited idea of what is 'sexy'.

Let's Talk About Sex

# IT'S YOUR DECISION

As a strong, young woman, you have to decide for yourself how much of this 'sex-sells' culture you want to buy into. You need to find a balance, and this can be difficult. It's hard not to get sucked in; after all, we're hugely influenced by the messages that our society gives us. Nevertheless, I'm encouraging you to stand back and take an objective look at both what's dictated to you by society and what you really feel yourself. If you think big boobs are everything and women licking their lips seductively are something you want to adhere to, then don't give yourself a hard time, at least you're being honest. If, however, you're the type of girl that isn't seduced by images in advertising and won't succumb to this 'sex-sells' business, then good on you, girl. Also, it's time we let go of the old views I mentioned earlier and realise that our sexuality is something to be celebrated and enjoyed. Sexiness is about being true to your individuality. Women who know who they are and what they want often come across as the sexiest of the lot, no matter what their vital statistics are.

## BAD EXPERIENCES

Unfortunately, one of things that can influence our sexuality the most is bad past experiences. These can be anything from being told we were rubbish in bed to being abused. (See I'm a Survivor p156) Our first experiences with sex can have a huge impact well into adulthood. My first serious boyfriend used to get upset with me when I didn't have an orgasm. He would tell me my vagina and clitoris were insensitive and he found it hard being with someone who he couldn't make come. His words had a huge impact on me, and I believed everything he said. I thought I wasn't as sensual as other girls and that if I didn't come my boyfriend would leave me. So it always became this huge pressure, and because I was thinking about it all so much it would make sex harder to enjoy. It wasn't until I found a lover I could trust and be relaxed with that I realised what this boy had said was untrue and I let go of the past.

Have you had any bad experiences? Maybe when you were a kid and you were experimenting with other kids? It might have gone too far, or you might have done something that didn't feel quite right. Do you think this experience is still affecting you today? If you think it is, spend some time thinking about it, and maybe even take some time writing it down. ✒️➤

Answer this question:

## How has [your experience] affected the way I feel about sex today?

Then go back to your answer and complete these three statements:

Once you get your feelings about this experience more out in the open, you may be able to begin to let go of it, and see that even though it might have been really painful or humiliating at the time, it doesn't mean things are always going to be like that from now on.

If you need to speak to someone further, please refer to the numbers in Sistah Support (pp208-221).

Understanding your own sexuality and being comfortable with it is very much a part of becoming a woman. Here are two questions to help you to understand your relationship with your own sexuality.

## Would you consider yourself a sexual person?

The way we hold ourselves and the way we look is a good indication of how we feel about our sexuality. Do you feel comfortable in your skin, and expressing yourself with your body? Or do you tend to hide yourself with baggy clothes and cover your face with your hair? Do you feel comfortable being seen dancing? Some of us may feel that showing others our sexuality is dangerous, so we learn to suppress it. We might have been brought up to think it's something to be ashamed of, so we hide it. Or you might feel proud of your sexuality and be confident about expressing that part of you. Maybe people have told you you're flirtatious. I've met women that seem to flirt with absolutely anyone, even people of the same sex. There comes a balance that's hard to define of whether you're sexually confident, or you're using your sexuality to get what you want.

## Are you aware of your sexuality and the effect it has on others?

Are you aware of your sexuality and do you notice how others react to it when they are around you? Do you lack confidence and feel that your sexuality falls flat on people you flirt with or fancy? Or maybe you're someone who's very aware of capturing people's attention when you walk into a room or flirt. You might know that by being sexual you'll receive attention from others, especially of the opposite sex. You might be completely in control of mesmerising people when you turn on your sexual power. There's a balance of being comfortable with your sexuality and proud of it but not using it to control those around you. Hopefully from reading this chapter you'll start to see the difference.

Let's Talk About Sex

# RIDDING YOURSELF OF SHAME

As you can see, there are lots of different ways our feelings towards sex and sexuality can be influenced. If you know you sometimes feel that sex and your sexuality is something to be ashamed of, here are a few things to keep in mind:

- Firstly, acknowledge that it's okay to really enjoy sex. Unlike most animals, women have an organ that is there purely there for their sexual pleasure: the clitoris. No other part of the human body has the sole function of giving pleasure. I don't think it's a coincidence that we've been designed like this – I think we've always been meant to enjoy sex.
- Remember, we all have different sexual desires and that what may seem completely normal to one person could seem strange or perverse to another. The only thing we need to know is that we mustn't harm others through sex. We shouldn't take advantage of others, or ever treat them disrespectfully.
- We've been told for centuries that sex is sinful. But just because sex is pleasurable and physical, it doesn't mean it's dirty or naughty. We often feel that pleasure is bad, but as long as we're not addicted to it, it can be an essential part of life.

# BEING SEXY AND LOVING

Understanding your sexuality and being comfortable with it is very much a part of being a woman.

- **Let's start with your appearance.** This is a great gauge on your outer sexiness. It doesn't mean we all wear the same things when we feel sexy, but we wear things we feel good in. If you're not sexually confident, try wearing clothes that are slightly more sexy than normal. I never usually wear high heels, but a few months ago I bought myself some very naughty, sexy high heels and have started wearing them out. At first it felt really weird and un-me, but after a few goes I've come to love wearing them and every time I do, I feel very sexy and womanly. Try it out for yourself with clothes that make you feel sexy. It may seem silly, but I guarantee it can make a huge difference to the way you feel.
- **Be sexy for someone in particular.** (This one can be great fun!) Go out on a hot date and get dressed up to the nines, knowing you're rocking his world. Maybe you won't wear underwear or paint your nails a shocking red. Whatever it is that makes you feel sexy, go for it, girl, and give your guy a night to remember!
- **Be sexy for yourself.** You can be sexy without flaunting it in people's faces. You don't have to flirt with guys to feel confident with your sexuality. There is a difference. Sometimes you don't want to be sexual for anyone but yourself; you're not looking for the attention of other people. There's nothing wrong with wanting attention and to feel good about yourself, so don't feel guilty if you do enjoy the wolf-whistles.

# IF YOU'VE GOT IT, FLAUNT IT?

As young women, it's easy to be seduced by the newfound power of our sexuality. Power is seductive. Why do you think so many of us attach so much importance to the way we look? Unfortunately, like anything that's linked to power, with it comes abuse and manipulation. A huge amount of people can't seem to avoid abusing the power that they have. You see it everywhere – policemen who take the law into their own hands, parents bossing their children, wealthy people trying to control everyone in their lives – and right at the top of the list is sexuality, and female sexuality, in particular. If we know it's a sure thing that our sexuality will bring us what we want – attention, men and power – who can blame us for using it?

But I think that if we use our sexuality as a secret weapon, we're underestimating our real feminine power. How do you use your sexuality? Do you start flicking your hair every time a boy enters the room? Do you wear short skirts when you're going for an interview? Are you the kind of girl that flirts at every given opportunity? If any of the above are true, it may be you're using your sexuality to manipulate situations to get what you want. The ironic thing is there are millions of books around, teaching women how to do just that – how to get the man they want, how to flirt and how to use their sexuality to their own advantage. Yes, it's important that we know how to be sexy and enjoy our sexuality, but not so we can get what we want. We don't have to use our sexuality to do that. We are so much more than just 'being sexy' and even though we've so often been told the exact opposite, it's time we realised the truth. We have brilliant minds, we have our humour, our courage and our openness. As women we have so many gifts that we don't need to manipulate anyone to get what we want. If we're being real when we're in relationships with others, we know that the love we receive from them is based on more than just our ability to be sexy, and therefore might last longer than the time it takes him to come.

**Be yourself and be comfortable with that. (Maybe even enjoy it!) That's when you're the sexiest you can possibly be.**

Girls and women who rely on their sexuality to get by have a hard wake-up call when they look in the mirror one day and realise that they're not as young and beautiful as they once were. They might become obsessed with staying young-looking, invest in plastic surgery and buy every anti-wrinkle cream available, but the inevitable is going to happen – ladies, we get old. Of course, old women are beautiful too, but let's face it, we're living in a society that is youth-obsessed. So think about that while you're young. You don't want to put everything into the way you look because it's not going to last for ever. Be loved and appreciated for you, not your body.

Let's Talk About Sex

# BEING GAY/BISEXUAL/TRANSSEXUAL

Here's a good place to apologise for relating everything to boys. I hope it doesn't put you off and it certainly doesn't mean I've forgotten the sisters that are into girls, not boys. I'm not really an authority on speaking about being gay or bisexual, so I've asked an older friend, Lisa, who is gay, to help out and answer the following questions.

## How do I know if I am a lesbian?

It isn't always completely clear (even though sometimes it is), but deciding whether you are a lesbian is a decision you have to reach yourself. It is important that you don't label yourself too early. Give yourself time. If you are still young, your emotions and feelings are still developing. When the time is right, you will know. You may feel you are attracted to other women, and maybe feel you don't seem to fit in as well with your other girl friends. When they are checking out other guys around, you might be thinking more about other girls. All this can be confusing. Just give it time and your sexuality will develop as you get older and start to experiment.

## When can I know for sure?

Different people discover at different times, and even then it's not fixed. Sometimes you can spend a few years with a woman and then decide that being with a man is what you want to do, and then back again. I always knew that I was gay from when I was 8 or 9, but my girlfriend only found out after spending 15 years in committed heterosexual relationships.

## Do you think it's important to tell close friends and family?

Very, as long as you are ready. You can't be yourself if those closest to you don't know how you really are — you will always be pretending to be something you're not in order to keep them happy, and it usually turns out that they want you to be happy, whoever you are.

## If you're still at school, should you tell people?

If you have a friend you can trust, then you should think about confiding in them. However, I think it's important to protect yourself until you're completely ready to 'tell the world' how you feel. When you have left school, people change quite considerably because there is less pressure to 'conform', which makes them less judgmental.

## Do you think our society is becoming more accepting of gay women?

Definitely. Many people in the entertainment business have started to be more open about being gay, and our favourite TV soaps are getting much braver at tackling the subject. We've even had some Big Brother winners who are openly gay.

## How do you deal with prejudices?

The first step is to feel entirely comfortable with the way you are. There is nothing at all different about being gay. If I don't judge others, then I presume they won't judge me. If they do, I let it wash over me and feel sorry that their lives are so restrictive. I certainly don't confront them with it, I protect myself and walk away.

## THE BOTTOM LINE

- The way we feel about sex and our sexuality depends partly on external influences such as parents, religion, the media and bad past experiences.
- Most of us feel shame and guilt around sex. We need to learn to let go of those feelings. Sex is great and sex is healthy. Learn to love and enjoy it.
- Enjoy being sexy, but don't use it as a secret weapon. Know that you have other things to offer.
- If you're gay, accept and love yourself even if you feel ostracised by others. Find support and other people that have been through what you're going through. If you feel ready, tell your family about it. They need to love you for yourself.

Let's Talk About Sex

# KNOWING WHEN YOU'RE READY

How do you know when you're ready to become sexually active? We know that sex isn't legal till we're 16. We're all different and what's right for one of us might not be for another. So we have to learn to trust ourselves and know that we're the ones who know best whether we're ready or not. It's not a decision your boyfriend can make, or your friends, who might have started having sex already. Nor should it be up to your parents, who will be worried about you getting hurt or pregnant. In From Girl to Woman (p26) I talk about asking yourself questions when you're not sure what to do or what you want. Do it now. When we develop this relationship with ourselves and get to know ourselves better, we're in a better position to make the right choice at the right time.

# LOSING YOUR VIRGINITY

This is a scene that most of us will experience (only once, mind you) – the old losing your virginity syndrome. From talking to other girls I believe that a lot of us rush into this one. Wham bam, it's gone for ever, never to be seen again. This can be for several different reasons – pressure from the boy, curiosity or simply wanting to fit in with the rest of your peers. Now this isn't where I get my long pointy finger out and start wagging it at you. Instead, it's where I ask you to take responsibility and ask yourself a few questions before you take the plunge. When we rush into things we often end up making mistakes.

So, if you can, slow down enough to ask yourself the following:

**ARE YOU READY TO LOSE YOUR VIRGINITY?**

Are you in a relationship?

How long for?

How well do you know them?

How much do you like this person?

Would they wait for you?

How much pressure do they put on you?

Are your friends sexually active? Do you ever feel left out?

How far have you gone with someone before?

Do you enjoy being physical with someone – how much do you enjoy it?

Do you know what you enjoy sexually (through masturbation) – do you reach orgasm?

What would you use for protection against pregnancy and STDs?

Where would you do it?

Would it be somewhere dodgy – like a public place – or have you got anywhere where you could you take time over it?

Why do you want to do it now?

Why with this person?

How do you think you'd feel afterwards?

I don't believe in bringing age into it too much. We've all had different life experiences. These questions are really to help you see clearly if you're ready and really want to lose your virginity. If you're someone who isn't in a relationship but still wants to start having sex out of curiosity or desire, I'm not going to tell you that's a bad thing and you should wait. Just please remember to use a condom and make sure the situation is safe, emotionally and physically.

Just as some girls feel bad for having lost their virginity, there are many others who feel bad for not having sex. It's a very personal choice and one that others don't have the right to judge either way. So if you want to stay a virgin you stick to your guns, girlfriend!

# FRIGID – OR JUST PICKY?

Guys know they can accuse you of being frigid just because you refuse to go the whole way with them. Don't let this word affect you – boys have been trying it out for years. If you're with someone who threatens to leave if you don't have sex with him, then maybe you should reassess how he really feels about you. If he really cared about you and respected your boundaries he wouldn't threaten you with abandonment. If he leaves you, you know he was only there for sex, not because he loved you. You can't judge a guy too harshly for really wanting to have sex – his late teens are when he's peaking sexually and he's got a huge amount of testosterone pumping round his body – but at the same time, you should never go against your own morals just because they don't fit in with someone else's. As girls, we are often overly keen to please and feel we have to do things to get people to like us. Many girls have sex with guys as a way of keeping them.

Remember, too, that sexual intercourse isn't the only thing you can do with your partner. You can have loads of fun and pleasure from kissing and touching each other. In fact, discovering and experimenting with foreplay is a fundamental part of becoming a good lover.

# SLUT, SLAPPER, HO, WHORE, EASY, LOOSE

I feel very strongly about any derogatory words that are used to make girls feel bad about the number of sexual partners they have. Girls still get stick if they want to have several lovers. They get called names and are judged harshly for their actions. It's the old cliché that guys pat each other on the back and get called studs if they sleep with lots of girls, but when we sleep with lots of guys we're called sluts. We should be allowed to have as many lovers as we want, without having to deal with rude comments from people. Make sure you never call other girls names like this, because if you do you're contributing to keeping this sexist screwed-up view alive.

If you're someone who has been called these names in the past, then I hope you know that you're not any of those things. People often call someone a slut because they're jealous or they feel threatened. When I was at school I was friends with all the boys and didn't pay much attention to the girls. The girls couldn't stand this and they use to call me names and spread rumours that I was sleeping with all the boys. It wasn't true. I was never physical with any of them, but the girls were jealous of me. See Da Sistahs, p117.

Choose not to buy into other people's ignorance and meanness. Stick to what feels right for you!

# PROTECTING YOURSELF

However many partners you choose, it's vital that you look after yourself, both physically and emotionally. You can do this by looking at your motives for being physical with someone. I've used some girls' experiences below to highlight and to show you how to protect yourself from any harm or future regrets.

 I was desperate for attention and love and knew that I could get it by having sex with different boys. I regret that now because they didn't fully honour and respect me; they only wanted me for sex. (Gemma, 19)

I've heard Gemma's experience repeated by many different girls. In the past, I've also had sex with guys because I wanted male attention and love. I kidded myself that in the time we were being physically intimate, I was important to this other person. It might sound blunt, but some boys' motivations are very clear – they want to get laid. If it means they have to lie to get what they want, they probably will. With this in mind, be aware of his motives as well as your own. You might be all he's thinking about while you're being physical, but it won't be long before it's over and if sex was all he was after, his attention will soon turn elsewhere. Giving a guy your body in order to receive love won't fulfil you in the long run. You deserve more than that. You deserve to make love to a guy who truly is into you, and not just while you're in bed.

I had lots of different lovers because I wanted to try everything as quickly as possible. I was often called a 'slag' by girls more than boys. Looking back now, I don't care about those people who called me names, but I wish I hadn't hurt so many boys by always being unfaithful to them. (Louise, 18) "

Sometimes we can be curious and want to devour all of life's pleasures as quickly as possible. You might be someone who's got a high sex drive. (Girls have them just as much as boys.) That's fine – you shouldn't judge yourself for that and neither should anyone else. Be aware, though, of how you're affecting others with your behaviour. If you know you're not going to be faithful, your partners deserve to know that. Even though I've said that boys are gagging for it, they also have feelings and the need to be loved and appreciated. You need to take these feelings into account and let them know where they stand from the start.

 I was always promiscuous when I was younger and I had a great time. Unfortunately, though, I got genital herpes, which was from not using protection and ultimately not caring about myself enough. I've had to live with that ever since. (Natalie, 26) "

Unfortunately, Natalie's story is all too common. We concentrate on not getting pregnant but forget about all the STDs we can get. Once you get something like herpes you have it for life, and you have the responsibility of telling every single partner you ever have about it because you can very easily pass it on to them (it's super-contagious). People are often embarrassed about telling a new partner something like this, but you owe it to anyone you sleep with to be honest. The reason you got it in the first place was probably because someone wasn't honest with you.

When you have sex with someone, you're, literally and metaphorically, letting a part of them in. You need to be aware of this with the partners you choose and also about your motivations for sleeping with them. You are sharing and giving someone an extremely precious, intimate part of yourself. As girls and women we often hold on to some of our sexual partners' energy for life. We have let them inside us.

 # THE BOTTOM LINE

- Before you have sex, figure out if you're ready for it. Don't do it just because others are, or someone else wants you to.
- If you're thinking about losing your virginity, slow down enough to ask yourself some questions.
- Don't let boys bully you into things by calling you frigid. There's nothing wrong with not wanting to go any further with someone.
- If you want to stay a virgin don't feel pressured into it. Stick to your guns.
- Don't call other girls names like slut, and be sure to ignore people if they do it to you.
- Protect yourself emotionally and physically. Use condoms and check your motivations for having sex.
- Be choosy, because your sexual partners can have a lifetime effect on you.

Let's Talk About Sex

# BACK TO BASICS

## Okay, ladies, now for the fun stuff. Let's get back to basics.

Discovering our sexual wants and needs usually starts with exploring our vaginas. Some of you may never have done this. Don't worry – there's no time like the present. Some women live their whole lives without ever looking at their vaginas in close detail. It's just a thing that lives down there, separate from the rest of us. Does that sound familiar?

If you're someone who hasn't looked at your vagina, why not have a go now? Go to your bedroom or an area of the house where you know you won't be disturbed. Take off your clothes and get in a comfortable position. Place a smallish mirror in between your legs, maybe backed up against a pillow. Prop up your back so you're angled comfortably and have a full view of your vagina. Then go for it. Explore every nook and cranny, inside and out. Probe gently, pull apart and look under. Change positions and get views from different angles. As girls we are used to scrutinising our bodies, so why leave out such an important part? Notice how you feel about looking at your vagina. Do you feel guilty, naughty, sexy or pleasantly surprised? If you feel that you can't look, that's okay. Be gentle with yourself and maybe start slowly, have a peek and then leave it completely till your ready to have another look.

The next step of exploration is touch, otherwise known as masturbation, frigging or jostling. Not the nicest words to describe giving yourself sexual pleasure. There's often a stigma surrounding masturbation, especially when girls do it. Even though this stigma still very much exists, I do believe we're slowly starting to approach a more accepting attitude towards this expression of our human nature. As strong women of the future, let's get rid of this negative misconception right now! Masturbation is good! It's healthy and you can do it as much as you want. It's an essential part of our journey into sexual bliss. How can we expect our lovers to know how to touch us if we don't know ourselves?

When you're ready, make a night of it. A good way to start is to take a long hot bath, with lots of nice smelly things in it. Wrap yourself up in your fluffiest, largest towel and find somewhere comfortable to lie down. When you're dry, massage cream or oil into different parts of your body. Take time to really relax. If you like, put on some sexy music and lie down on the bed. If you're someone who likes fantasising, close your eyes and think of your sexiest fantasy. Start slowly, caressing your breasts, circling your nipples. Wander slowly down to your thighs; gently squeeze them, stroking around your vagina. Try different speeds and pressures, rubbing, caressing, stroking and squeezing. Don't let a part go untouched, in between your buttocks, your anus, all over your clitoris.

Be patient. Try things you wouldn't think of normally. Change positions on the bed; go on all fours then on your front. If you find something that feels great, stay there for a while soaking it in. Feel yourself getting hotter and hotter and your breath changing. Enjoy yourself, your freedom; love your touch and relish the fact that you're pleasing yourself. No one can teach you how to do it, you have to discover yourself. Take responsibility for pleasuring yourself. If the first time you try it out nothing much happens, and the earth doesn't move, that's okay. Be patient with it. Our bodies are all different and the most important thing is not to worry. Worry and pressure on yourself may make it harder for you to enjoy sexual pleasure, as you won't be fully relaxed.

If you're inexperienced in the lovemaking department, don't fear. Luckily for you, I remember very clearly not knowing what on earth I was meant to do with a penis. I'd beg older girlfriends to tell me and even though I was shown a few good examples on carrots, no one really ever gave it to me straight. I wanted details. I wanted step by step diagrams with fully comprehensive instructions. Once you know what to do, you kind of assume everyone knows the basics, forgetting that you too were once completely unaware of a penis's desires. So with true empathy and sisterhood I give you the following information.

A quick tip before I give you some basics on how to pleasure a guy is that there are two types of penis: circumcised and uncircumcised. So don't get shocked if you see one penis that looks completely different from another one. A circumcised penis has had the foreskin taken away so you can see the head of the penis clearly and there's no extra skin. Usually, you'll grow to have a preference, and both will require slightly different handling.

## HAND JOB, TOSSING OFF, JOSTLING

Unless the guy you're with is particularly into pain, an important thing to remember is to get rid of the rings. It can be really helpful if your boyfriend is confident enough to show you how he handles his tool. Some boys prefer fast and furious, others will be more turned on by slow and sensual caressing. Frankly, most boys in my experience like a bit of both. The really sensitive part of the penis is around the dome at the head. There are hardly any sexual nerve endings along the shaft, but the testicles (balls) will probably be very sensitive (or even ticklish! Careful!). Boys' preferences for hand jobs are as varied as the penises themselves. Once again, communication is the key. An unashamed sexual dialogue is the fastest and surest way to satisfy each other's every need.

## BLOW JOB, SUCKING OFF, GIVING HEAD, GOING DOWN

A good way to start is to lick the penis with as much of your tongue as you can, then put it in your mouth and start sucking. If you use your hand as well, as you do when you're giving him a hand job, it's a sure winner. Experiment. You can't really go that wrong (as long as there's not too much teeth action). And you need lots of variation – most repeated actions become unfeelable after more than 30 seconds. A lot of pleasure is based on temperature changes, and wet and dry.

I know you've probably been told this in millions of girlie mags, but I'm going to say it again. Unfortunately, most of us won't give the perfect blow- or hand-job the first time; we learn by trial and error. As long as the error isn't too life-threatening (i.e. no penis gets shredded) then a guy is going to be pretty satisfied. Trust yourself enough to go with it. If you're enjoying yourself, your partner is going to sense that and it's a guaranteed turn-on.

Let's Talk About Sex

# TURN IT ON!

Okay, I've given you a few techniques, now here are some tips on pleasuring your guy in other tantalising ways:

- **Spend ages teasing him** by kissing his whole body gently and then more passionately. Give some extra attention to his erogenous zones (other than the obvious one – his penis) and if you don't know where they are yet, listen carefully to his breath for some vital clues.
- **Pounce on him** when he least expects it. Be the one to make the first move. Show him who's boss.
- **Tantalise him** when you're out in public, but subtly so he's the only one that knows. A soft whisper in his ear or a slight glimpse of your thigh.
- **Nibble at his neck** for a while – this drives most guys crazy. But don't leave a mark. Love bites are seriously un-classy.
- **Turn it into a game.** Play strip poker with him and take your clothes off one piece at a time.

These tips are really a bit of fun to try out. At the end of the day, all you really need to know is that the biggest turn on is letting your partner know how much you fancy him. Just show him how much you're into him (and his body) and you'll have him lapping at your feet for more.

## TALKING DIRTY

Having a fulfilling sex life has a lot to do with letting your partner know what you want. We all like different things to turn us on, and without a bit of guidance our partners won't necessarily know what these things are. If you feel particularly shy about being sexually verbal with your partner, then a few hints through your body language will usually put the message across. Make a few more mmm sounds when he's touching you in the right way and guide his hand to the places you want him to touch. If he's ignorant of your hints then you could suggest to him that you take it in turns to show each other how you like to be touched. You could even go one step further and masturbate for each other. Watching is always a great way to learn (and who knows, you may even like it!).

## SEXUAL SATISFACTION

We hear about the female orgasm a lot more now than our fore-sistahs ever did. Pick up any magazine and there'll be an article promising you bigger and better orgasms. Well, that's all well and good, but what if you haven't even got to the stage where you can have orgasms at all (even on your own)? If you're reading this, then you're probably at the age where if you come with your partner, you're in the minority. However, I've also heard of girls being able to reach orgasm as young as eight. Whichever category you fall into, there is no normal age at which you can have an orgasm. Being able to have orgasms has a lot to do with your emotional state. That's why we usually first have orgasms on our own while we're masturbating, because there's no pressure to perform or please anyone.

**FAKING IT**

I asked some girls why they fake having orgasms.

If I'm not really enjoying myself and want it to end, I know that it's a great way to do just that. (Lizzie, 17)

I've faked orgasms to avoid the Spanish Inquisition with my boyfriend as to why I haven't come. (Sam, 18)

My boyfriend hates it when I don't come, so sometimes I fake it to make him feel better. (Jennifer, 16)

Very few girls have told me they've never faked an orgasm, but hopefully we're not faking them every time we make love. If we are then we'll never find out how to truly have one with our partner. If you find yourself regularly faking orgasms, try talking to your partner more openly about what you want so that in the future your orgasms will be for real.

## THE BOTTOM LINE

- Explore yourself physically, on your own and with a partner. Find out what makes you go wild.
- Get into being sexy – build your sexual confidence and love it.
- Trial and error. If you're worried about how to please a guy, know that just enjoying yourself and showing him that you're into him is usually more than enough.
- Communicate with your partner about your needs and let him know how you like to be touched.
- Having an orgasm is very much a state of mind. Make sure you're relaxed and don't feel pressurised to come by yourself or with him or it'll be even harder.
- Explore your erogenous zones. You might have some where you least expect. Your biggest erogenous zone is your mind.
- We've all faked it, but don't make a habit of it.

Let's Talk About Sex

> **❝** I love wearing sexy clothes but other girls always call me a slut and boys seem to only want one thing from me. Is it wrong to wear sexy things? Is it true that I'm sending off the message that I'm a slut and that all I want is sex? (Natalie, 17) **❞**

**There's nothing wrong with wearing sexy clothes,** but there are certain consequences (as you've discovered) that come with that, like immature people putting a label on you. It's sad but people (especially when they're young) often take any opportunity to be cruel to someone. They do it to protect themselves from being the one that is being bullied. You sound like you are expressing yourself and you happen to be a sexy chick. Other people might dress all in black and be into heavy metal. One thing I would say, though, is be aware that the way you dress will cause more boys to look at you and some of these boys might not just call you names. Always keep yourself safe and in public, especially at night, don't ever go out on your own.

> **❝** I've been having sex for over a year and I've had three partners. But I've never enjoyed it and in fact most of the time it really hurts. When I masturbate I get really wet but with a partner my vagina always stays dry. What am I doing wrong? (Alex, 16) **❞**

**It can be quite common to tense up** when you're making love, especially if it's still a relatively new experience. If you are stressed every time you're making love it's more than likely that it's not going to be an enjoyable experience, and that's why you're staying dry. One thing I would suggest is that the next time you are being intimate with someone try using some lubrication. Go really slowly and don't panic if you're not getting wet straight away. Also, saliva is a great lubrication. Ask your boyfriend to give you oral sex – you'll definitely get wet then. Relax into it and if it hurts make sure you stop or it will just get more painful.

> **❝** I always wear really baggy clothes and people call me a tomboy because I don't wear make-up. I've never had a boyfriend before or even kissed a boy. Sometimes I think I must be a lesbian because I don't really care about boys and sex but I don't fancy girls either, so it's confusing. Am I just weird? (Louise, 15) **❞**

**You are not weird,** you're still 15 and some people don't become sexually active until a lot later in life. What is important is that you don't push yourself into a situation just to fit in. It also doesn't necessarily mean that you are a lesbian – you may just not have discovered your sexual identity yet. Carry on trusting that you will at some point in your life, but there is no rush to be sexually active now.

I gave a guy my first blow job the other day and I heard through a friend that he's told everyone that it was really bad. I feel so embarrassed and I don't ever want to do it again. How can I know what to do? (Karen, 16) **"**

**That must have been difficult** but what might have felt bad to one guy might feel great to another. He also might have said it to show off or because he felt embarrassed. One thing to remember when you're giving a blow job is to enjoy yourself; it's by far the sexiest and most important ingredient. Experiment and try different things, use your hand and your saliva. Ask him what he likes, and don't forget to try and have a good time, because he'll know. Also remember that he might not have even said it and your friend has got her information wrong.

Well, my lovelies, you've made it to the end of another chapter. Hope you enjoyed it and are finishing it with more of a sense of your sexual wants and desires. Sex and sexuality is something to celebrate and enjoy; don't be ashamed of that part of yourself. SEX IS GOOD. Do protect yourself, though, because we girls often have sex for the wrong reasons and this can affect us later on in life. Never use it to hurt or control others. Know that you don't need to do that. You are more than that.

If you've been hurt in the past and it still affects you today, get help (see I'm a Survivor, p172). Talk to someone that you can trust about it and, most importantly, never blame yourself for something someone else did to you. You are innocent.

# BOYZ

Hmm, ladies, this is a subject we love to talk about. We've sung more songs, written more books and made more films about relationships than anything else. Why are we so obsessed by relationships and what does being in love really mean to us? Is it all down to the chemicals in our brains and the survival instinct to keep the race going or are we all trying to find that one person who we'll be with till death do us part? This chapter attempts to show you what you want from a relationship, how to remain true to yourself and new ways of communicating. We'll also look at ways to control our — and their — jealousy.

Things to remember when you're in a relationship:

**R** – Respect each other

**E** – Enjoy each other

**L** – Love one another

**A** – Assist each other

**T** – Talk to each other

**I** – Inspire each other

**O** – Open up to each other

**N** – Nurture one another

**S** – be Sexy with each other

**H** – be Honest with each other

**I** – Involve each other

**P** – be Patient with each other

# IT'S ALL NEW

If having a boyfriend is a relatively new thing for you or something you haven't done yet, then don't worry, you're not going to get left behind. You might not be interested in having a relationship or you may have yet to meet someone you really like. Don't feel that just because you've reached a certain age you have to jump straight into the dating pond. Some girls (and I know I was one), place all their energy into finding the right guy and having the perfect relationship. I missed out on focusing more on my schoolwork, friendships and my relationship with myself because of it. Here's a similar story.

> " I wonder what I could have achieved by now if instead of putting all my energy into the guy in my life I had put it into my work. The one thing I would go back and change is getting into my school work and career instead of those boyfriends that were often losers anyway. (Lisa, 25) "

But if a boyfriend is something that you really want, and you're tired of listening to your friends endlessly talking about theirs, maybe it's time you made the leap and asked that certain someone out. Aaargh! You may think, 'No way am I going to make the first move.' Fair enough, it's a scary thing to do, but what if the guy you like is equally as shy? It takes guts to ask someone out, whether you're male or female. And anyway, you don't have to storm in there and ask him straight out for a date; you could take the more subtle approach and start by getting to know him as a friend. Gradually drop some hints and 99 per cent of the time you'll figure out whether he likes you or not. That way you can find out if he's interested, without being turned down or embarrassed.

If that's not for you and you still feel desperately shy, perhaps you could ask a friend to ask him who he fancies. We're girls, for God's sake! We know how to find out the information we need. If you find out he likes you but you don't know how to follow through, here are some tips to remember:

- He may be even shyer than you, so try and get him on his own (when your friends aren't surrounding you).
- If you don't want to go straight out and ask him out, find out what he's doing at the weekend and casually go along with a group of mates.
- Use your body language to express yourself if you're too shy to use words. Body language is a great way of telling someone how we feel. Look out for any signs in his body language (especially held eye contact).

**Remember, though, that as far as relationships are concerned, quantity doesn't necessarily mean quality.**

# DATING RITUALS

Okay, now that you have arranged a date with a guy that you fancy, where do you go from here? There are no rules to dating except to be yourself and to try and relax and enjoy yourself. But if you really are at a loss, remember these guidelines.

- Choose something to wear that you feel sexy in but also comfortable. Don't make toooo much of an effort.
- Make sure you have plenty of eye contact – it's the quickest and most effective way to get close to someone fast.
- Even if you're shy, make conversation. Ask him about himself.
- If you decide during the date that you don't actually fancy him, don't be pressured into having a snog. You'll just be giving him the wrong signals.
- Don't lie to him, or always agree with him, just because you're nervous and trying to make a good impression. Or he'll just be falling for someone that isn't the real you.
- Try and do something with him that requires some movement. I find it easier to relax and talk if I'm moving, e.g. walking, bowling, ice skating, etc.
- Oh yeah, most importantly, if you go out to eat, never order spaghetti. It's very hard to stay looking cool while slurping spaghetti into your mouth.

These tips are really only a bit of fun. Be yourself, girlfriend, and have a good time!

# THE BIG C

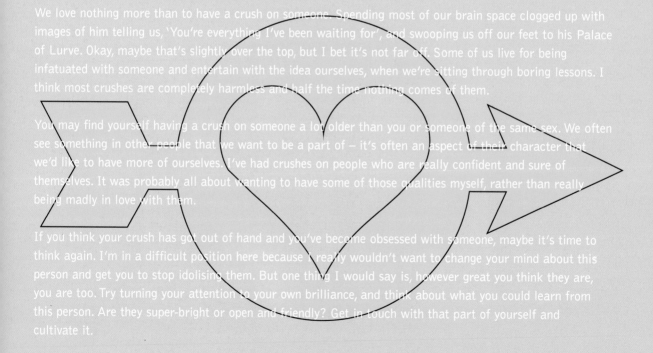

We love nothing more than to have a crush on someone. Spending most of our brain space clogged up with images of him telling us, 'You're everything I've been waiting for', and swooping us off our feet to his Palace of Lurve. Okay, maybe that's slightly over the top, but I bet it's not far off. Some of us live for being infatuated with someone and entertain with the idea ourselves, when we're sitting through boring lessons. I think most crushes are completely harmless and half the time nothing comes of them.

You may find yourself having a crush on someone a lot older than you or someone of the same sex. We often see something in other people that we want to be a part of – it's often an aspect of their character that we'd like to have more of ourselves. I've had crushes on people who are really confident and sure of themselves. It was probably all about wanting to have some of those qualities myself, rather than really being madly in love with them.

If you think your crush has got out of hand and you've become obsessed with someone, maybe it's time to think again. I'm in a difficult position here because I really wouldn't want to change your mind about this person and get you to stop idolising them. But one thing I would say is, however great you think they are, you are too. Try turning your attention to your own brilliance, and think about what you could learn from this person. Are they super-bright or open and friendly? Get in touch with that part of yourself and cultivate it.

# THE REAL THING

## WHAT DO YOU WANT FROM A RELATIONSHIP?

We've been having relationships since forever, and some scientists would argue that we've been designed this way to keep the human race alive. But I don't think we're just in it to make babies. Why do you think you want a boyfriend?

Here's what other girls said.

Companionship – someone to be able to do things with

Friendship

Sex

To feel loved and loveable

Fun and laughter

Partner in crime (not literally, but someone who's on your side against the rest of the world)

To learn more about myself

Money and financial security

Emotional support

# The What you want and are you getting it? exercise

Time for writing your own list. At the top, write 'I want the following from a relationship...' Once you've written your own list think about the relationship you're in at the moment (if you're not in one, think about the last one). Next to each WANT, put a mark from 1 to 5, with 1 meaning you don't feel you get very much of this WANT and 5 meaning you are completely fulfilled with it. Then count up how many WANTS you have and add up all the marks. Divide the total number of marks by the amount of WANTS you have and you're left with an average. Now look at the scores below.

## An average of 1

Seems pretty obvious to me, lovely, that your relationship isn't exactly fulfilling. In fact, it seems downright shoddy! My advice to you is either tell your guy that you're not happy, or get the hell out of there.

## An average of 2

Hmmm, still not very impressive, but at least you've got one more than 1. If you think you can improve on what you've got then great, give it a try. Maybe by the end of this chapter you'll be able to see ways of increasing your average. If not, don't waste your time – get out!

## An average of 3

Well, that's more like it. Bang in the middle. You are obviously fulfilled in some areas of the relationship, which is great. Still room for improvement, though. Concentrate on what you want more of and communicate that to your partner (if you feel you can).

## An average of 4

That's brilliant. You're well happy and fulfilled in your relationship. Not really much room for improvement – maybe you could ask him to do the same questionnaire and see if he comes up with anything different. That could be very interesting – hopefully he'll get a 4 too. If not, tell him to read this chapter.

## An average of 5

Wow girlfriend! Aren't you the lucky one? Nothing I can really say about that – you might as well skip to the next chapter. Just joking, there's always room for improvement. One word of warning, though, make sure you're not kidding yourself and that you are really as happy as you think.

Whatever you scored, hopefully you'll be able to see more clearly what it is you want in the first place and if the relationship you're in (or were in) gives you that. Don't worry too much if it looks as though your relationship isn't really making you very happy. Read on and maybe you'll begin to make different choices (like dumping him or improving what you've got).

Your list of things may seem like a lot to want, but, then again, if you don't know what you want in the first place, you might not get it.

# THE BiGGEST WANT OF ALL

The most common answer I've had from girls when asked what do you want from a boyfriend? is, 'to feel loved and loveable'. Often, the reason we want that from a boyfriend is because we don't already have those feelings towards ourselves. So even if the relationship isn't that fulfilling in other ways, we at least get to feel wanted. It's great to feel wanted and desired by someone else but we also need to feel loved by ourselves. Otherwise we end up in relationships for the wrong reasons and pick guys that usually aren't right for us. Hopefully, this book will help you along the path of realising that the person you need to be loved by the most is you.

# DOES HE MATCH UP?

Looking at what your boyfriends are like can help you see how highly you rate yourself. So ladies, time to look at who the guy in your life is. Is he kind, open and generous, or insensitive, mean and closed-minded? Are your boyfriends loving, giving and together, or self-obsessed, arrogant and selfish?

In the past, my choice of boyfriends has been pretty self-destructive. I've been with boys who were everything from drug addicts to violent, from mentally unstable to sexually messed up. I've also had a pattern of being with boys that I've supported and looked after. Now I look back and can see that I wasn't at all happy in these relationships, but that's because I didn't know what I wanted in the first place. When I started to get to know myself better (and like myself more), my new relationship reflected the new way I felt about myself. If you're someone who seems to end up with guys that aren't really that nice or loving, it's a sign that you need to start believing that you deserve more. The better you feel about yourself, the better choices you'll make when it comes to guys.

Boyz

# HE'S SOOOO AMAZING, ISN'T HE?

This is a common one. Seeing a boy in terms of his possible future potential, rather than what's really in front of us. It's a great quality to have, seeing the best in someone, but let's not kid ourselves. Sometimes they just aren't as great as we think. I'm not saying he doesn't have the potential to be great, just that he isn't quite there yet. Most of my relationships have been with boys who are potentially fantastic but haven't started to realise and live it yet. I'd put a huge amount of energy into trying to make them fulfil the potential that I saw. I'd focus on how great they were, and tell them so constantly. Hours of talk and energy spent on trying to get them to see their brilliance. It was always a let down in the end, though.

I once went out with someone who was quite heavily into drugs, and I believed it was up to me to get him to stop. I'd spend hours talking to him about how great he was and turn all his problems into solutions. I tried to fix everything in his life: his relationship with his dad, his drug habit and his debts. I would see glimpses of change and hang on to them for dear life. But it never lasted. He might stay sober for a day and look like he was getting his act together, but then, in another day or two, he'd be right back to square one. He wasn't ready to change and he wasn't ready to stop being so self-destructive. Nothing I could do could change that. It wasn't about me and what I wanted him to be like. It was his path, that he alone was responsible for. Once I'd accepted that, I left him and left the responsibility behind me.

We can, however, think positively about our boyfriends and want the best for them. Ask yourself these questions:

❶ Do you want him to change for your sake or his?
Ask yourself why you want your boyfriend to change. Is it because you want him to have a more fulfilling enjoyable life? Or is it so that you can be with someone who will give you a more fulfilling, enjoyable life.

❷ Does he want the best for you, too?
It's vital that just as much as you want the best for your boyfriend, he also wants the same for you. Some people don't want their boyfriends to live out their potential because they're scared they might be left behind. Some people are so scared of their partners exceeding them in looks, intelligence, popularity, etc, that they choose people they can have the upper hand over.

❸ Can you accept that it's not your job to save them?
We can get trapped in playing out the role of saviour and enjoy being the martyr, the good one, the therapist. We often enjoy the feeling of being needed as it gives us a sense of purpose. People might not want to be helped, though, and we have to accept that it's not up to us to save them. If one of us takes on the role of saviour, giver, therapist, it can stop there being room for other dynamics between the two of you. You might even be avoiding dealing with some of your own problems. Constantly focusing on someone else's problems means we can get away with not looking at our own.

Hopefully, after answering these questions you'll be clearer about your motivations. Be realistic about your guy and don't place him on a pedestal unnecessarily.

# ENCOURAGING POTENTIAL

I've talked a lot about just seeing someone for their potential and wanting our boyfriends to change when they aren't necessarily ready to. Well, the other side of it is that if we're with someone who we feel is great and has the potential to be even greater (all of us can be), then it's important that we encourage each other to grow and fulfil our potentials. By this, I really mean wanting the best for each other, encouraging each other to go for our dreams and explore life to the full. Hold the highest thought for someone by believing in them, and you'll be giving them huge encouragement to succeed and reach their potential.

Three ways to do this:

- Give them positive feedback about the little things. Let them know you think they're great.
- If they're scared of doing something, such as taking an exam or trying for a university place, encourage them to go for it. Let them know they're capable.
- Praise their work and their achievements.

# GIVING, GIVING, GONE

We've probably all done it at some point – given too much of ourselves to someone else, or to the relationship. In the early stages of a relationship, it's natural to be slightly obsessive and spend every waking moment thinking about or being with the other person, especially if you're really into each other. You're overwhelmed by these new feelings and you want to give everything you've got to this one person. That's normal and you should enjoy it; the high you get when you first fall in love feels fantastic. But if you've been with him for a while and you're still giving him your everything, you might end up feeling washed out. It can also be draining for the person you're giving so much to. You've probably put him on a pedestal and it can be tiring for him to have to live up to your ideals.

It's also important to keep some energy back for yourself. You can relate that to work, friends and family. You need to find a balance between all the things in your life or the other things will get neglected. There are obviously times when you have to get your head down and focus on your work, or give extra help to a family member who's sick, but I'm talking about a general way of living. Often there is fear when it comes to relationships that if you don't give give give, the guy isn't going to stick around. Nine out of ten times that's the opposite of what happens; the guy ends up feeling stifled and leaves the relationship needing some space. He will respect you and therefore want to be with you more if he knows that you're confident and that you have balance in your life. He'll appreciate the time you make for him if it's not just 'given' that you'll be there every spare moment.

Over-prioritising him and the relationship can also affect our friendships. Friends start feeling excluded and say things like, 'You never ring me anymore,' or 'Why don't you ever go out with us anymore?' I'm not saying you should feel guilty about this and run after them; just think about it, and decide whether you want to spend more time with your friends or not. The worst thing you could do is be with them while constantly thinking and talking about him. But make sure you're not neglecting them out of fear that if you take your eye off your new love for a moment, he might vanish. The fact is, if you truly are inseparable, good friends will usually deal with it. Their time will inevitably come, when they're madly in love. The great thing about good friends is that you can go without seeing them for months and when you re-connect it's as though you saw them yesterday.

Have a look now at how much of your energy you're giving to your relationships. Do you think it's out of balance? Has your school work started slipping? Do you ever see your family anymore? Do you think of anything else? I'm not here to tell you to change any of that; I just want you to be aware of it for yourself. Common remarks I've heard from older women include 'I wish I'd given the same amount of time to my school work as I did to my boyfriends – maybe I'd be a lot further in my career today,' and 'I can't believe I gave so much to so many losers. I mean what was I thinking of?'

 **THE BOTTOM LINE**

- Have crushes on people but don't go too overboard. No one is worth becoming a crazed stalker over.
- The whole dating experience might be completely new for you. If it is, you might want to consider asking that certain someone out. If you're not ready, or not interested in having a relationship yet, though, don't rush into it just to fit in. Quantity doesn't equal quality.
- Really there are no rules to dating. Just be real with him and say no if you don't feel like finishing the evening with a snog.
- Find out what it is you really want from a relationship. If you don't know you might never get it.
- Encourage each other to be great, but know when you're fighting a losing battle. Sometimes people just aren't ready to change and reach their potential.
- Never give all of your energy to one person. Keep some back for other areas of your life.
- The most important relationship is with yourself.

# THE GREEN-EYED MONSTER

Whether we're on the giving or receiving end, jealousy isn't a pleasant feeling to deal with. But unfortunately, it seems to be something most of us have to confront at one time or another. It usually stems from our insecurities about our boyfriends or girlfriends cheating on us. The notion that we could be cheated on is a hard thing to contend with, and that's why it's such an important area to be clear about with one another. Yes, we know people are sometimes unfaithful and people do cheat but instead of focusing on the lack of trust, start building on the trust that you do have. Trust is essential to making the relationship work and for your sanity's sake.

One thing we do instead of being honest about our insecurities and jealousy is to become possessive of one another. We start trying to control and literally possess each other. This is not a good path to go down. We can't control one another and usually the more we try to, the more we'll end up pushing them away. The more you can allow each other the freedom to do and be with whoever you want, the stronger the relationship can become.

## THE DOS & THE DON'TS

Do be clear with each other about where you stand on faithfulness. Do you want to have a closed relationship where you are both committed to being faithful, or do you want a more casual, open one? Tell each other your boundaries and what you're prepared to put up with.

Don't pretend that you don't really care either way. Don't fake being strong because you'll get more hurt in the long run.

Do be vulnerable. It's one of the hardest things for most of us, being vulnerable with another. We're scared that we'll be seen as weak but actually being vulnerable is one of the bravest things we can do, and it often gives your boyfriend the signal that it's safe to be more honest himself.

Don't waste time and energy pretending you're not jealous if you are. Tell him that you feel threatened or worried, but be calm and don't blame him for the way you feel.

Do be honest with him about where you've been and who you've been with. People can usually sense when you're not being fully honest.

Don't lie to protect yourself or avoid a discussion, because if he finds out later, he'll trust you even less. When we cover things up they end up looking more suspicious in the long run. It also makes your true trustworthiness seem doubtful. Trust is such a hard thing to rebuild when there's doubt around.

If you've done all this and your boyfriend is still breathing down your neck, asking you where you're going or why you're wearing that sexy dress when you're not going to be out with him, then you've got a problem. Some people have had their trust broken and therefore find it harder to trust again. Some are insecure by nature and can't really believe someone is going to stay with them. Others have watched parents be unfaithful to each other. Even when we're relatively young, we enter our relationships with our unique baggage (some of us have a trunkload!). It's up to you how much of your partner's insecurities and lack of trust you can put up with. If you love him and want the relationship to work, here are some tips on how to help him trust you:

- Tell him in your own words that whether you're together physically or not, he is always with you. Look him in the eyes and let him know how much you care for him and that he's always in your heart.
- Talk to him about his past. If he's been cheated on by an ex-girlfriend, talk to him about it. The more you talk about both of your past hurts, the easier it will be to let go of them.
- If he's really on your case and you know you haven't done anything wrong, try not to get caught up in a fighting match. Be gentle with him and tell him calmly that you need your freedom and space or it will eventually destroy the relationship.

We aren't all perfect, though, and sometimes this trust does get broken. Being in a relationship where one of you has been unfaithful is a hard one to mend. Namely because when the trust is no longer there, you've got nothing to build on. I've been unfaithful to boyfriends before and we've tried to keep the relationship going. It's never worked because I've always ended up feeling guilty and my boyfriends have never been able to fully trust me again. I've learnt the importance of staying faithful. I know how unrewarding it is and how rubbish it makes you feel if you aren't, and also how important that trust is making the relationship work. If I wanted to be unfaithful badly enough to actually go through with it, I would break up with my boyfriend instead of hurting him.

# ARGUING

We all feel differently about this. Some of us are natural born arguers and others cringe at the thought of it. Personally, I like a good old barny – I think it's better out than in (but then I also believe in burping and farting openly). But if you're someone who bites your tongue every time anger creeps in, I might have some tips for you. When we react too quickly we can get swept away in the moment and say things we don't really mean, hurting the other person and often making them defensive. I've learnt a thing or two from arguing so much with my boyfriends. I still sometimes get swept away by the moment, but now I try to not get too caught up with pointing the finger and blaming him for how I feel. 'You didn't pay me enough attention,' 'You never say you love me,' 'You're always out with your mates.' Are you getting the picture? We need to start by changing our language and instead say, 'When you didn't pay me much attention I felt hurt.' Or 'I feel sad when you go out with your mates a lot. I want to spend more time with you.' It's essential that we start taking responsibility for how we feel instead of making out that it's always somebody else's fault. I promise you, people will respond differently and not be so quick to jump back at you with a thousand excuses of why they did what they did. When that happens, no one's really getting anywhere. You're just trying to prove to each other that you're the one in the right.

Being controlled like this might seem a bit contrived to start off with, and it's definitely a discipline that needs practice. When we take responsibility for how we feel, we're showing another part of ourselves – the part we usually protect by hiding. This takes courage because it means being vulnerable instead of acting like the tough guy. I promise you it's worth it, though. You'll open up a discussion where the other person doesn't immediately feel 'got at' and go straight into defence mode.

> **So, the next time you are upset or in the middle of an argument remember:**
>
> ❶ Don't go straight into blaming mode. Don't start shouting or raising your voice or swearing.
>
> ❷ Try and take deep breaths and calm yourself down.
>
> ❸ Where you would normally say, 'You always…' or 'You never…', say 'I feel like this when you do that.'
>
> ❹ Remember that you actually normally quite like, or even love, this person and you want things to work out, so don't get mean.
>
> ❺ We often think the other person is evil when they've upset us, but actually a lot of arguments come from misunderstandings. Give them a chance to explain themselves before you start jumping down their throat.

At the end of the day, if someone's actions are causing you pain or anger you have a choice to leave them. If the other person isn't going to change, that's their prerogative. They don't owe you anything — no one does — but that doesn't mean you have to stick around. I see so many girls hanging on because they're scared that there is no one better for them out there. It's not true. There will be someone better out there for you. You just have to believe it.

# HOLDING IT ALL IN

Some of us, because of our conditioning, believe that we can't show our needs or upsets to others. We're scared of confrontation and the possibility that we'll not be liked as much if we're honest with someone when they've done something that we're not happy with. Instead, we play it safe and hold it in and, as with a pressure-cooker, the pressure eventually gives way and makes something explode. I know some people are scared to even raise their voice, so I'm not saying, Go out there and have a barny with the first person that crosses your path. I am saying, the next time you feel upset or angry, try telling that person how you really feel. As long as it's not just a string of blame, they won't feel attacked so they may remain calm enough to tell you their side of things. The most important thing is not to be scared that you'll be disliked if you're honest.

Being honest with each other like this can be a great way to learn about yourself. For example, I can be very brattish (I know, it's hard to believe) and when I'm on my own there is no one to tell me 'Jessica, stop being such a brat.' But when I'm in a relationship, I'm forced to face parts of myself that I might not like.

# GETTING YOUR NEEDS MET

There is a fine line we walk in terms of our needs. There are two completely contradictory schools of thought and I believe in both of them. One says you should have no attachment to anything, you shouldn't need anything from another person to make yourself feel good, i.e. you have all the resources in yourself to be happy. The other says that we're all human and most of us do have attachments outside ourselves. When we have relationships there are certain things we probably want like love, respect and attention, and it's okay to want them.

I've heard many stories from girls about feeling unfulfilled in their relationships. A common thread through all of them is the shame they feel in having these needs in the first place and the fear that if they express them, their boyfriend won't stick around. I have a story of my own.

When I lived in Australia, I typically got myself an Australian boyfriend. He was cute, dangerous and wild but he didn't fulfil my needs at all. He worked in a bar, often doing the late shift which would finish at midnight. Well, at this stage, I wanted him to jump on his motorbike and get back to me as quickly as possible. But he rarely did. He would stay at the bar after closing time with his mates drinking and hanging out. I would be gutted, eagerly waiting all night for him to walk through the door. When he did it was often after 3 a.m. and instead of saying, 'Why are you back so late?' I would act as though I couldn't care less. I thought there was something wrong with me and that he would see me as needy and possessive if I told him how I really felt. Meanwhile, it was all building up on the inside. One night I got completely wasted and ended up snogging his best mate. I did it because I was so hurt inside that I wanted to pretend to myself that I didn't care and hurt him back in some way. If I had been honest with him, I would have given him the choice to come home earlier or to carry on staying out late. Then if he'd decided to carry on staying out late, and I'd decided I wanted more, I could have left the relationship. The relationship ended because I decided to move back to England. Once I'd left, he found out that I'd snogged his best mate and it devalued our entire relationship. I really regret letting it get to that, instead of just being honest with him from the start that all I had wanted was for him to spend more time with me.

It's common to believe that our needs are unhealthy and we should put a lid on them. We can be worried that if a guy sees this neediness in us they'll find it unattractive and leave. Some guys claim that they don't want to feel pressured or made to feel like they are doing anything wrong. Girls in relationships with boys like this will be even more likely to pussy foot around him and ignore their own needs. Some girls' believe that they're wrong to have needs in the first place. Like I said, it's a fine line. We can't make others change for us, but we can choose for ourselves what we want from our relationships.

## WHAT ARE YOUR NEEDS?

You've already done an exercise to help you find out what you want from a relationship and whether you're getting it or not. But needs are slightly different, they are more emotionally led. Like wanting his time or him to listen to you, etc. Find out for yourself what needs you think you have and which ones are realistic or not.

| | |
|---|---|
| TELLING YOU EVERYTHING, INCLUDING HIS SECRETS | PHYSICAL AFFECTION |
| TELLING YOU HE LOVES YOU ALL THE TIME | LISTENING TO YOU |
| BEING THE MOST IMPORTANT THING IN HIS LIFE | RINGING YOU A LOT |
| COMPLIMENTING YOU | BUYING YOU PRESENTS |
| NEVER LOOKING AT OTHER GIRLS | HIS TIME |

### A score of 0–10  You're Miss Independent

You're probably fiercely independent, and you rely on yourself to feel good. You don't need a boy to make you happy – you already know that you're great and you don't need a guy to tell you. It's great that you're like this, but my only warning is that even though you're so independent it doesn't mean your boyfriend is, so give him a bit of slack if you ever feel claustrophobic because he seems to need so much from you.

### A score of 11–30  You're Miss Needy from time to time

You are somewhere in the middle. You definitely have needs within a relationship but they don't completely control you or your emotions. Make sure that you're honest when these needs come up but don't give him a hard time about them. Be realistic about how much one person can give to another and try and give yourself some of what you want your boyfriend to give you.

### A score of 31–50  You're Miss Needy Pants!

Oh dear, sweetheart, you really are pretty high-maintenance aren't you? You look for your relationship to make you happy, instead of feeling good from all of the other aspects of your life like your friendships and family. Usually we're really needy when we don't feel very good about ourselves, so we look to our boyfriends to make us feel good. When you start feeling good regardless of what your boyfriend gives you, and I promise you'll start to feel less needy. When we have so many needs we usually aren't satisfied, and so end up feeling hurt and let down a lot, and that's hard. But it's not really up to your partner to be so totally devoted to you and make you feel good. Promise yourself that you'll be more realistic about what your boyfriend can give you and start giving more to yourself instead.

# MOVING ON

It's all very well my writing a few sentences on ending a relationship, but we all know that in reality it can be an extremely hard thing to do. However unhappy you are, at the end of the day you might still love them. The problem is, we get addicted to relationships like we do to everything else. They give us a sense of security, make us feel loved and most importantly, not alone. These are hard addictions to give up. What we need to know is that there's a life without that person. But we can't really know that until we start distancing ourselves and getting fulfilment from other things in our lives. Not an easy one!

Okay, let's imagine that you've made the decision to leave him. How do you go about it? You have a choice to do it the cowardly way, i.e. through a friend, on the telephone, or just stop ringing him. Or you can be brave and tell him straight. However badly you think he treated you or however much you know that it's going to hurt him, tell him the truth. If you aren't clear and honest with him, he's going to get mixed signals and end up getting more hurt in the long run. One thing to avoid is the never-ending split, on one day and off the next. For most of us there's nothing more of a turn-on than when we've split up with someone and they've suddenly become unavailable. Often, breaking up with someone can make him seem even more attractive and it creates an exciting new spark between you. Hard as it may seem, you should avoid going down this road, if not for yourself, then for your now ex-boyfriend. Blowing hot and cold can be very painful for the person you're leaving. He'll just stay in denial about the fact you're leaving him and focus all his energy into getting you back. More often than not he won't succeed, but the boundaries between you will have become unclear and it might be harder for each of you to move on.

Lastly, tell your close friends that you've finished with him so that they can give you extra support; let them take you out and have some fun. It might take a while to adjust, but you'll get used to it, and who knows, you may even end up loving being single again.

Relationships often break up when one person changes and grows and the other doesn't. You can see with your friends that you sometimes grow apart and change interests – it's the natural way of life: change. It's not your responsibility to carry each other or stay back for them. The best thing you can do is be honest with them or eventually let go of them all together.

# BEING DUMPED

There's no nice way of phrasing this one – being dumped. There are also not many words that can make it easier. Let's get to the point. It can be so painful your heart feels like it's being ripped apart. It's something most of us can't avoid in our lifetimes. Heartbreak. Having the person you love more than anything in the world, no longer loving you back. You know the minute it happens; you can decide to ignore it and hope it goes away, but inevitably it will come back. He gets slightly short with you, he stops ringing you every day, his kisses seem cold. Every time we decide to love we take that risk of getting hurt and the more we allow ourselves to love, the more hurt we can get.

The most important thing for you to know is that it doesn't mean there's something lacking in you, personally. It doesn't mean there's something wrong with you or that you're 'not enough'. We often fall into the trap of believing it's all to do with us, especially when we watch them fall in love with someone else.

## MY FIRST HEARTBREAK

I was in love. I was 16, he was 18 and I adored him. He was intelligent, good-looking and confident. Where I was lacking in self-esteem he made up for it, for both of us. We would spend hours in bed talking, making love and eating ice cream. I would listen to every word, soaking in his profound words. I was in love.

After about six months of our being together, I noticed a difference. I noticed it straight away, but I chose to ignore it. I accepted that he couldn't see me on Saturday night as he had 'other' things to do. I accepted that his kisses felt flat. I accepted that when he was with me he seemed elsewhere. I accepted all of this until it hurt too much. I had to make a choice – stay with him and pretend that his feelings for me hadn't changed, or give him the easy option and break up with him.

I broke up with him. I rang him and bit my lip. I told him that it just wasn't working for me any more and I thought it best if we were just friends. He sounded relieved, if not a little shocked. More than anything, his ego was bruised that someone had finished with him. I put down the phone and in simple terms 'I lost the plot'. I threw everything I could in my bedroom, I screamed, I cried, I practically hyperventilated. And then I rang my grandmother. She promised me that there would be other boys queuing up to go out with me. She told me that the pain would go and that I would probably go through it many times over. I couldn't listen to a word she said. The pain stopped me from hearing or seeing anything.

I went through months of believing I was rubbish and that no one would ever want me. I kept asking myself what was wrong with me and compared myself to a girl I knew he now fancied. I didn't get any answers quickly, but one day through all my tears it dawned on me. It had nothing to do with me, it was my compatibility with this other person. It didn't mean I was crap; it meant he couldn't fully see my greatness because we were both coming from different places. This other girl wasn't better than me, but she might be more suited to him. Other guys would love me and the next time I'd be with a guy who really saw me for myself, instead of trying to change me into someone that he wanted me to be. I felt great and I felt strong. I had used that pain to go into a deep place inside myself and discover much more of who Jessica was. I had resurfaced loving and accepting myself even more.

Another thing we do when we're heartbroken is choose to remember all the good times. Our memory becomes very selective and we draw on the times that back up our pain of being left. Try and remember what it was really like; the times you thought he was a dickhead and promised yourself you were going to leave him.

If you've been hurt by love before, you might try and avoid ever being in love again. It can seem too scary and painful. Once we've been hurt our barriers are quicker to go up and we don't let people so far in. Hopefully, though, we'll meet the right person who can help us let down some of those barriers and we can start to feel love again. It's better to love and be hurt than never to have loved at all.

Boyz

> "My boyfriend is ten years older than me and my mum and dad have told me I have to split up with him. The age difference doesn't mean anything to me, though, and I really love him. I'm turning 16 in a couple of months and I'm tempted to move out and live with him, but I don't want to fall out with my parents. I just want them to accept him. What should I do? (Lisa, 15)"

**It can be really frustrating** and upsetting to have your parents not supporting your choices. Even though the age difference is quite large, it doesn't mean that your relationships can't work. Your parents probably feel protective of you, and at the end of the day, they think they know best. What you could try doing is arrange a dinner for your boyfriend to meet your parents and let them get to know him a little bit. Tell your parents that he deserves a chance at least. Don't rush into moving out — you are still quite young and if you break up with your boyfriend, it will probably be your parents who let you back into their home to live.

> "My boyfriend is really possessive and jealous whenever I so much as talk to another boy. I've done everything to persuade him that it's him I love and then recently I found out he has been unfaithful to me with another girl. I confronted him about it but he denied it. I really love him and I want to believe him but I'm sure he's lying. Should I leave him anyway? (Phoebe, 16)"

**This is a hard one to answer** and something that you ultimately are going to have to decide for yourself. I would try and find out for a fact if he has slept with her or not and not just rumours. If he doesn't admit to it you might still find it hard to trust him. At the end of the day, you need to decide whether you want to be with someone who doesn't trust you. Don't let him bully you. Listen to your inner voice (see Girl to Woman, p23).

> "My boyfriend broke up with me about a year ago and I was devastated (understatement of the year). All my friends kept telling me I would get over it as time went by, but a year later I still hurt as much as I did when he broke up with me. Recently I saw him with a girl at the cinema and I left in tears. Will I get over him, and, if so, how? (Julie, 16)"

**We usually do get over people** but it can take time. Have you tried being with anyone since him? Meeting someone else who you find gorgeous and fun can be a great way to get over an ex. At the end of the day you do need to move on as he obviously has. One thing we usually do when we're heartbroken is think that we're never going to find anyone we love as much ever again. It's not true — there are so many great compatible boys out there, but you're not going to find them if you're inside moping all the time. You could also try getting into something you find enjoyable to take your mind off things. It's not easy, though, and there aren't any real answers. Make sure you have good friends around you to keep you company.

 My boyfriend went out with his previous girlfriend for two years. She broke up with him and I know she broke his heart. He's told me that he never wants to fall in love that deeply again because he'll just end up getting hurt again. I really love him and I'm jealous that this other girl got all the love from him that I don't. I'm also worried that he still loves her and that's why he hasn't opened up to me. Sometimes I think I should leave him rather than always feeling upset because he doesn't fully love me. (Jessica, 17)

**This must be really hard for you.** You deserve to be with someone who loves you as much as you love them. You have to look at why you're with someone who has said they can't fully commit themselves to you. Do you think it reflects how you feel about yourself? Do you know that you deserve someone who loves you totally? If it's still really hurting you, you could tell him that you want him to love you as much as you do him. Otherwise you shouldn't be together. Don't threaten him, but be clear and tell him how painful it is for you. If you feel like you can stay with him even though he won't love you totally, then be patient with him. You have to show him that you are fully trustworthy and that you're not going to hurt him, and he needs to know that you're worth taking that risk for.

The most important thing in any relationship is trust. Without trust, a solid foundation for a relationship can't be built. To be able to be honest you need to have a strong sense of who you are and know what you want. Don't try and be someone you're not just to please another. If you're being loved for being someone you're not, then you're not really being loved, are you? Don't give up years of your life to someone just because you're scared of being on your own. I hear too many girls say, 'It's easier to stay in the relationship than to leave,' meaning that they're comfortable and secure but not fulfilled. This is no way to live, if we do things because we're scared, then we're blocking new, more exciting things from coming our way.

Boyz

# DA SISTAHS!

# S Support

# I Inspire

# S Share

# T Together

# E Everything

# R Real

# SISTERS

The words I've chosen for Sisters show you why I called the book and the website, *Sisters Unlimited*. When we come together and combine our experiences and wisdom, we create the possibility for an unlimited and awesome life for ourselves. We realise that we're not alone and that others can help us, just as we can help them – even if it's just by listening.

Our friendships with other girls are an important part of our lives – staying up all night talking, sharing new experiences and having a shoulder to cry on are all brilliant aspects of our relationships with each other. My relationships with other girls have always been a fulfilling part of my life, though they haven't always been easy. In this chapter, we'll explore the complexities that exist within the dynamic of our relationships with one another. We'll look at ways we can support each other and find out what our female friendships mean to us. There are also some fun rituals you can do together.

## WHAT DOES FRIENDSHIP REALLY MEAN TO YOU?

You probably all have at least a few close friends, but have you ever thought about what friendship really means to you?

Here's what other girls said:

Having fun

Talking about personal things

Trust

Someone to look out and after you when you're down

Someone to do stuff with

Laughing

Someone who loves you for you

Someone to cry on and tell all your worries

Someone who you feel has the same tastes, opinions, beliefs

Sharing secrets

Dressing up – going shopping

Someone who you can be comfortable with in silence

Someone you can be completely yourself with

To help you discover what friendship means to you, do this simple exercise:

Picture your closest three friends and then think about why you are friends with them. Write down the name of each friend and then write next to her name three reasons why you are their friend. ✒

It's good to know why you're friends with people, because you can then appreciate what your friendship with them adds to your life. If you ever have a fight or feel annoyed with one of them, remember the reasons why you're friends in the first place and hopefully you'll be able to let it go or forgive them.

**Treat others how you'd like to be treated – stick to these friendships rules.**

**F** - forgive each other for your mistakes
**R** - rescue each other when you need help
**I** - include each other in things
**E** - enjoy each other's time together
**N** - nurture and look after each other
**D** - differences – accept each other's
**S** - secrets – keep each other's

Da Sistahs!

# ARE YOU BEST FRIEND MATERIAL?

Have a go at this fun quiz to detect just how good a friend you are.

**1** Your friend rings you crying because her boyfriend has dumped her again – (they keep getting back together). Do you

**a** tell her you're in the middle of watching EastEnders and you'll try and ring her later, after dinner?

**b** take some time to listen to her on the phone and tell her you'll talk to her about it tomorrow at school?

**c** get straight on a bus, go over to her house with some chocolates and listen to her all night.

**2** It's your best mate's birthday. Do you
**a** forget but give her a big birthday kiss?
**b** bring her in a card and a pressie?
**c** plan a huge surprise party for her?

**3** You win two free tickets to see your mate's favourite band. Do you

**a** not tell her and take your boyfriend instead?

**b** take her, but on condition that she pays for the ticket?

**c** take her and lend her your new dress?

**4** It's your friend's birthday. How much do you spend on her present?
**a** you give her a card, if she's lucky.
**b** about a fiver – or you give her something of yours you've never used.
**c** at least £30 – you've been saving up.

**5** You're meant to go and see your friend in a play on her opening night but at the last minute you find out your boyfriend has tickets to a gig you've been really wanting to go to. Do you

**a** pretend you're ill and go to the gig?

**b** ask her if you could come to the play another night and go to the gig?

**c** tell your boyfriend to take a friend. You know how much it means to your friend that you're there.

**6** Your friend's boyfriend comes on to you one night when you're drunk. Do you

   **a** snog him. You've always fancied him and she'll never know.

   **b** tell him to back off and let your mate know straight away that he made a move on you?

   **c** turn it into a joke with him and tell him to behave himself or he'll risk losing a very cool girlfriend?

**7** You are shopping with a mate and you see a great outfit. She sees it and loves it too. Do you

   **a** tell her that you saw it first and you hate it when she copies you?

   **b** tell her that you should both buy it but try not to wear it on the same day?

   **c** let her buy it – there will be plenty more cool things to buy?

**8** What is most important to you?

   **a** boys.

   **b** getting good grades.

   **c** friends.

Now see if you answered mostly As, Bs or Cs.

## Mostly As – you're more like an enemy

Mmmmm, you're not really a very good friend, are you? You always put yourself first and you never sacrifice anything for your friends. You're not very trustworthy either, and in fact you're more like an enemy than a best mate. Have you got any mates?

## Mostly Bs – you're a good mate

You're quite a nice person and your friendships are pretty important to you. But whether you'd drop everything and be there for your friends depends on your mood. You've probably got lots of friends but not that many really close ones.

## Mostly Cs – you're a best buddy

You're definitely best buddy material. You'd do anything for a friend and always put her first. You're never selfish and you enjoy giving to people. You probably have a tight circle of really close friends and definitely a very close best friend. All I'd say is, make sure people don't take advantage of your huge heart.

# NOT SO FRIENDLY

Although female friendships are important, never let us forget that they can also be competitive, mean and bitchy. When teenage girls are asked what they worry about most, friendships are the third highest on their list (coming after looks and families). The following section highlights the negative dynamics we can have with one another and how we can start changing them. Here we have another opportunity to set new standards for the younger sistahs.

# SHE'S MY BEST FRIEND

Our relationships with other girls can start to get difficult as early as nursery school. When my boyfriend's daughter had just started school at six, she experienced competitiveness over best friends. When my boyfriend told me he was worried about her, it took me back to my own school years and my experience of other girls at that age. Thinking back, practically every day a girl would break down in tears because of a fight over best friends. I explained to him that what his daughter was going through was normal and that it might continue throughout her whole time at school. He couldn't fully understand it. That's because although boys have their own bullying and fights, they tend to be about different things from the ones that girls fight about. I've rarely heard of fights between boys that have been over best friends and who gets to be partners with who!

You might have grown out of the 'She's my best friend' phase but you wouldn't be alone if you hadn't. It usually continues until we're well away from the school playground. It's as though we have mini-relationships with one another, which we transfer on to boys when we're older.

I asked girls why best friends mean so much to them. Here's what they said.

We feel **secure** in knowing that someone likes us more than anyone else.

It's bonding to create a partnership – to have a **partner in crime**.

We're **complicated** creatures and we get wrapped up in the whole friendship thing.

We're **rehearsing** for later on in life when we'll have boyfriends.

If you still find yourself getting jealous because the friend you want to sit with or be partners with, already has a partner, remind yourself that it's really not that important. Spread your wings and get to know other people in your class. There might be a whole group of girls you've hardly ever even spoken to. Don't assume that you're not going to get on with them – go and chat to them and find out for yourself what they're really like. At school, most of us tend to hang out with one particular group. There's nothing wrong with that, but if you want to avoid petty fights and competitiveness about 'best friends', make sure you have lots of mates. Remember, you enjoy different things with each person.

The good news about all this best friend stuff is that once we get older and leave school (or the education system), it usually changes. You might still have a best friend, but you will both allow each other more space to have new friends, too, and you won't live in each other's pockets anymore.

Being at school can be hard. You want to be best friends with someone who already has one and then you feel left out.

# COMPARING AND COMPETITIVENESS

Are you someone who compares yourself with other girls all the time? Do you find yourself scrutinising other girls' looks, intelligence and popularity? How do you feel if you meet another girl who is beautiful and smart? Do you feel threatened and jealous? Or do you give yourself a hard time for not being more like her? It's natural to compare yourself to others and we all do it. It can become unhealthy, though, if you do it obsessively and feel crap when someone else is better than you at something. There will always be someone who is more beautiful, more intelligent, more talented and more popular than you. Human beings were not made to be all the same; it's what makes us so interesting.

We need to learn how to celebrate each other's inner and outer beauty. It can be hard, though. I find that when I meet powerful women I feel redundant and think I don't have anything to offer. In situations like this we need to remember that there is enough love and attention for everyone.

# GOSSIP

Gossip, gossip, gossip. Mmmm, ladies, what's our angle on this one? I know in my heart that gossiping isn't right, but I am definitely prone to having a gossip now and then. If you are a bit of a gossip, there are a few things you should think about the next time you're about to:

❶ Try not to say negative things about a person to someone who's never met them before, if there's a chance they will meet. We should meet other people with an open mind and then decide for ourselves how we feel about them. After all, one person might not get on with someone but that doesn't mean you'll have the same kind of relationship.

❷ It's important for people to feel they can trust you, especially friends. If they've asked you not to repeat something, then don't. Otherwise, people get hurt and will eventually stop telling you things.

❸ If you repeat something to someone, don't do it to stir up trouble. Check where your motivations are coming from and what the long-term effect of your repeating it might be. Are you doing it to create friction between people, and will it end up creating more problems? If you think someone needs to be told something, then approach the person who's involved. Tell them that they should confront the other person, or if they won't, you will. Give that person the initial chance to come clean.

Gossip can be harmful if you're gossiping about something that is very private to someone. Things can get out of hand and stories always get exaggerated the more they're passed on. It's important to respect people's lives. Remember, you wouldn't want your private life splashed around for everyone to judge and talk about.

You could find yourself in a situation where you've found out something that concerns a friend but you know they'll get hurt if you tell them. I once found out that my best friend's boyfriend was two-timing her. I knew that if it were the other way around, I'd definitely want to be told. When I finally did tell her she went straight to her boyfriend, who said that I was talking rubbish and I was just jealous. She became angry with me and chose to believe him. I was really hurt, but kind of understood that it would be less painful for her to believe him. When we'd made up about a month later we went out to the cinema and guess who we bumped into? Yes, her boyfriend and the other girl he was two-timing her with. In the end I was glad that I'd been honest with her, even though she'd chosen not to believe me. I owed it to her.

# BITCHY BITCHY

When we think of someone being bitchy we usually think of girls or women. That's an awful thing to say, isn't it? But unfortunately it's true. Some of us do have a mean, spiteful streak and this can be even more prevalent when we're young. We say hurtful things, gang up on each other and we even sometimes have physical fights.

Complete this questionnaire to rate your own level of bitchiness.

## ARE YOU A BITCH?

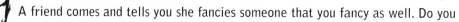

**1** A friend comes and tells you she fancies someone that you fancy as well. Do you
- **a** tell her you do too but you'll let her go for it?
- **b** tell her you do too and say 'May the best girl win'?
- **c** go and find him to make your move first without telling her?

**2** Have you ever purposely not invited someone somewhere to make them feel left out?
- **a** never – you always try and include everyone.
- **b** occasionally, but only if they have been really mean to you beforehand.
- **c** regularly – people should know when they're not wanted.

**3** You see a beautiful girl walking down the street. Do you
- **a** admire her beauty and think how lucky she is?
- **b** think, It's not fair. Why did she get to be so good-looking?
- **c** think that she must be anorexic, have had plastic surgery, and be wearing lots of make-up (and, anyway, she's not as good-looking as you).

**4** You know a really juicy secret that everyone would love to hear about. Do you
- **a** not tell a soul?
- **b** just tell your best mate?
- **c** tell everyone. Who cares if it's a secret – you'll get loads of attention from telling it?

**5** Have you ever been mean about someone, then nice to their face?
- **a** no, you never say mean things about people.
- **b** once or twice but you felt bad about it afterwards.
- **c** all the time – there's no point in making enemies.

**6** You and a good-looking girlfriend are with a group of good-looking boys (one of whom you fancy), and your friend has a big gunk of food stuck in between her teeth. Do you
- **a** discreetly let her know about it?
- **b** not tell her for a while, then eventually let her know?
- **c** not tell her for ages then announce loudly in front of everyone that she has some disgusting left-over lunch in between her teeth?

**7** You are at your house with a girlfriend, getting ready to go out, and your friend is wearing something dreadful. Do you

**a** offer her your latest unworn cool outfit to borrow?

**b** tell her you think she should wear something else, then lend her something of yours that is a few years out of date?

**c** not tell her anything and let her go out looking rubbish?

**8** Someone you think is 'geeky' asks you to dance. Do you

**a** dance with him? What harm can one dance have?

**b** tell him you're not interested and turn your back on him?

**c** laugh in his face and say, 'Did you really think someone like me would dance with someone like you?'

To find out if you're a bitch or not, count how many As, Bs and Cs you scored.

## Mostly As – You are Miss Nicey Nicey

Well done, you are a genuinely nice person. You don't have an ounce of bitchiness in you. Be aware, though, of always putting others ahead of yourself. You might find that people take advantage of your niceness and walk all over you.

## Mostly Bs – You are an Occasional Bitch

Mmmm, you've definitely got some bitchiness in you. You know how to be a bit catty now and then. Make sure you're aware of other people's feelings as you can hurt people more than you realise. Keep a handle on your bitchiness or you could end up being a mega bitch.

## Mostly Cs – You are a Mega Bitch

Woh there! What got stuck up your arse to make you such a bitch? You always put yourself before others, usually treading on them along the way. I'd stop and think about how mean you are, or you'll end up a very lonely person.

The questionnaire above is really a bit of fun. Hopefully, not too many of you scored a lot of cs. You know in your heart whether you're a bitch or not. If you aren't happy with being bitchy to people, then decide to change. Be more aware of other people's feelings – people can be more sensitive that you realise (think about how you react to even the smallest things.). It's a lonely path to walk. You will alienate people and probably not have many real friends. People are usually mean because they're unhappy.

# FIGHTING OVER A BOY

I hope it never happens to you, but unfortunately it doesn't escape many of us – fighting over a boy because both you and a friend fancy the same one. It's not an easy situation to be in and I've messed up before by choosing boys over friends. I learnt from my mistakes, though, and realised what my priorities really were and that it's never worth it in the end.

I was about 14 at the time, and boys were still a new thing for my girlfriends and me. One of my close girlfriends really fancied a boy I knew (a very good-looking boy). We were at her house, getting ready to go out and she was getting very excited about seeing him that night. I think she even rang him to ask if he was going to be coming out. We arrived at 'the hang-out' where I proceeded to get horrendously drunk (I'm not using that as an excuse though). I remember snogging someone I didn't even particularly like and the next thing I remember I'd bumped into this guy that my friend fancied. I flirted with him outrageously and we went off down an alleyway together and kissed. I told him that my friend was really into him and that we shouldn't be kissing. He ignored me and said he didn't care about her. My friend ended up finding out about it and was really, really hurt by what I'd done. She was meant to come away with me that summer and had even booked her plane ticket. She cancelled it and told me she didn't consider me her friend anymore. I felt awful. What an idiot I'd been.

I know I'm not the only girl to ever do this. Looking back on it I can see why I did something that mean to a close friend. I felt powerful when boys fancied me. This feeling of power was new and I liked it; I'd started living for it. The feeling of power was doubled if the boy was popular and fancied by other girls. Who would he shine his torch of attention on? It would obviously be the better girl, the prettier one, the cooler one. It was about feeling powerful and in control. I wanted to prove to myself that I could win him and that it would be me that he chose. In some dysfunctional way, because of my feelings of inadequacy, I did it to feel good about myself. But obviously, it's an awful thing to do just to feel good about yourself and it actually leaves you feeling empty and more crap about yourself than before.

It's all connected to the competitiveness we have with each other. Since this incident, I've encountered over and over again other girls trying to assert their power over me by flirting with my boyfriends and often picking up my sloppy leftovers. It's not really even about the boy; it's more about the girl that you're competing with. We want her to know that we're the more desirable, beautiful one. (Because it's actually the last thing we really believe.) Again, it comes down to the need to feel powerful. If you ever come up against these feelings in yourself, try and be honest about them. You don't need a boy to make you feel good about yourself. I can promise you, he's not worth it. At the end of the day, it doesn't say anything about you if a boy chooses to be unfaithful to his girlfriend and get off with you. Boys are easy to catch and they'll often be tempted by anyone who pays them enough attention.

If you've had a girlfriend steal your boyfriend or snog him, then it's up to you whether you choose to forgive her. If you think the friendship is worth saving, then you'll need to have an honest chat with her about it. Ask her why she felt she had to do that to you. Does she really like him? How does she feel about what she's done? Ask her if she feels that she needs to compete with you and assert her power over you? (That'll get her thinking). You'll soon know if she's being honest and she realises what a huge mistake she's made.

Another thing that can happen is that you and a friend meet someone at the same time and you both really like him. Who's going to back down? Once again, talk about it. Don't leave things unsaid with one of you ending up getting hurt. Friendships are not worth breaking up over a boy. I know this might sound patronising, and I would have probably hated someone saying it to me when I was younger, but I'm going to say it anyway – there are many more boys out there. One thing there is no shortage of is willing boys to go out with. You probably won't even remember why you liked the guy when you're older. (Told you it would sound annoying.) If I were you, I'd let her have him. Tell her you'll let her have him, but if he isn't interested, she's got to let you try afterwards. And vice versa. True sisterhood is not about being competitive, but about supporting each other. Good luck, though – it's never easy.

Da Sistahs!

## SPEAKING UP

When you're upset with friends it's important to speak up and let them know. This can be quite scary. I know I spend a lot of my time avoiding confrontation with others. I don't mind standing up to establishments or bullies, but standing up to close friends or family can be difficult. Do you ever feel that by confronting someone there seems to be a lot at stake? A risk of having someone deciding that they don't like you any more and taking their friendship away? The truth is, it'll probably never happen, especially with a good friend.

With your closest girlfriends, try your hardest to let them know if you're upset by something they've said or done. It can be really difficult being honest with a close friend because you have to strike the balance of not accusing them but getting your point heard. In any friendship it's important we tell each other when we're upset with one another. Anything we hold on to will only magnify itself and, however deep we think it's buried, it will inevitably rear its head later on.

# MAKE UP, MAKE UP, NEVER NEVER BREAK UP

If you do end up having a big row with a friend, then hopefully there'll be a time when you decide to make up. Most strong friendships can survive a row now and then. I actually think it can be healthy to argue occasionally, because in a way you're saying that you know the friendship is strong enough to be able to have a fight and still be best mates at the end of it. It's like when we fight with family members. We know that even if we absolutely hate them in the moment (and even fantasise about a few nasty things happening to them), we'll end up making up and loving them just as much as we did before.

It depends what the fight was about, but here are a few things to remember when making up.

- Listen to each other's sides of the argument. Take it in turns to speak and to listen.
- Be willing to forgive the other person if they are genuinely sorry. Don't hold on to things and don't make them beg.
- You be the one who approaches your friend to make up. It takes a mature, cool person to step forward first.
- Try and laugh together about the silliness of the fight and turn it into something light hearted.

# LETTING GO OF FRIENDS

Most of us experience close friendships that change. It's a familiar story. You've known each other since you were toddlers and have always done everything together. You've always liked the same things, worn the same clothes and listened to the same music. Then, gradually you find that your tastes seem to be becoming more and more different. You hang on in there, though, because you've been friends for such a long time and you feel guilty about moving on. We all change as we get older – sometimes when we're teenagers we might change more in a year than in the five previous ones put together. Sometimes you have to accept that a friendship has changed and even though you might still love this person dearly, you no longer share the same interests. It's okay to know that you can move on from these friendships and create new ones. Who knows? You might see them again in a few years, and get on brilliantly again. But if you know that you have friendships like this, why don't you start making new friends as well.

There are also so-called friends in our lives that aren't really very good for us. They might bully us or try and get us to do things we don't want to do. The people you surround yourself with reflect how you feel about yourself. The very fact that you're reading this book is a sign that you are ready to start loving and respecting yourself more. When you have more respect for yourself you might begin to move away from certain people because you realise that you deserve better friends than them.

# THE BOTTOM LINE

- Have a think about what friendships mean to you and set yourself some standards that are important to you. Stick to them and you'll be a good friend.
- Although friendships with other girls are great, they can also have a few negative dynamics, like fighting over best friends. We don't need to be so possessive over each other and we can all share our friendships.
- Girls tend to be competitive with one another when they don't need to be. There is enough love and attention for everyone.
- Instead of being competitive, we need to encourage each other's inner and outer beauty.
- Try not to gossip, and if you do, be very careful what you say. Don't hurt people with gossiping.
- Don't be a bitch. You'll end up lonely and with no mates.
- Don't lose friends over boys. They're not worth it.
- Tell each other if you're upset or hurt with one another. It takes guts, but real friends will be able to handle it.
- Learn to forgive each other for your mess-ups. But don't let people walk all over you.
- Sometimes we change and so do our friends. Allow each other to move on and make new friends.

Da Sistahs!

# SUPPORT DA SISTAHS!

> Celebrate the friendships you have with your female friends

This section highlights how we can be there for one another and support each other even more!

There comes a time in all of our lives when we need extra support and love. You might have broken up with your boyfriend, got into trouble at school or had a fight with your parents. At times like this, the people who can usually look after you the best are your mates. And knowing that your friends will be there for you is a great comfort – we all have times when we need someone to bring us tissues, make us cups of tea and let us cry for hours on end with total understanding.

Hopefully, your friends know that you will also be there to do the same for them; being there for them in any way they need you. When someone is hurt or in pain, it's important not to judge her. I've had girlfriends who have come to me in tears because their boyfriends have mistreated them in some way. I want to say, 'You should dump him he's a loser', but that might not be what they need to hear right at that time. You're being a better friend if you listen and let her get out everything she needs to say. Most of the time she doesn't even want to hear your opinions; she just wants you to listen. Once she's finished letting it all out ask her if she wants any advice and then offer it, but remember to be tactful. The worst thing you can do is to tell someone what a mistake they've made and how you've been telling them that for ages.

# BE A GOOD LISTENER

There are good and bad listeners. Some of us love listening to others and learn loads from being able to listen well. Others of us are more interested in hearing our own voices so we miss out on this.

You're a good listener if you

- Listen beyond the words. Anyone can hear the words someone else says, but are you really listening to what that person is trying to tell you?
- Observe their body language. When we talk we use more than words. Our whole bodies tell a tale.
- Stay focused. Sometimes it takes focus and energy to listen to another person. Don't become distracted.

You're a bad listener if you

- Interrupt the person while they're talking.
- Think about what you can say next while someone's talking.
- Don't respond directly to what she's said once she's finished, instead coming back with a bigger and more interesting story that's about you.
- Are constantly looking over your shoulder to see if anyone more interesting is around.

People can tell subconsciously whether you're a good listener or not and if they think you aren't, they'll eventually stop sharing things about themselves with you. Don't give yourself a hard time if you think you're a bad listener. Just remember, when you're next talking with a friend (or anyone else for that matter), to consider the above pointers and listen well. Listening is a skill, and something that needs to be developed. If you want to be a good 'people person' and have a career where communicating is important, then good listening is vital.

My only warning about becoming a great listener is that people will often notice this quality in you and start to use you for it. We get so much from being listened to that it's easy to see why people want good listeners around them. Protect yourself and when you've had enough of listening, stop, otherwise you'll end up getting drained and tired. It takes a lot of energy to listen properly, so you have the right to choose who you want to give that energy to.

# MAKE THE EFFORT

It's amazing how much it can mean to someone when you perform even the smallest kind gesture – bringing people back presents from holiday, remembering to call on someone's birthday, sending someone an email. But don't just give to make people like you. Reminding people how much you gave them later shows that it wasn't really giving.

If one of your friends moves to a new school or city, remember that she's the one that has had her life uprooted and will have to make new friends. Be there for her. Ring her and stay in touch with her. Let her know that you miss her, and even make the effort to go and visit her. People really appreciate that extra bit of attention and love, more than we tend to remember. Now, with the use of email, it's so easy to stay in touch with friends wherever they are.

# ENCOURAGE EACH OTHER

For me, a big part of being the woman I want to be is encouraging the women around me to be their best – thinking highly of them and really wanting them to succeed. We can help another girl feel good about herself by letting her know how truly great she is. So if you have a great friend and can see what her gifts are, help bring them out. Encourage her to develop her gifts and let others know how much you respect her. Compliment her in front of others (especially boys) and help others see her brilliance. We spend so much time doing the opposite because, once again, we're scared it means there will be less attention for us.

The girls I respect and look up to the most are the ones who live by this rule. They will comment on how beautiful and wonderful you are even in front of their boyfriends. They're comfortable and secure with their own beauty, boyfriend and intelligence, so they don't need to feel they have to diminish yours. You'll notice that these girls don't feel the need to hog all the limelight and will instead bring you into the light with them. They'll make you feel comfortable and welcome and open their hearts to you. These are our true female role models.

Da Sistahs!

# MOON MAIDENS

Full moons are a very potent time for doing any kind of ritual, but are especially powerful if you want to bring new things into your life. A woman's own cycle matches the moon's, both are around 28 days long. The moon is thought of as feminine energy, whereas the sun is thought of as masculine energy. The best time to come together and do a ritual is the night before the moon becomes completely full. This is when the energy is most powerful and rituals are most effective. You might have already noticed a change in yourself around this time before; and once you start getting in touch with the moon's cycle, it's very common for people to start feeling different. The weather often becomes wilder and things can become really intense. If you feel at all connected to what I'm talking about with the full moon energy, check out the ritual below.

Fiona Horne, Australia's most famous witch and author of *Teen Witch* has this ritual/spell for you to do at the time of the full moon.

The full moon is a great time to do magic of any sort, but particularly for girls it is a time to unleash and honour your inner goddess. The magic that is created by doing this can then be used to fuel goals, desires and dreams so that they come to fruition.

## FULL MOON MAIDEN RITUAL

### Time:
Midnight of the Full Moon

### Preparation:
Create a bath fit for a goddess by adding 1 cup of camomile tea and 9 drops of lavender oil to the running water in your bath. Sprinkle scented white flowers and petals on the surface (say, jasmine, gardenia or white rose). Take your time and soak in the water, allowing the stress of the day to dissolve away, so that you are ready to enter the world of feminine magic and enchantment.

After your bath, dress in white, put white flowers in your hair in honour of the Maiden face of the goddess, and if possible be barefoot.

### The Ritual:
Outside, in the light of the full moon, place the following.

### You will each need:
A white, drip-free candle and holder
A piece of white paper and silver pen
A small fire, or cauldron, in which a fire can burn
A couple of handfuls of dried lavender
Food (say crescent-moon shaped biscuits) and drink (sparkling grape juice or champagne)

Light the candles, stand in a circle around your fire or cauldron with your objects in front of you, then each throw a handful of lavender (sacred to the Moon goddess) into the fire and raise your arms in the air gazing at the moon. Joyfully intone the following:

*Goddess of the Moon,*
*Radiant in our eyes*
*Glowing in our hearts*
*Shining in our spirit*
*We honour your presence*
*Within and without*

Feel the glorious lunar energy flow into you through your outstretched arms and illuminate your feminine lunar energy within. Now, all hold hands and still gazing at the moon, say:

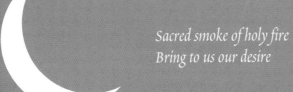

*We honour each other*
*Each Goddess manifest*
*We seal this blessing*
*Sent with a kiss*

Now kiss each person to the right of you, and as you do so, say: 'Thou art Goddess'.

When everyone is blessed, sit and create a petition by writing your goal, desire or dream on the piece of paper. When you're all finished, throw your petitions into the fire at the same time, followed by another handful of lavender each. Hold hands and together say:

*Sacred smoke of holy fire*
*Bring to us our desire*

Chant this over and over again as the smoke carries your wishes up into the sky, blessed by the powerful energies you have conjured as Moon Maidens. When the energy peaks, seal the spell by saying 'So Mote it Be', drop your hands to the earth and ground any excess energies.

Stay and enjoy food and drink together, pouring some on the earth as libations to the goddess.

When you leave your circle, carry the beauty of your ritual in your hearts to illuminate and bless all your endeavours in the coming days and always know that you are sacred and special! – a divine earthly expression of the universal feminine forces of magic.

Da Sistahs!

I found out recently that my best friend snogged my boyfriend while I was away this summer. She says she's really sorry and it didn't mean anything, but I don't know whether I can forgive her or not. Do you think I should? I haven't broken up with my boyfriend and I'm more upset with her because she's an old friend. (Vanessa, 16)

**I'm surprised that you so easily forgave him** but not her. We tend to get more angry with the girl because we feel like she now has power over us. If she's a really good friend, I would try and patch it up and not let a guy get in between the two of you. Friends are really important and I'd always give someone a second chance. You decide whether she's normally a good friend or not, and ask her why she did it. Was it to be competitive with you, or just because she was drunk, or because she really liked him? Ask her to be honest with you and then make your decision. You might just need space from her and then let her back in your life when it's less painful.

 One of my closest girlfriends is always being competitive with me. In front of boys she turns into a really flirtatious, silly girl and puts me down at every given opportunity. I've tried to talk to her about it before but she just tells me I'm being silly. It's really annoying me and I'm thinking of just not hanging out with her any more. Do you think I should stop being her friend? (Samantha, 14)

**I don't know if you need to be as drastic** as that, but maybe you could decide not to hang out with her when boys are around. It's a shame girls feel they need to do this to each other, but it's because she's insecure and obviously feels threatened by you. Otherwise she wouldn't feel the need to put you down. Get her to read this chapter and maybe she'll get some insight into how being nice to each other is important, and that there's enough attention and love to go around for all of us.

 I can't help feeling really jealous of my best friend. She has it all. She's really beautiful, smart, funny and talented. Next to her I look like a plain Jane and whenever we go out she gets all the attention from the guys. Recently I did something really bad. I spread a rumour about her that makes her look bad, and now people have started being mean to her at school. I feel really guilty, but don't know what to do to fix it. (Monica, 16)

**If you can muster up enough courage, you should tell her** what you've done and why you've done it. You need to be prepared for her to be angry with you, but at the end of the day she will hopefully respect that you've been honest with her. It's not her fault that she's beautiful and intelligent and that boys like her – she obviously likes you and thinks you're great as well, or she wouldn't be your friend. You might even be surprised to hear that she's jealous of you about certain things as well. I envy different aspects of all of my friends and I'm sure they do with me as well, but these very things we're jealous of are the same reasons why we're probably friends with them in the first place. Your friend hasn't done anything wrong and she doesn't deserve to have everyone against her. You need to deal with the consequences and set that right. Start concentrating on your own gifts instead of hers.

My best friend has made friends with these girls in the year above me and she's started spending less and less time with me. I told her that she's leaving me out but she denies it and tells me to stop being silly. I feel really sad that we're growing further and further apart but I don't know what to do. (Laura, 15)

It is sad when friends start moving away from us and make new friends. Have you tried to make new friends with these older girls as well? I don't see why she can't include you as well. Or do you think she doesn't want you to be a part of it? If this is the case, maybe you should spend sometime getting to know some new people yourself. Let her do her thing – that's also the role of a good friend. She might be trying to prove something by hanging out with older people, and if you can give her some space to explore these new friendships then I would.

I'm just about to start a new school and I'm really worried that I won't be able to make any friends. Everyone will have already known each other for three years. I'm also really shy so it takes me a long time to make friend. Do you have any tips? (Elaine, 14)

I've started lots of new schools before and even though it can be nerve-racking, you will find people to be friends with. They'll probably be happy to meet someone new. Sometimes when we're shy we need to pretend that we're not, as though we're acting at it. Then, before you know it you'll find it easy, once you get used to talking to people. Try and be open with people and look them in the eyes. Go up to people and introduce yourself; tell them that you're new and you don't know anyone and would they mind showing you around the school. It will probably happen naturally and before you know it, you'll forget altogether that you're the new girl.

Well Sistahs!, after reading this chapter you'll hopefully cherish your friendships even more, and recognise the importance of supporting each other rather than competing with one another. All friendships have their ups and downs, but we all need good friends and being a good friend to someone is important. Don't let feelings of jealousy and competitiveness get the better of you – enjoy each other's inner and outer beauty and let each other know how great you think they are. A real friend and real woman loves other women and supports them in the best way she knows how. This world can be a lonely place and without good friends we can end up lonely. So treasure one another and celebrate your friendships; they're the most important things you have.

Da Sistahs!

# ARE ALL FAMILIES MAD?

As we grow up and change, our relationships with our family members can change too. This can often lead to rows with our parents, or feelings of distance from them. It's natural. We're becoming more independent and want to have more control of our lives, and parents often seem to be blocking that path. Some of us also begin to see the mistakes our parents have made – often hurtful ones – and this can lead us to question their decisions, and even disagree with their religious and moral beliefs.

There are loads of other challenges at around this time, too. We live in an age where the 'nuclear family' (mum, dad and 2.4 children) is no longer the norm. More and more of us are having to deal with parents splitting up, step families, and seeing less and less of one or other parent. And as well as all this new stuff, we've still got to deal with getting on with our siblings, leaving the security of our homes, and all the other crazy things that being in a family can bring. Phew!

# PARENTS AND CHILDHOOD

This chapter encourages you to look at your relationships with your parents and hopefully let go of any unhealthy self-beliefs you've picked up from childhood. It also talks about the challenges of family life and ways of communicating – without those rows!

The important thing for all families is to be willing to be honest with each other and TALK about any problems.

## THE COMMUNICATION BEGINS

Have you ever thought about why you are the way you are? Why you like certain films or songs? Why you get on with the people you do? Why you react in different ways to things? Do you believe your personality traits have been passed on to you by your parents' genes, or that you're a product of your experiences and the influence of the people around you?

Whichever theory you believe (for me it's a mixture of both), one thing's for sure: that we are all closely linked to our parents. If you haven't been brought up by your birth parents, the same applies to the parental figures in your life. All this doesn't mean we necessarily become like our parents (even though we often do, and we don't always like it); it means we are moulded by their decisions, mistakes and general behaviour.

### THE KEY YEARS

Our first years on this planet are hugely influential on the rest of our lives. This is our first impression of the world, and as children we absorb everything. We believe our parents are right, however harsh or neurotic they may really be. So if they regularly say 'You're so clumsy, you're so stupid', we'll believe them and hold on to that limiting belief about ourselves later on in life. Some parents are extremely loving, but always over cautious. 'Ooh, don't do that darling. You might fall over', or 'No, I don't want you going out because you might get hurt.' Sound familiar? If so you might have grown up feeling that the world is a scary place and may always feel slightly nervous and on edge. Parents (and guardians) affect us both positively and negatively. That's something I've learnt, now that I'm a stepmum and I work with children – however well-meaning and loving you are, you can't get it completely right. The important thing is now that you're becoming a woman it's time for you to decide for yourself what kind of person you want to be, rather than being dictated to by your parents. We can't avoid being moulded by them to a certain extent, but we can pick and choose the bits we want to take with us into adulthood.

## Why looking at your childhood is important

- It teaches you more about yourself.
- It helps you to shed light on unhealthy beliefs you might have about yourself that aren't true.
- It helps you get in touch with what you want out of life and your gifts and passions.
- It can help you start to tell the difference between the things that your parents want you to do and the things that you want to do for yourself.

**Looking and learning about your past helps you be a better person in the present.**

Some parents might feel scared about the prospect of you looking at your relationships with them. When I started looking at my own relationship with my parents and my childhood, I could tell by their reactions that they were frightened — my mum immediately said, 'You're not going to start blaming everything on me are you?' and my Dad sent me a newspaper article which argued that the way you turned out was 'nothing to do with how your parents treated you, it's all to do with your peers'. (I wonder what he was trying to hint at by that.) Before we go any further, I want you to know that it's okay for you to feel angry, hurt or pissed off with them. You might have been brought up feeling that you couldn't question any of their decisions — well, now is the time to know that you can. And, yes, it might be scary for them because they could be forced to look at their behaviour and not be ready to change it. But the most important thing to remember is that this is about you. It's not about getting them to agree with you or apologise for everything; it's about you allowing yourself the space to feel these different emotions and, hopefully, starting to let go of some the pain you've felt in the past (and the present). If you don't start now, you could get more set in your ways and find it even harder later on in life.

　　　　　　　　Are All Families Mad?

I want to make the point, that however much our parents screw us up, they also usually give and teach us a lot of good stuff. This section is about looking at some of the hurtful things we have been told by our parents and understanding that it doesn't mean they didn't try their best.

We know that most parents want the best for us, and sometimes they try to give us the opportunities they never had. But this can sometimes bring a huge pressure for us to be high achievers in everything we do. When you get your report at the end of term, how important is it that you take it home showing them straight As? Do they expect you to work hard and achieve goals you feel are out of your reach? Sometimes if parents never fulfilled their own dreams, they try and pressure their kids into doing it for them. You could, for example, have a mother who wanted to be an actress but had children and gave up her career for her family. Or you might have a dad who was brought up in a poor family and never had the opportunities you've been given. He might push you and use the fact that he never had anything when he was a kid, against you. If this is how it is for you, explain to them that you find the pressure hard and you'll try your best, but you'll do it for yourself and not for them. You might also need reassurance that they'll love you whether or not you get an A on your next exam.

As well as school and work pressure, they sometimes also enforce their religious beliefs, morals and opinions on us. This can extend to the clothes we wear, the friends we hang around with and the music we listen to. It's important to be honest with your parents when you feel you're being bullied or pressured into doing things you don't want to do. They have to understand that you might be different from them and you don't necessarily want the same things. It's up to parents to encourage us to express our individuality from a young age. It's up to us to remind them that our lives are about us and not them (in the nicest possible way, obviously!).

## DADS: DISTANT AND DIFFICULT?

Here are some of the 'Dad' problems you mentioned you have

> 66 My Dad is **really strict**. He hates my boyfriend and hardly lets me see him and he never let's me go out with my friends at night. He doesn't trust me at all and it's driving me crazy. I used to get on with him brilliantly but I can't stand him any more. (Natalie, 15) 99

> 66 I never get to see my Dad now that he's got a new family. He's moved to the countryside with them and I feel that most of the time he's forgotten we even exist. (Harriet, 15) 99

> **"** My Dad no longer plays silly games with me and he rarely ever hugs me any more. I think he feels **uncomfortable** now that I'm becoming a woman and he doesn't quite know how to be around me. (Bianca, 15) **"**

> **"** I love my Dad but I don't get to see him very much. He's **always working** and because he and Mum aren't getting on very well, he spends the rest of his time down the pub with his mates. (Katherine, 17) **"**

From talking to girls and women and from my own experience, it seems that many of us feel that during our adolescent years we lose some of the strong bonds we had with our fathers when we were children. Going through puberty and adolescence is a weird time for us and it can be weird for them too. We're growing up and becoming women, and we're no longer Daddy's little girl. Some dads find it difficult watching us become independent and starting to date guys. They might also feel awkward about being affectionate while we're discovering our sexuality. One minute they are bathing us, and the next we're locking the bathroom door behind us. On the other hand, part of us might still crave that bond. And our dads probably do too. Dads sometimes need reminding that although we're growing up we still need to know that they love us and are proud of us. If your dad no longer lives with you, which is becoming more and more common, keep the lines of communication open and tell him if you want to see more of him. Dads might assume that you've got better things going on now that you're older – why would you want to spend time with your boring old father? How do we let him know that he is still an important part of our life?

- Make an effort to spend time with him. Try and find some time together when it's just the two of you.
- Talk to him honestly about what you're up to. He's probably been there himself.
- Be affectionate towards him. Give him a cuddle or a kiss when you see him.
- Let him know that you feel you've grown apart. He probably feels the same way, but hasn't wanted to step on your toes.
- If you think he's overly strict with you, sit down with him and calmly explain that you're growing up and you need him to give you a bit more freedom. Tell him that you want to prove to him that you are sensible and that you can be trusted.

Are All Families Mad?

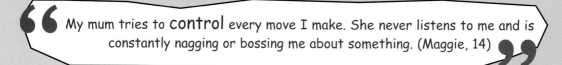

# MUMS: FEISTY AND SMOTHERING?

I also spoke to some of you about how you feel about your mums

> " My mum tries to **control** every move I make. She never listens to me and is constantly nagging or bossing me about something. (Maggie, 14) "

> " My mum's a **pain in the butt**. She is always meddling in my business, telling me what to do. She never lets me stay out as late as my friends' mums let them.
> (Louise, 17) "

> " I know my mum really loves me but I wish she'd stop worrying about me all the time. She's been like that since I was a kid, **always scared** I was going to hurt myself or mess up. (Susannah, 14) "

> " She **shouts** at me at every given opportunity and freaks out if I dare to shout back. It's becoming unbearable, living together, and I'm thinking about moving out.
> (Rachel, 18) "

If you're someone who never sees your mum because you've always slammed a door in her face or walked off in a huff, don't worry, you're not alone. It is very common for us to start fighting with our mums when we're teenagers. Both want control and both think they know what's best. Our mums (usually) ultimately want what's best for us and they don't want us to make the same mistakes they did, whereas we want to start being more independent and be allowed to make our own decisions (even if they're sometimes wrong).

- Mums need to understand that our mistakes usually make us stronger and can hopefully help us make different decisions in the future.
- We need to understand that they want to protect their babies from all the bad things that could happen to them.
- Both sides will need to leave each other a lot of space to avoid massive blowouts. I know for me and most girls I've spoken to, arguing is just a phase, and once you're a bit older and have maybe moved out of home it calms down (a bit!) For techniques as to how to avoid the blazing rows, see p146.

## LOOK AGAIN — THEY'RE REAL PEOPLE TOO

Now that you've looked a bit more closely at the relationship you have with your parents and how they've influenced and affected you, it's time to think about ways you can be more accepting of them as individuals. You can start this by taking a closer look. We often see our family members simply in terms of their family roles, 'Mum', 'Older sister', 'Dad', etc. We might think we know our parents brilliantly as Mum and Dad, but do we know them as individuals? Do we see beyond their family roles? Becoming a woman includes removing these titles for a moment and acknowledging your parents as more than these things, by acknowledging the roles they play with other people – friends, work colleagues, etc. Once we take away the 'Mum' and 'Dad' tags we get the chance to see that they're actually people in their own right, with their own dramas, pasts, hopes and dreams.

A good way to start seeing your parents as individuals, with their own unique stories, is to ask them about their childhoods. What kind of relationships did they have with their parents? Were they naughty at school? What were their friends like? I'm sure they'll be more than willing to talk about their lives and it will help you understand them more as people. Seeing them more clearly will help you to understand the patterns that may have led to them to making certain choices in their lives.

Are All Families Mad?

## THE LETTER EXERCISE

Now that you've explored different ways your parents have affected you, it's time for you to get some of those old resentments, anger and pain off your chest. The exercise below gives you a chance to express some of those past hurts and wounds, and to open up a dialogue with your parents about them.

Start off by finding some time when you know you won't be disturbed. Sit in silence, with your eyes closed and check in with yourself about how you're doing.

I now want you to address two letters to your parents or your guardians. If your parents are separated or you want to write to them individually, that's fine.

When you're ready, ask yourself, 'If I could write a letter to my parents, being really honest with them about things they've done or said that have upset me, what would I say?' Don't hold back! Write a letter to them that gets everything off your chest. Try and go back in time to the first upsetting thing they did that you remember. The letter might take you a while to write. Don't worry if you think you're writing too much or you feel guilty about what you're writing – let it free flow. If you feel emotions coming up such as sadness, frustration or anger, then allow yourself to really feel them. The more we feel our emotions, the more we can release them and stop them controlling our behaviour in the future.

When you've finished, sit back and give yourself some time and space to allow your emotions to settle. Writing the letter may have been harder to do than you thought. It might have brought up a lot of feelings for you. Find the place in your body where you can feel they're stuck or swelling up – usually the stomach, solar plexus, heart or throat. Breathe into these areas and feel them gradually release and relax.

The second letter I want you to write is a letter expressing your gratitude to your parents. Everything they've done for you or said to you that has made you feel good and loved. All the ways they've supported you. Decide if you want to write this letter straight away or wait a couple of days till the experience of writing the first one has died down a bit. So, address another letter to your parents and this time write a thank you letter. Once you've finished, sit back and take in how you're feeling.

## What to do with the letters:

> ## You have several options
>
> - You can give them to your parents.
> - You can give one to your parents and hold on to the other one until you feel ready to give it to them.
> - You can burn one or both of them. Writing someone a letter is sometimes enough in itself without having to actually deliver it.

### THEIR RESPONSE

If you give your parents the letters, it may have more of an impact on them than you expect. Be prepared for this. Also be prepared to not get the response you wanted or expected. Just because you're expressing your feelings to someone, doesn't mean that they'll be ready to hear or understand it, especially when your anger and upset is directed at them. Also, remember that just because one person remembers an experience a certain way, it doesn't mean that that's how everyone else remembers it. It's a hard one, because everyone likes to think they've remembered things the way they actually were but in the moment we all read things differently.

I wrote my Mum a letter like the one you've just done when I was younger, and she wasn't ready to hear what I had to say. She dismissed it, saying she didn't have time and that I clearly already had everything I could possibly want. This ended up hurting me even more because she couldn't even start to listen or accept how her absence was hurting me.

But that was a risk I had to take and I would do the same again. She actually found the letter again recently and told me how much it had made her cry. So even if your parents aren't ready to respond now, they might be in the future. Just by writing it, though, you have stepped into your power and acknowledged that your feelings are worth expressing, regardless of your parents' reactions. You have started to look deeper into your relationship with your parents and, even though that can sometimes be painful and frustrating, I promise you that in the long run, it will be liberating for both of you. However, if you feel it may upset them too much then simply burn the letters. It will still be a very empowering exercise for you and you can always talk to your parents rather than hand them a letter.

Are All Families Mad?

## ACCEPTANCE AND FORGIVENESS

In From Girl to Woman (pp18-38), I discuss how forgiveness plays a part in becoming a woman. We often have pent-up anger and old resentments towards our parents and even if we're right, the only person it's going to hurt is ourselves because we're carrying that pain inside us, not them. I'm not saying that sometimes it isn't right to cut off from a parent, and I'm not blind to the fact that parents sometimes do things that aren't forgivable. But if you feel that you're ready to start to forgive them for their past actions, it's important to start now. By forgiving them we're able to move on from our past and carry less baggage with us into the present.

This might not be the right time for you to forgive, and that's fine. Maybe you've even been hurt too much to ever forgive. If you can, though, I encourage you to come back to it at a later time when you feel that you are ready to forgive. Don't worry about when that will be; you'll know when the time is right.

The aim of this chapter is to help you improve your relationship with your parents (if you feel you need to), but I want you to be realistic too. The mistake I made, and I've seen many others make, was to try and change my parents into the way I wanted them to be. You're totally within your rights to want parents who treat you right and love you fully. But unfortunately some parents' best is not enough. You might wish your dad would sometimes tell you that he loved you, or that your mum would sometimes put you first, but however much you try to honestly tell them what you'd like from them, they can't give it to you and they might never do. It can be like banging your head against a brick wall, and sometimes you have to accept that they won't ever be the parents you want them to be. It can be really painful if you put too much energy into trying to change things, and it can be a disappointing road to go down. At some point (and it doesn't have to be right now), you need to accept them for who they are and start to let go of some of the stuff you emotionally want from them. Instead, concentrate on building beautiful, fulfilling relationships with friends and people that do treat you well and give you what you need.

 # THE BOTTOM LINE

- Parents and guardians have a huge influence on the way we are.
- Looking at your childhood and how it's affected you is vital for letting go of unhealthy self-beliefs and learning more about yourself.
- Be clear about what you're doing for you and what you're doing for them. You might have different views to them on how you want to live your life.
- Dads aren't always around as much as we'd like them to be. Let them know that you're still their little girl.
- If your mum keeps going on at you, try and understand that it's probably because she wants the best for you.
- Take some time to get to know your parents as more than just 'Mum' and 'Dad'. You might start seeing why they are the way they are.
- Start the dialogue. Let your folks know any past hurts you're holding on to, especially if their behaviour is still affecting you.
- Don't expect them to turn around and apologise for everything. They might not be ready to see the pain they've caused you or they might be angry with you for expressing it to them.
- At some point you might make a decisions to forgive your parents for the things they've done. If you're not ready or able to do this, though, don't worry. Sometimes people do things that are unforgiveable!
- At the end of the day, you might have to accept that your parents are never going to be exactly how you want them to be, which can be hurtful but will help you stop feeling disappointed.

Are All Families Mad?

# FAMILY PROBLEMS

I chose this chapter title really to make light of the fact that all families have their secrets, idiosyncrasies and general mad dysfunctional behaviour. This doesn't have to be something extreme, like drug addiction or abuse; it also includes families who sit around the dinner table and never have any truly meaningful communication, or parents who force their religious beliefs on their children even after they're old enough to make up their own minds. All of us have 'mad families', to some extent – there are just different degrees of dysfunction. Even seemingly perfect families have their own share of madness (and sometimes, even more). The families that can be open and talk about their problems are healthier than the ones that hide them.

## DIVORCE

I found my parents' divorce very painful and difficult. I was one of the last of my friends to have parents that split up so I found it harder to show anyone my pain. I thought I didn't have a right to be upset because everyone else had been through it before me. Because I was suppressing how I felt, I compensated by getting into drugs, booze and boys. I had always been naughty and wild, but when my parents separated I reached a new level of self-destructiveness. I was 14 at the time and just starting to come into my sexuality and have boyfriends. What I really needed was a safe place to show my feelings, and to have more communication with my parents about how I felt.

If your parents have split up (even if it was a long time ago), it's okay for you to be upset about it, even if it is becoming the norm. It is a very painful thing to go through and you're having to adapt to a completely new family unit. We all have different needs at times like this and it's important to vocalise them to our parents. Often, they're going through so much themselves that they don't realise you're finding it hard as well, and they might even lean on you for support.

- Tell your parents how you're feeling through it all; if you have a sibling, maybe confide in them too.
- You friends will rally round if you let them know you need them.
- Speak up and even get outside help if you need to.
- If you feel angry, allow yourself those feelings – it's your right to be pissed off. Don't try and protect your parents from your feelings – they are valid and important.
- Tell your parents that you don't want to feel like you're in the middle of their arguments. Tell them you don't want either of them to bad-mouth the other one to you.

Even if everyone you know has been through their parents splitting up, it's doesn't devalue your pain and hurt. It is a really hard thing to go through.

## WICKED? STEPMOTHERS (AND STEPFATHERS)

In fairy tales it's always the wicked stepmother who tries to hurt the innocent beautiful young princess. But why are stepmothers always portrayed as wicked? They're obviously not all evil (I'm one, after all) but when there's upheaval at home and new family members come on the scene, it's not always easy. A home consists of different people's personalities mixed together. The loud, abrasive teenage boy, the naughty mischievous toddler or the bad-tempered, overworked dad. You've got used to the vibes in your house when all of a sudden a new person comes along and everyone's got to shift around to fit them in. This could be a stepbrother or sister, a stepmum or a stepdad. For some people it's completely harmonious and everyone gets on happily ever after. For others, it's not such an easy ride.

My parents split when I was 14 and I inherited a stepmother. She was a close family friend so I knew her already, but when my dad moved into a new home with her and I was meant to spend weekends there, I spent as little time there as possible. I never felt I was in my own home, more like I was a guest. Even though my family hadn't exactly been conventional, it was the only one I'd known. It was hard to suddenly adjust to a new family member, one who had symbolically broken up the unit. I felt very distant from my father and bad for my mother. It's easy to blame a step-parent for the break-up of your parents' marriage and for any change in the relationship between you and a parent. But most of the time it's not anyone's fault. If our parents can't live together any more, we wouldn't want them to spend the rest of their lives feeling lonely, would we?

## BETRAYING A PARENT

Sometimes we can really like a new step-parent, but we feel that if we show it we're betraying our other parent in some way. They might not be able to stand this person but you find yourself liking them. Well, maybe don't shove it in your mum or dad's face that you get on brilliantly with their ex's new partner but also don't be mean to the new person for your abandoned parent's sake, or give yourself a hard time if you genuinely like them. Having an extra parental figure can be a great gift. It can mean having another person in your life who loves you and who looks out for you. It might sound far-fetched, but this new person could even be a blessing.

## Remember:

- You are the child in this situation and you don't have to feel responsible for everyone else's feelings.
- Try and be polite to the new person, but don't feel you have to be their best buddy just to please your parent.
- Don't play games with your parents by bad-mouthing one to the other or telling one private things about the other's new life.
- If you feel you don't get enough one-on-one time with the parent that left and now they have a new partner, let them know.
- Don't blame yourself if you find yourself liking your new step-parent. It's not your job to hate them.
- Remember, the new person in your life could even improve your relationship with your parent — if they're cool, that is!

Are All Families Mad?

If you have a brother or a sister, you'll probably be familiar with the term sibling rivalry. It's when siblings compete with each other — usually the closer the age gap, the more they'll fight. We all have our moments, but if you feel like you can't even stand the sight of your brother or sister, you're not alone. Our siblings can get us riled up more than anyone else. They know just what to say to each other to hurt and provoke, better than anyone else. I fought horrendously with my brother when I was younger (we still have our moments now), and I was always told by adults that when we were older we'd get on better. I didn't believe a word of it.

Just as our parents have a huge influence on who we are, so do our siblings. If you have a sibling who always calls you names and is mean to you, after a while you might start to believe them. So be careful what you say to each other, and when you're making up after a fight; acknowledge that you didn't mean what you said or you might grow up having deep complexes. My brother always used to tell me I was fat and I used to always tell him he was short. Lo and behold, we grew up with major complexes, with me thinking that I was fat and him thinking that he was small. Luckily today, neither are true, but I think somewhere deep down in both of us we still hold on to these insecurities. The reason most siblings fight is because they are competing for their parents' attention (that's why it's called 'sibling rivalry'). Each is afraid the other will get it. This can be especially hard if you're the eldest child. You're used to having all the attention and then suddenly you've got to share it with a younger 'annoying' brother or sister. There's no rule stating that all siblings should get on, but it's a shame when they don't. The love between siblings isn't one you should miss out on if you have them. So make the effort; include your little sister and don't torment your older brother. Be there for each other and look out for each other, especially if you go to the same school. Know that one day your kids will probably all play with each other, and by showing them that you love and get on with one another, they'll hopefully follow your lead.

# LETTING GO OF THEIR LITTLE GIRL

Often it's even harder for our parents to let go of us than for us to let go of them. They've spent the last 18 years or so putting all their love and energy into us, and then suddenly one day we're moving out. We might be everything to them and just as they've given us everything, we've also given them companionship, love and, above all, the feeling of being needed. It can be especially hard for single parents. Single parents form extremely intense relationships with their children, and if there's no partner to fall back on they might be scared of being alone. If this is the case in your family, it won't be easy because you probably don't want to cause them any pain. It's vital, though, that you make decisions for yourself. At the end of the day, they're the adult, and they'll get through it. Now it's your turn to live your life and to be free. How many of you have said that you often feel like your parents' parents? It's ironic, but we often end up looking after them and feeling responsible for their wellbeing. If this is the case for you it might be even harder for your parents to let go, as they're leaning on you for emotional support. You need to encourage them to find support from other areas of their life.

 # THE BOTTOM LINE

- Divorce can be very painful even if all your friends' parents' are divorced as well. Allow yourself the space to grieve the loss of your parents no longer being together.
- Accepting step-family members can be hard, but remember it's not their fault that your parents split up.
- Don't feel guilty if you get on with a step-parent; your other parent should be mature enough to know that it's a good thing if you all get on, and not feel threatened.
- If you have siblings, don't always be competitive with them. Instead encourage each other and include each other in your lives.
- Your relationship with your siblings might be bad now, but often our relationships with them change as we get older.
- They might find it hard letting go of their little girl but they have to let you go at some point. Don't be trapped into feeling guilty that you're growing up and moving on. They need to be responsible for their feelings.

Are All Families Mad?

# COMMUNICATION - THEIR SIDE

I talked to several parents about their relationships with their daughters. This is what a couple of them had to say.

> She never listens to me. She thinks she's always right and that I'm a Neanderthal from the prehistoric ages. I sometimes wish she would actually stop and think that maybe I actually want what's best for her. I know of the dangers involved with sex, drugs and going out, and **I don't want her to get hurt.** (Wendy, 48)

> I used to be really close to my daughter but ever since she's become a teenager **all we do is fight.** She's even started swearing at me and storming off when we're arguing. I feel like she's out of control and one of these days I won't be able to handle her and she'll leave. I just want my sweet little girl back. (Susan, 44)

# COMMUNICATION - YOUR SIDE

I also spoke to you about your side of things.

> My mum is the biggest control freak I've ever met. She has to know my every move and it drives me mad. She's constantly nagging and she ignores anything I've got to say. I wish that she'd get a life instead if trying to control mine! (Jasmine, 17)

> My dad has turned into an opinionated, patronising, boring old fart. He's so paranoid that something bad is going to happen to me that he never stops to think that maybe I know how to look after myself. He never trusts my side of it and always tells me that I'm too young to understand. (Lisa, 16)

The problem is that both sides feel that the other doesn't respect or listen to their opinions. If there's no respect there in the first place, it's very hard to communicate. Even though you're the younger one, try and be as an adult should be and stay calm and blame-free. It's when we start feeling got at and not listened to that a lot of the fighting begins – for both of you.

# RESPECT

Respect between a child and a parent is very much a two-way street. If either of you believe it's just you that deserves respect then it's going to be hard to get real. You wouldn't be normal if you didn't disagree with your parents sometimes. What you want for you and what they want for you are sometimes two completely different things. They'll say they know what's best, they've been there before and they're older. You'll say that it's different now, they're overprotective and they're trying to control you. These arguments have been going on since time began and your parents probably had the very same ones with their own parents. But if we don't respect and listen to each other's opinions we'll never get anywhere.

If you have a parent who you think never listens to your side of things, then decide today that you're going to make time to talk to them about it, and not while you're angry but when you're feeling calm and – dare I say it – respectful.

- Try and get them on their own. Choose a moment when there isn't chaos going on around you and talk to them from the heart.
- Compromise is usually the key. Both of you will have to budge a little bit and agree to review things every month and maybe re-evaluate things.
- Talk about all the different things you want to discuss with them – i.e. boys, staying out, where you can go, money, clothes you can wear, keeping your bedroom tidy – separately.
- Make deals with them. If you promise to keep your bedroom tidy and help with the chores, can they give you a bit more pocket money? If you come home on time for a whole month, can you stay out half an hour later?

### Remember to: ←

- Explain to them that you don't always feel you get heard and that you think your opinions are worth listening to.
- Tell them that you do respect their side of things but you feel like they need to consider your side too.
- Acknowledge that they have their reasons and they're also worth taking into consideration.

The way we communicate is essential to sorting things out. In Boyz (p102) chapter I've talked about ways to avoid screaming matches with boyfriends; well it can also be applied to how we talk to our parents.

Oh, yeah. Never say to them, 'But everyone else's mum/dad lets them' – it **NEVER** works and usually ends up annoying them even more!

Are All Families Mad?

# SAYING I LOVE YOU WITHOUT THROWING UP

This might sound obvious but we often forget to tell the people closest to us how much we love them. Do you have a mum who is constantly juggling a hundred things? Do you have a dad that goes to work early every morning and returns home exhausted late every evening? Show them and tell them that you appreciate them and love them very much (without vomiting please!).

If you have siblings, give them encouragement in their lives. Tell them you're proud to be their sister and how great you think they are. If you're the older one, take them out occasionally with you and your mates and let them know they're included.

# CONVERSATIONS WITH THE ELDERS

Take time to get to know the elders in your family – maybe spend one day a fortnight with them helping them do the gardening or bake a cake. Find out what your grandparents enjoy doing and then spend some time doing it with them. Both of you will get so much from spending time together, and old people like nothing more than being asked questions and reminiscing. Ask your grandparents about your family history: what was your Mum or Dad like? (You might be lucky and even get some gossip on them.) Try asking them soul-searching questions about love, relationships and family; you might be surprised at how much they open up to you and how much insight they have. Make time to connect with the older people in your family before you miss the chance and spend the rest of your life wondering what your grandparents were like.

# GATHER YOUR OWN TRIBE

When I say this, I mean gathering your own set of close friends and creating a family between you. Have you ever met someone and felt like you're part of the same family? They might look similar to you or have the same interests. These people don't come along every day so honour their friendships and create your own family with them. This can still include real family members; it's people who you feel really at ease with and understood by. In this day and age, I think it's vital to create your own family, your tribe. People that you can let it all hang out with, cry, fart, be silent with and share a bed with. This is especially important if you're someone who doesn't have great relationships with your own family. You need a loving supporting group around you and sometimes you have to DIY. These are people you will be able to ring at any moment and know that they'll be there to help in a second. Choose them carefully and honour the specialness of this kind of relationship.

 # THE BOTTOM LINE

- Communication is KEY. You need to be able to talk to your parents and them to you with MUTUAL respect. Sometimes we need to make compromises.
- It might sound obvious, but remember to tell each other that you love and appreciate each other. Put some time aside to have fun and enjoy each other's company.
- Listen to the elders in your family. They hold a lot of wisdom and story about your families past. Ask them questions and you might be surprised by some of their answers (especially the intimate ones about your folks!).
- Create your own tribe, especially if you feel you don't have a great connection with your family. Your tribe will see you through the good and hard times.

Are All Families Mad?

> **"** I know it's an awful thing to say but I really hate my mum. She's an alcoholic and when she's drunk (which is most of the time) she starts being really abusive and telling me how worthless I am and that having me ruined her life. My dad and her split up when I was two and I hardly ever see him and I don't have any brothers or sisters. I'm thinking of moving out but because I'm only 15 I'd have to move into care or out onto the streets. What should I do? (Christine, 15) **"**

Do you have another family member like a grandparent or an aunt that you could talk to or live with? Maybe you could even tell your Dad what's going on. He might not have been a very good father to you in the past but maybe he's ready now. You definitely need to get some outside help and I can understand that you don't want to go into care, but sometimes it can work out brilliantly. You can stay with foster parents until your Mum has sorted herself out. You can even visit her on the weekends. Even though your Mum says really nasty things to you, it is the alcohol talking and you need to know that they aren't true. However, it is abusive to talk to a child like that and you need to be in a safe environment and looked after properly. In the long run if you move out it might influence your Mum to get better, which is ultimately the best thing. You need to get outside help.

> **"** My parents never listen to me and I'm fed up with it. They assume that because they're older than me they know everything and they stop me from doing anything that I want to. I wish I could make them at least listen to me, but they have no respect for me at all. How can I do this? (Kate, 14) **"**

It is important that our parents listen to us as much as we listen to them. They need to know that you are worth listening to and compromises should be made. They sound really overprotective, so why don't you agree to get a mobile phone and tell them you'll ring them regularly when you go out to let them know you're safe. Explain that you'll soon be old enough to move out and make your own decisions, so why don't they start giving you a little bit of freedom now. Tell them kids who have really strict parents are often even wilder when they get older because they've been so restricted most of their life. I'm sure that might make them think again about being so strict.

> **"** My parents recently split up and it completely messed me up. My dad had been having an affair with the woman he's now living with. What I hate is that my mum constantly tells me how awful my dad is and my dad keeps trying to get me to spend more time with him in his new home, but I know how much it will upset my mum. This Christmas my dad has invited me to go away with him to Thailand, which I would love to do but I don't know if I can leave my mum on her own. I hate always feeling responsible for her and wish she wouldn't lean on me so much for support. How do I tell her? (Rachel, 15) **"**

It's common for parents to turn to their children when their marriage has split up but it really isn't fair. We're having to deal with our own feelings as it is, without feeling responsible for theirs as well. If you want to go to Thailand you should. It's an amazing opportunity and your mum should want you to go. She should make fun plans herself so she can let her hair down and start to get over your dad. Tell your mum that you don't like it when she's mean about your dad; she might not even realise she's doing it. You obviously love your dad as well and you have a right to continue having a close relationship with him.

 I used to have a really good relationship with my brother but he's started getting more and more distant. I think he's doing drugs but when I asked him he told me to leave him alone. He's really changed and even the clothes and music he now listens to are different. I really want him to be honest with me about what he's up to. How can I get him to do this? (Milly, 13)

You might be right that your brother is getting into drugs, but there's nothing you can do if he doesn't want to tell you. You don't want to betray him and talk to your parents, so tell him that you're worried about him. Give him the opportunity to be honest and then respect whatever he tells you. He might just be smoking pot or hanging out with a different group of mates. Also, when boys go through adolescence they can often seem more distant and moody. Ask him how he feels about drugs as a whole and if he's against them or not. It's very hard to get involved with someone's personal stuff if they think we're going to be against what it is they're doing.

In this chapter I've mostly focused on things we can improve within our families. I'm not cynical, though, I know that there are families where the children get on, Mum and Dad are still together and the whole family love each other very much. Some parents are doing a great job and most parents are trying to do their best, and I give them huge credit for that. (Bringing up a family isn't easy, especially doing it well.) Hopefully, though, one or two things in this chapter will have rung true for you and will help you get along and understand each other even more. Remember, however much you fight or think you hate them, your family will always be there for you and that is priceless.

Are All Families Mad?

# I'M A SURVIVOR

This chapter is essentially about looking after yourself, and learning to respect and love yourself enough to be safe. It offers ways to protect yourself from outside harm and is a resource for you to find out information and read about issues such as drugs, suicide, depression and eating disorders.

As young women, we are in the highest bracket for inflicting self-harm, both physical or mental. Statistics are rising when it comes to eating disorders and drug addiction in young girls. Many of us seem prone to self-destructive behaviour and show low levels of respect towards our bodies. Maybe this is due to the lack of self-love many of us have and the pressures society puts on us to achieve highly at school, look and act a certain way, and to map out our futures.

# ABORTION

Emotionally, abortion can be a huge ordeal and not just for the female involved. Boys, who can often be a lot less mature, especially with their emotions, can also find this time painful and complicated. They are completely powerless in a decision so big it could change their entire lives. Remember that there are two of you involved and going through this with someone else can make it easier to deal with. Don't try and go through this completely on your own; talk to people that can support you and be there for you.

If you are worried that you might be pregnant, you can do a test straight after being late for your period. Some of the signs of pregnancy usually appear two to three weeks after conception. They vary from woman to woman, but may include: missing a period, a shorter, lighter period than usual, swelling or tenderness in the breasts, frequent peeing, feeling tired, nausea or vomiting (known as morning sickness, though it doesn't always happen in the morning), feeling bloated or having period-like cramps, changes in appetite and mood changes. If you notice any of these symptoms, have missed a period or are in any way worried, you can either do a pregnancy test yourself at home, or you can have one done free at your local GP, family planning or sexual health clinic, or a young person's clinic such as Brooks. Pregnancy tests are about 99 per cent accurate. Please find out as soon as possible, and even if you are under 16 it will be kept confidential.

If you end up deciding you want to have an abortion you can have one done up to 24 weeks of being pregnant, but if you decide to go down this route, it's best to have one done at 12–14 weeks. The abortion can be done either free on the NHS, or privately. If you decide you don't want your parents to know and you're under 16, the doctor can keep it confidential if she is sure that you are aware of the procedure and confident that you understand the decision you are making. She might advise you to see a counsellor or that you bring an older relative, such as an aunt or older sister, with you for the operation.

My own personal story regarding abortion is not a rare one. I have had two, the first when I was 16 and the second when I was 19. The first one was especially hard. I found out I was pregnant literally just after I had broken up with my boyfriend. We were not getting on any more and the relationship had become unhealthy. I decided to tell him that I was pregnant, though, mainly because I needed the support. Our relationship continued and remained on and off throughout the pregnancy and the termination. I found it hard because at first I couldn't decide whether I wanted to keep the baby or not. I realise now that the part of me that did want to keep it was an unhealthy part of me; the part that needed something to fill the big hole left from the break-up and general unhappiness in my life. I thought a baby might make me feel better. I'd have someone I could focus all my attention onto and who would love and need me in return.

Understanding that parenthood is a full-time job is easily forgotten when we're young. I once watched a TV chat show in which five young girls were interviewed about wanting to be young mothers. They each spent a day with a 'pretend' baby, that cried, urinated and needed to be fed every couple of hours. It had amazing results. Most of the girls realised what a full-time and tiring job motherhood was, and decided to wait till they were older.

For Sexual Health and Pregnancy issues, call The Family Planning Association (see Sistah Support at the end of the book), who will put you in touch with your local family planning or sexual health clinic. These clinics can see anyone over 16 without informing their parents – and under 16s who are deemed competent to make their own choices.

## THE FACTS ABOUT ABORTION AND TEENAGE PREGNANCIES

Teenage pregnancies are rising. In 1997, 96,000 teenage girls became pregnant and the following year the number rose to 101,500.

More than 8,000 girls under 16 got pregnant.

Nearly 40 per cent of teenagers who became pregnant had abortions (33,200 abortions).

Almost half of the girls under 16 who got pregnant had abortions (3,800 abortions).

About 90 per cent of teenage abortions were carried out before 13 weeks.

(Source: Office for National Statistics)

I'm A Survivor

# ABUSE

Not all our families want what's best for us – in fact some of us are born into families where there is mental, emotional or physical abuse. I work with children in foster care and regularly see children who have been neglected. Because their parents are either incapable of looking after themselves, let alone their children, or are deeply screwed-up, so they lash out at their children. Either way, a child has the right to be loved and taken care of. Most families have their problems but no child should be abused, ever. Foster care in the UK is improving and I feel very positive about my experiences working in the foster care system. Obviously, it's far from being perfect, but there is a lot of love and care taking place that we don't usually hear about.

If you feel you have been, or are being, abused by a family member it's essential that you speak up about it. You need to protect yourself and be safe from any further harm. You deserve to be looked after properly. If you speak up, it also gives others more courage to speak up and get help. Is there a teacher at school you can approach? Someone you can confide in who is not part of your family. You can also ring the childline number in Sistah Support at the end of the book. Please don't sit in silence, however scared you are. There are lots of people out there to help you and give you the love and attention you deserve. If you know someone who is being treated badly at home, encourage them to take action and get help.

# BULLYING

Any form of bullying is one of the worst things one human being can do to another. I wish schools dealt with bullies in a more effective way. It's society's fault if we don't stop this terrible practice and give both bully and victim the attention they need. People usually bully because they're acting out in some way – they might be getting bullied themselves, be unhappy at home or be crying out for attention. I don't excuse bullying but neither do I think that simply punishing the bully makes the problem to go away. Parents need to be told, teachers alerted and schools should in no way tolerate their behaviour. Some schools have started trying new anti-bullying systems like having 'bully boxes' where you can leave notes about any bullying that is taking place, or student meetings, where bullying is discussed and dealt with out in the open. All different sorts of people experience bullying at school and some very successful adults were bullied when they were young. It is encouraging to know that it is possible to succeed, in spite of being tormented at school. Even celebs like Kate Winslet and Tom Cruise were bullied in some way at school.

I spoke to Michelle Elliot the founder and director of Kidscape – a charity set up to prevent bullying – and she gave the following advice for what you can do if you're being bullied. Numbers and website details are in the Sistah support section at the back of the book.

## Tell a friend what is happening
Ask him or her to help you. It will be harder for the bully to pick on you if you have a friend with you for support.

## Try to ignore the bullying or say 'No' really firmly, then turn and walk away.
Don't worry if people think you are running away. Remember, it is very hard for the bully to go on bullying someone who won't stand still to listen.

## Try not to show that you are upset or angry.

Bullies love to get a reaction – it's 'fun'. If you can keep calm and hide your emotions, they might get bored and leave you alone. As one teenager said to us, 'They can't bully you if you don't care'.

## Don't fight back if you can help it.

Most bullies are bigger or stronger than you. If you fight back you could make the situation worse, get hurt or be blamed for starting the trouble.

## It's not worth getting hurt to keep possessions or money.

If you feel threatened, give the bullies what they want. Property can be replaced – you can't.

## Try to think up funny or clever replies in advance.

Make a joke of it. Replies don't have to be wonderfully brilliant or clever, but it helps to have an answer ready. Practise saying them in front of the mirror at home. Using prepared replies works best if the bully is not too threatening and just needs to be put off. The bully might just decide that you are too clever to pick on.

## Try to avoid being alone in the places where the bully is likely to pick on you.

This might mean changing your route to school, avoiding parts of the playground, or only using common rooms or lavatories when other people are there. It's not fair that you have to do this, but it might put the bully off.

## Sometimes asking the bully to repeat what they said can put them off.

Often bullies are not brave enough to repeat the remark exactly, so they tone it down. If they repeat it, you will have made them do something they hadn't planned on and this gives you some control of the situation.

## Keep a diary of what is happening.

Write down details of any bullying incidents and your feelings. When you do decide to tell someone, a written record of the bullying makes it easier to prove what has been going on.

If you're being bullied yourself, please don't let the bully get away with it. I know it can be scary to stand up for yourself or get others involved, but by being brave you might stop the bully from hurting others in the future. It's not your fault if you're being bullied. People that bully are wrong and need to be stopped. Don't be worried that by bringing adults in to it you might be bullied more. Keep getting people involved until it stops.

The more we bring bullying out into the open the more it will decrease. We live in a dysfunctional society where teachers are underpaid and don't have enough time to deal with everything. Bullies often get away with it because others don't confront them enough. Help change that, and help abolish all forms of bullying.

**SPEAK UP!**

I asked some girls how well they think bullying is dealt with at their school.

> 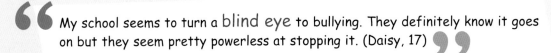 My school seems to turn a blind eye to bullying. They definitely know it goes on but they seem pretty powerless at stopping it. (Daisy, 17)

> I think our school is trying to improve ways of dealing with bullying but their efforts aren't working. In fact, bullying is increasing. (Catherine, 16)

> The teachers at my school are so busy that they just don't have the energy to stop bullies. It's a shame, though, because I've known a kid who committed suicide because of it. (Rachel, 15)

# COUNSELLING

I spoke to Rachel Creeger, School–Home Support Worker of the East London School's Fund, based at Daniel House Pupil Referral Unit, who gave me the following advice on counselling that is available in schools.

Your school might have a counsellor that you can speak to. They have to treat what you say with confidentiality, and having someone to speak to who is a complete stranger can make it easier to open up. Many schools have facilities that provide counselling for students. In secondary schools counselling is often topic specific, e.g. drugs / women / abuse / ethnic groups / ESL (English as a Second Language).

Schools also have to have a designated child protection teacher. In theory you should be able to speak to them confidentially. However, problems may arise if the issue discussed is against a specific school policy, e.g. drug addiction. Many schools now, however, employ a generic counsellor or a School–Home Support Worker, youth workers and project co-ordinators to make up a team for referral.

Counsellors who work in a topic-specific field can usually work with their clients around any issue as long as that topic features somewhere in their life, e.g. school drugs counsellors can see a young person who uses Ecstasy but really wants to talk about their family problems. You can talk to a generic counsellor about anything in confidence, apart from a few exceptions that apply to all counselling clients, which will be discussed with you beforehand. The exceptions are as follows:

- If the client is under 18, and their life is in danger because of a child protection issue, e.g. sexual/physical abuse. However, this is not immediate and a procedure is in place to actually empower the young person to report this themselves and to support them through the whole process.
- Genuine fear of harm to themselves or others – if the counsellor believes that their client is suicidal or violent and poses an immediate risk – the usual procedure is via the GP.
- Acts of terrorism / serious crime. If the client threatens to commit one of these, the police have to be informed.

Most importantly, there are no instant solutions and it is vital that you give your support or therapy a serious chance before giving up. Even then, rather than give up, you should consider why it wasn't helpful and try somewhere else.

## DEPRESSION – A HOLLOW; A DIP; A SINKING; DEJECTION; DESPONDENCY

Depression is something that isn't really talked about, but something a vast number of us experience. It's a place we go to on our own internally and it is a very low place to be. Think back to when you may have felt down for a long period of time. Did you feel that you were never going to be happy again? That no one could reach you? Did you not smile or laugh for a long while? You'd be surprised at how many of us do feel depressed at some point or another in our lives. When I was about 16, I fell into a depression which lasted about six months. I felt like I had reached the end and that there wasn't much point in continuing. I went around with an invisible cloak wrapped around me, making it hard for others to see in and me to see out. When you are depressed it is hard to see a way out and sometimes you think this is the way it's going to be for ever. Friends and family can assure you it'll pass but no words can penetrate your darkened emotions.

I spoke to some young women who talked to me about feeling depressed.

> " I had always been a really happy child, but something happened to me when I entered my teenage years. I suddenly felt like I was carrying the weight of the world on my shoulders. Every time I saw the news there was something dreadful happening to other people in the world, and I just couldn't understand why there was so much suffering. I found it really hard to talk to anyone and I spent most of my time on my own. In the end my parents sent me to a therapist who really helped me see that there was a lot of pain in the world but there was also a lot of joy. He opened my eyes and I stopped being depressed. Now I know to spend more of the time concentrating on the good stuff. (Kate, 17) "

> " I had always felt really special and even as a child I knew I was going to be a powerful successful person. I was an amazing pianist, I was pretty and I had lots of friends. People were always telling me how great I was, and I believed them. When I left home and went to university it all changed. No one seemed to care about who I was and I found it hard to be away from my friends and family and make new friends. I felt like an outcast and was suddenly no longer the brightest in the class, but somewhere in the middle. I felt like a 'nobody' and I entered a huge depression. I spent days on end without seeing or speaking to anyone. Until slowly I started making new friends. I realised that we're all special and you don't need to be THE MOST popular or talented to be happy. All of us have something to offer. I feel a lot better nowadays and I haven't been depressed since, but I can tell others that it was definitely a huge wake-up call for me and I think I'm actually a lot happier now than I've ever been. (Alex, 22) "

I'm A Survivor

I believe depression for most of us is a valuable part of the growing-up experience. When we are young we have huge ideals of how life is going to be. We think we're invincible and that we can do anything, and even change the world if we want to. Somewhere this innocence can be lost, either through constant knocks from life or from a diminishing of self-esteem. You realise it's not as easy as you thought and, even more painfully, that you aren't as important as you thought. In *The Hitchhiker's Guide to the Galaxy*, the author writes about the worst torture you can receive for your crimes in the future. The torture is being shown just how small and irrelevant you are in the scheme of it all, and the largeness of the universe.

## Here are a few things that might help when you are feeling depressed:

- Talk to people about what's going on for you. Don't close off to the point of always being on your own; it will only feed your depression.
- Read soul-searching books. One might not have the answer but reading a few might help you see you're not on your own and that life can get better.
- Seek professional help if you have to. Depression can be a serious thing and there are people out there who can help you.
- Remember, it will end. However bad you're feeling now, you will feel good again.
- It's easy to forget humour. Try and do or see something that will make you laugh.
- Do something to help other people who are worse off than you. It will give you a fresher perspective on your troubles, and it's really empowering to have your gifts gratefully received. It's hard to be down on yourself when you've been really giving that day.

If you suffer from prolonged and recurring depresssion you may have a medical condition called clinical depression, which can sometimes run in families. It can be treated. Consult a doctor if you're concerned or you know that your family has a history of mental health problems.

## ANXIETY

Anxiety can range from feeling slightly on edge to full-on panic palpitations, sweaty hands and shallow breathing. Anxiety is quite a taboo in our society and I was surprised when I talked to girls who had experienced it. Some had it regularly while others had only experienced it once or twice. But the one thing I noticed is how most of them hadn't been willing to speak about it because they thought people would think they were odd.

If you suffer from anxiety, try these tips:
- Concentrate on listening to your breath. Focus on each breath in and each breath out. The sound it makes. The rise and fall of your chest.
- Distract yourself. Call a friend or get one to come over, or put on the TV. (Do something brainless.)
- Taunt your anxiety. Pretend with phrases like: 'Come on, then! Show me what you got, sucker! You ain't shit!' (People might think you're nuts but it does work.)

# MOODS

At one time or another we all feel sad, fed up and lonely. The emotional rollercoaster of life is something that most of us are familiar with. However, some of us are more inclined to strong mood swings than others. Do you find yourself feeling energetic and positive one minute and heavy and lethargic the next? Do you sometimes not know how to justify your large mood swings – there isn't even any particular reason for them? Being moody is a stereotypical image of a teenage girl. That's because we've got hormones pumping around our bodies, we've got our periods every month to deal with, and there's a lot going on for us.

# DRUG ADDICTION

Taking drugs brings with it the huge risk of drug addition – an extremely painful path to walk down. Please remember, if you do drugs you're running the following risks:

- Dying
- Losing your friends
- Becoming homeless
- Losing your mind and becoming mentally ill and unstable
- Becoming physically very ill – drugs can destroy your body
- Stealing to support your habit
- Getting into trouble with the police and put in jail
- Dropping out of work/school
- Getting into dangerous situations – like being raped.

Really, the list of risks you take with drug addiction are endless. Being an addict is a mental illness.

How do you know if you are addicted to something?

- You start to lie to people about how often you're doing it.
- You do it when you're on your own or during the day.
- You take the drug every day and if you don't for a day or two you feel completely messed up.
- You start stealing to support your habit.
- You stop having any interest in any other areas of your life. Taking the drug and getting wasted is your only priority.

There are lots of support networks to help young people get off drugs (p215). You don't have to be a hardcore junkie to get help. Even if you think you want to give something up or stop doing it so much because it's starting to control your life, there is help out there for you.

If you have a family member, close friend or boyfriend who is a drug addict, there are also places you can go to, to support what you're going through. It's very difficult to have a parent who is an addict and you need to get support, even if it's just listening to other people with similar stories. There are numbers you can ring at the end of the book (see p215).

# DRUGS

Drugs are illegal and there are severe penalties for those who are found in possession of them. Drugs can have devastating and long-term effects on your life and the lives of those close to you. The most important thing is to be educated about the effects and dangers associated with drug-taking (see also Drug Addiction p161). Most of the information you find on drugs will tell you about their effects. Here, you will also read about the real-life experience of drug taking.

In many ways I feel lucky to not have been seriously hurt as a result of my experiences with drugs. If you asked, 'Do you regret doing any of it?' I'd say 'yes'. Drugs have affected me and probably killed about a billion of my brain cells. They've also made me more insecure. I'm not telling you to try drugs or not try them, but if I had a second chance I wouldn't have done them to the excess I did. I've been very lucky in escaping long-term damage to my body and mind. (No symptoms so far!) Other friends I know have had strokes, fallen off walls and lost their minds through that spontaneous decision of, 'Why not? It'll be a laugh'. Please remember these warnings and guidelines and keep yourself protected at all times. If you decide to never do drugs you won't be missing out on anything. Life has enough stimulus and intrigue without them.

## POSITIVES

All your problems slip away

It's great fun

It's mind expanding

You make new friends

You can dance all night

Sex can be brilliant

## NEGATIVES

They come back

It makes you forget all the other ways of enjoying yourself

It numbs your mind

You've forgotten their names the next day

You know you don't need drugs to do that

But mostly he can't even get it up!

If you ever make the decision to take drugs, remember the following guidelines:

- Always take them with people you feel comfortable with.
- Be in an environment that is safe and relaxing.
- Make sure people you trust have tried that particular batch of drug before. Don't be a guinea pig!
- Start slow and be cautious of the amount, especially if you're not used to it.
- Make sure there is someone sober around, or who knows of your whereabouts and who will look after you if you're in trouble.

## ALCOHOL, BOOZE, DRINK, BEVY, SHOT, SPIRITS

Alcohol is an illegal substance for people under 18. It can be addictive.

### Effects

- It can help you to relax and feel more sociable.
- Depend on the strength of the drink and how fast it's consumed.
- Speech can become slurred, co-ordination affected and emotions heightened.
- A hangover (the after-effects of alcohol) can leave you feeling ill for a day or so.

### Warnings

- It is a depressant drug and you can end up feeling very down.
- Overdose can lead to loss of consciousness. Users then risk on choking on their own vomit. This can kill.
- Overdose can also cause alcoholic poisoning, which can be fatal.
- Long-term use can lead to serious liver, heart and stomach problems and breast cancer.
- More than 25,000 deaths in the UK each year are alcohol related.
- Mixing alcohol with other drugs is SERIOUSLY DANGEROUS.

Alcohol is the most commonly used drug and also the most socially acceptable. It's usually the first drug young people will use – unfortunately sometimes to an extreme excess. Even though the legal drinking age is 18, most people try booze way before then. When we drink our inhibitions tend to go away and we say and do a lot of things we might not when we're sober: for example, have sex with someone, tell someone a secret, talk to people you don't know. Some say it's the truth drug because it makes people open up a lot more, but I know from my own experiences that I mostly talk a lot of rubbish when I'm drunk.

If you are drinking, be in a safe environment and look out for each other. I would be cautious of always using alcohol to have a good time. If you do, you'll forget how to have fun without it.

Never ever drive when you are drinking. You are risking other people's lives as well as your own.

------------------------------------------------

> " I've done more things I regret drunk, than on any other drug. I've felt and been the most out of control when drunk. I've felt the most screwed up the next day after being drunk than with any other drug. (Sophie, 17) "

> " It can be a great way to loosen up and it helps me feel free and at ease in social situations. (Elisabeth, 17) "

I'm A Survivor

Amphetamines, or speed, can be highly addictive and are illegal.

### Effects

- Excitement – the mind races and users feel confident and energetic.

### Warnings

- While on the drug, some users become tense and anxious.
- It leaves users feeling tired and depressed for one or two days and sometimes longer.
- High doses repeated over a few days may cause panic and hallucinations.
- Long-term use puts a strain on the heart.
- Heavy, long-term use can lead to mental illness.

> **"** I was in Australia travelling when my life was changed. I'd always taken speed before by bombing it or snorting it. But I spent one night with a group of nutters who were all injecting it. I decided to join in and go for it. I had an amazing evening dancing all night and feeling fantastic, until we got home. When everyone had left or gone to sleep, I suddenly didn't feel right. I couldn't move. I finally woke someone up who immediately rang the hospital. I was having a stroke. I ended up staying in hospital until I was well enough to go back to England. I had been two days away from going to Thailand. My body will never be quite the same again and drugs could be lethal if I ever took them again. I learnt the hard way that drugs aren't to be messed with. (Tamsin, 19) **"**

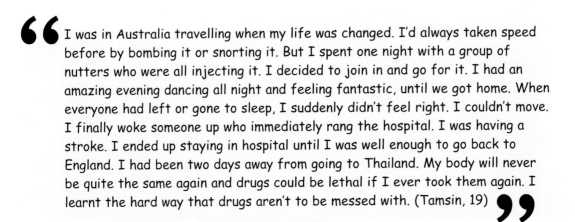

## CIGARETTES

It is illegal to sell tobacco to under-16s. The nicotine in tobacco is highly addictive.

### Effect

- Nicotine is a powerful and fast-acting drug.
- When smoke is inhaled, the nicotine effects hit the brain about eight seconds later.
- Nicotine speeds up the heart rate and increases blood pressure.
- First-time users may feel sick.

### Warning

- Smokers are more likely to suffer coughs and chest problems.
- A long-term tobacco habit can lead to cancer (and not just of the lungs), emphysema and heart disease – all of which can kill.
- Tobacco contributes to at least 2,000 limb amputations and 111,000 premature deaths in the UK each year.

Tobacco makes your teeth go yellow, your breath, fingers and clothes stink, and can give you lung cancer. It also costs a fortune! (And it doesn't even get you high!!) Why do it?

More teenage girls than boys smoke. People can start because their mates are doing it or they think it makes them look older. You can become addicted to it very quickly, though, and it's not a cheap habit to take up. Sometimes people smoke because they feel nervous and it gives them something to do with their hands. It's like eating because you're nervous; it distracts you from your nerves. But there are other ways of calming your nerves, like fiddling with something and chewing gum. Eating is better than smoking, so eat nuts and healthy snacky things.

I smoked when I was a teenager and I'll tell you how I stopped. I was smoking about a 20-pack a day and when I was about 18 someone who I didn't know very well but looked up, to told me that they were shocked that I was a smoker. I asked them why and they told me that it was because they had thought I was intelligent. It got me thinking, but I didn't stop until a week later when another older person, who I also looked up to, also said they couldn't believe I smoked. When I asked why, they told me exactly the same thing – because they thought I was smarter than the kind of person who would smoke. Well, from that day on I stopped and I haven't looked back. Something clicked in me that made me realise just what an idiotic thing it was to do, and nothing as disgusting as tobacco was I going to be a slave to.

The people you're giving your money to when you smoke are laughing – they've got you hooked on the most revolting, pointless drug possible and they're getting fat off your money, while you kill yourself. If I had my way, smoking would be illegal.

## COCAINE, ROCK, BLOW, COKE

Cocaine is another illegal and highly addictive drug.

### Effects
- Users have a sense of wellbeing, alertness, confidence.
- The effects last roughly 30 minutes.
- Users are often left craving more.

### Warnings
- It is addictive.
- It leaves users feeling tired and depressed for one or two days and sometimes longer.
- It can cause chest pain and heart problems that can be fatal.
- Heavy use can cause convulsions.
- A habit can be expensive and hard to control.

People who take cocaine ramble rubbish all night, not realising they're boring the hell out of everyone around them. They usually take it to give them a false sense of confidence – cocaine users tend to be deeply insecure! While they're on it, people can be extremely boring and tend to love the sound of their own voices. Cocaine bulldozes through your bank balance and can make you paranoid and insecure. It also destroys your nose.

I'm A Survivor

## ECSTASY, E'S, PILLS, DOVES, MDMA

Ecstasy is illegal and is a Class A drug. It is not addictive.

### Effects

- Users feel alert and in tune with their surroundings.
- Sound, colour and emotions seem much more intense.
- Users can dance for hours – the effects last from three to six hours.

### Warnings

- It can leave users feeling tired and depressed for days.
- There's a risk of overheating and dehydration if users dance energetically without taking breaks or drinking enough fluids (sip about a pint of non-alcoholic fluid such as fruit juice, sports drinks or water every hour).
- Use has been linked to liver and kidney problems.
- Some experts are concerned that using Ecstasy can lead to brain damage, causing depression in later life.

Ecstasy is the drug I've taken most of in my life. I like it mainly for the physical feeling, the rush that goes through your body. Also the energy it gives you and the fact that all your problems slip away and turn to mush. You become a pure manifestation of love. Ecstasy can be really fantastic, but like all drugs, it can be extremely bad, too. Ecstasy kills off brain cells at a fast rate. It tinkers around with the part of your brain that supplies you with concentration and focus. (We already have to deal with being part of the MTV generation that can't focus for more than three minutes at a time.) If you are worried about your ability to concentrate, don't take E. The feeling E gives you is very addictive and easy to rely on for a good time. Don't get caught in that trap. Life becomes dull and you spend most of your days getting over the come-down. Don't take too much of it at once – it's easy to do – it screws up your body and you don't want to experience an E overdose. I have a few times. It's scary and it's extremely dangerous.

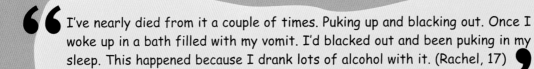

> I've nearly died from it a couple of times. Puking up and blacking out. Once I woke up in a bath filled with my vomit. I'd blacked out and been puking in my sleep. This happened because I drank lots of alcohol with it. (Rachel, 17)

> I used be a complete raver. I'd go out two or even three times a week and get off my head on pills. I loved it at first but after a while I started feeling really depressed during the week, until I'd get off my head again. I found myself in a deep depression and old friends kept telling me how different I was. In the end I gave up taking it, but it took me ages to get over the depression I'd sunk into. (Louise, 18)

People have taken just one pill before and died, so you are taking a huge risk.

## HEROIN, BROWN, SMACK

Heroin is highly addictive. It is illegal and a Class A drug.

### Effects
- Small doses give the user a sense of warmth and wellbeing.
- Larger doses can make them drowsy and relaxed.

### Warnings
- Heroin is addictive (even when smoked).
- Users who form a habit can end up taking the drug just to feel normal.
- Excessive amounts can result in overdose, coma, and in some cases, death.
- Injecting can damage veins.
- Sharing needles puts users at risk of dangerous infections such as hepatitis B or C and HIV/AIDS.

Heroin is a drug I thought I'd never try but I have twice, by smoking it. I didn't enjoy it. It made me feel sick and really apathetic. I listened to a friend drone on at me for hours, too deadened to care either way. There is a huge amount of stigma around heroin, and rightly so. It's killed a lot of people and screwed up a lot of people's lives. I understand why it is judged harshly and I can only advise you to really be careful in your decision and look at the facts about the drug before considering it.

Don't buy into the 'heroin chic' image. In the last few years heroin has been made glamorous through the media and films. I promise you, it's not. It destroys lives.

> I first tried heroin when I was 16 and I fell in love with it straight away. I thought I had it under control but before I knew it I had dropped out of school, was living in a squat and stealing to support my habit. I became clean when someone told me about Narcotics Anonymous meetings. I've been clean ever since I went to my first meeting a year ago, and I'm back at school and living with my parents again. (Amy, 19)

## LSD, ACID, TRIPS, BLOTTERS, MICRODOTS, TABS

LSD is not addictive. It is a Class A drug, which means it is illegal.

### Effects
- Effects are known as a 'trip' and can last up to 12 hours.
- Users will experience their surroundings in a very different way.
- The sense of movement and time may speed up or slow down.
- Objects, colours and sounds may be distorted

I'm A Survivor

## Warnings

- Once a trip starts, it cannot be stopped.
- Users may have a 'bad trip', which can be terrifying.
- 'Flashbacks' may be experienced, where parts of a trip are relived some time after the event.
- It can lead to mental health problems and complicate mental health problems.

I have mixed feelings about acid. I know people who have taken it for years and never had anything but an amazing time. But I know others (and this is more common) who have taken it and it's made them paranoid and even slightly loopy. It's a gamble. On the one hand, acid showed me that nothing is black and white. It made me aware of more than just what we see, and it opened my mind to spirituality. But on the other hand, I had a really bad trip that I still get paralysing flashbacks from.

I was 15 and at the time acid was my drug of choice. I took it on my own at school and with mates. My friends all either took a lot of it or dealt it – including my boyfriend at the time. One night we were all hanging out and I decided to take two trips at once. Soon after, a heavy acid-taker who had already taken one, said in a panic that he wished he'd taken half. My alarm went off. I freaked big time. The trip went downhill from there. I won't go into the gory details; you just need to know that it was really scary. I thought I'd lost my mind for ever. The evening dragged on until, finally, eight hours later, it started to end. I believe that trip scarred me for ever. A door had been unlocked; a world of unadulterated insanity was opened up for me to walk around in and have in the back of my mind – permanently. It didn't stop me from indulging again, but it was never the same after that. Acid always turned sour for me. I knew that dark world I could enter and I couldn't help revisiting it.

Acid definitely needs a **LARGE WARNING SIGN**. It really needs to be treated with respect. If you're absolutely sure you want to try it, always take small doses and make sure there is someone completely sober, who understands the drug, to look after you in a crisis.

## MAGIC MUSHROOMS, MUSHIES, SHROOMS

While it isn't illegal to possess raw magic mushrooms, it is an offence to posses any preparation of them (e.g. when they're dried or stewed). Then they are considered a Class A drug. They are not addictive.

### Effects

- They have similar effects to LSD, but the trip is often milder and shorter (about four hours).

### Warnings

- They can cause stomach pains, sickness and diarrhoea.
- Eating the wrong kind of mushroom can cause serious illness and even fatal poisoning.
- They can complicate mental health problems.

Mushrooms are similar to LSD in their effect but they naturally grow from the earth. They can be great fun but be careful of the dose as a few can go a long way. Many believe that mushies are the truth drug and once on them you can't avoid seeing anything but the truth.

Marijuana has recently been classed as a C drug, which means the government and law now recognise it as less harmful. It isn't addictive, but if you smoke it with tobacco, the tobacco is addictive.

### Effects

- Users feel relaxed and talkative.
- Cooking the drug, then eating it makes the effects more intense and harder to control.
- May bring on a craving for food (often referred to as the 'munchies').

### Warnings

- Smoking it with tobacco can make users get hooked on cigarettes.
- It impairs the ability to learn and concentrate.
- It can leave people tired and lacking energy.
- Users may lack motivation and feel apathetic.
- It can make users paranoid and anxious, depending on their mood and situation.
- Smoking joints over a long period of time can lead to respiratory disorders, including lung cancer.

Marijuana has had a lot of bad press, especially in recent years. It seems that whenever a young person dies of a harder drug, people point their finger at Marijuana, claiming that smoking it makes young people go on to do harder drugs. You could say that as alcohol is more commonly the first drug to be tried, it's alcohol that promotes other drug usage, but of course, no MP would ever admit that because the government gets so much money from taxing alcohol. Also, most of the people who make the law enjoy a brandy or two when they get back from the office. Whatever the reason, alcohol has caused far more damage to our youth and society at large than marijuana ever has or ever will. Yet the irony is, one is legal and socially acceptable, while the other is illegal and stigmatised.

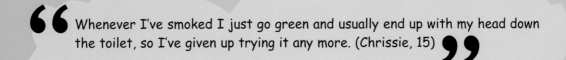

66 Whenever I've smoked I just go green and usually end up with my head down the toilet, so I've given up trying it any more. (Chrissie, 15) 99

66 I love ganja and I'm an everyday smoker, like how other people might drink every time they go out. I have a spliff instead. It completely relaxes me. (Rachael, 19) 99

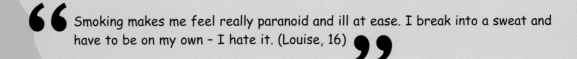

66 Smoking makes me feel really paranoid and ill at ease. I break into a sweat and have to be on my own – I hate it. (Louise, 16) 99

66 I just fall asleep when I smoke, so my friends have stopped giving me any. (Sabena, 17) 99

I'm A Survivor

## SOLVENTS, GLUE, AEROSOL

They are illegal to sell to under 18s when abuse is suspected.

### Effects
- The effects feel similar to being very drunk.
- Users feel thick-headed, dizzy, giggly and dreamy.
- Users may hallucinate.
- Effects don't last very long, but users can remain intoxicated all day by repeating the dose.

### Warnings
- They cause nausea, vomiting, black-outs and heart problems that can be instantly fatal.
- Squirting gas products down the throat is a particularly dangerous way of taking the drug.
- There's a risk of suffocation if the substance is inhaled from a plastic bag over the head.
- Accidents can happen when the user is high because senses are affected.
- Long-term glue abuse can damage the brain, liver and kidneys.

Solvents were hugely popular at a boarding school I went to that gave the students random drug tests. It seems obvious that youngsters who are restricted from doing drugs are going to find an alternative. I only ever tried it once but didn't get a high off it at all, even though those around me seemed to. It can be very dangerous. The high mainly consists of extreme hallucinations and disorientation.

# EATING DISORDERS

When I was researching this book, I came across an inspirational book called Ophelia Speaks, compiled and edited by a young American woman called Sara Shandler. Sara asked young women from the ages of 12 to 18 to write short stories concerning important issues for them. What surprised me was the subject that was written to Sara about most: eating disorders. It seems that so many of us are unhappy about the shapes of our bodies. Girls I have talked to have been of all shapes and sizes and I have yet to hear, 'I love my body.' There are many causes for this dysfunctional relationship with our bodies, which I've spoken about in more detail in the Bod-ease chapter. Somehow, together, it's our job to change this belief that our bodies are horrible and 'wrong' for our younger generations.

Eating disorders come in several guises, from bulimia (where you make yourself vomit) to anorexia (where you starve yourself). And there are hundreds of different types in between.

I interviewed Claire Beekan, author of *My Body, My Enemy*, and founder of the Luton-based eating disorder charity, Caraline.

## How can you tell if someone has an eating disorder?
You will notice that they avoid eating and probably get into a panic if they eat food containing fat or sugar. Physical changes such as a rapid loss of weight and withdrawal take place very quickly. Another common symptom is constantly thinking of food, which is a sign of hunger.

## Do you think anyone can have one?

It depends on life's experiences. They used to say it was a middle class disease but girls from all different family settings get it. It usually affects the 'addictive personality' – the same sort of people who go down the path of drug addiction. Also, very self-destructive people who need an emotional escape.

## Do you think the media has influenced how girls feel about their bodies to the extent of them having eating disorders?

I'm asked this question a lot. I don't think the media is entirely responsible. When you start getting ill you aren't really thinking about weight that much. Then you lose lots of weight and look at magazines with skinny models, and it reinforces your belief that you look good. I will say that I don't think it's healthy for grown up women to be walking down the catwalks looking like 12-year-old boys.

## What more could society do to help?

I believe that eating disorders are the poor relations of addictions – eating disorder charities like ours get less money and are taken less seriously by doctors. I would like society to not see eating disorders as slimmers diseases, and to realise they're deep-rooted psychological disorders that have serious physical complications. Eating disorders have the highest mortality rate (10 per cent) of all the addictions, yet we are given the least money to treat it.

## What would you say to girls who were worried about their body shape?

I would ask them what's made them worry and suddenly bring attention to their body shape. Then I would try and get them to focus on positive aspects of themselves, ask them what people like about them. I'd get them to make a chart and literally divide up every aspect of themselves to show them how small the importance of their body weight is in comparison.

## What would you like people to know that they might not about eating disorders?

I'd like them to know to what extent they harm your body. Here are just a few things they can cause:
Anorexia: Headaches, tiredness, depression, lethargy, skin problems, excess body hair growth, insomnia, constipation, permanent damage to the digestive system, and in some cases infertility.
Bulimia: Kidney damage from the constant vomiting, rotten teeth because the stomach acids you're bringing up attack the enamel.

## Lastly, what can you do to help if someone you know has one?

One thing you can do is find a number for a helpline and ring it. Approach your friend gently and tell them that you are worried about them and that you have rung the helpline. Give them the number and suggest they ring it. That way they can't be cross with you, and most of the time they'll probably go away and use it.

People develop eating disorders like anorexia and bulimia for all sorts of different reasons. Most people think it's about food but it isn't – it's do with much deeper psychological problems.

I'm A Survivor

# RAPE AND SEXUAL ABUSE

If you have been raped and in any way feel guilty for what has happened, or are trying to protect someone, please find the courage to speak up. You are innocent and if you allow this guy to get away with it, he might attack someone else.

The Rape Crisis Federation gave me permission to use the following information taken from their website – www.rapecrisis.co.uk

**Myth:** She didn't struggle so she was not raped.

FACT: Most women are too afraid to struggle because of threats of violence if they make a sound.

**Myth:** Rape only occurs at the hands of strangers in dark alleys, at night, behind bushes, in lonely places.

FACT: Research shows that in the majority of cases the rapist is known to the woman. He may be a friend, a workmate, relative. About 50 per cent of rapes occur in the home of the woman or attacker.

**Myth:** Women 'ask for it' by hitching lifts, wearing short skirts and make-up, leading men on.

FACT: No woman ever deserves to be raped, abused or assaulted, no matter what the circumstances. Most rapes are planned. What a woman is wearing makes no difference.

**Myth:** It cannot be rape unless there has been an act of physical violence such as beating, cutting, or using a weapon and in some way physically injuring the woman.

FACT: Some attackers badly beat and severely injure the woman; others don't. However, in any rape the man violently takes away the woman's control over her life and her sexuality and she suffers psychological trauma. The emotional after-effects of rape can include eating disorders, sleeping disorders, agoraphobia, depression, suicide attempts and sexual difficulties.

**Myth:** Rape is only when a penis penetrates a vagina against a woman's will.

FACT: The law currently defines rape as the non-consensual penetration of the vagina or anus by penis. However, acts such as forced oral sex, and the penetration of the vagina or anus by a foreign object are also experienced by women as rape. The law defines these acts as sexual assaults. In addition, touching, fondling and sexual contact against a woman's will are all forms of sexual assault. Legislation on Sex Offences is currently under review by the Home Office.

**Myth:** Women say 'no' when they mean 'yes'.

FACT: While some women may have been socialised into believing that it is wrong for them to want sex, and that they should play hard to get, when a woman says 'No' she means 'No'. This is no excuse for disregarding a woman's 'No' to sex.

**Myth:** She wanted it really.

FACT: This is part of the idea that all women want, need and/or enjoy being taken by force, and that she only says no to take away the need to feel guilty. Women do not want, need or enjoy being threatened, beaten or being afraid for their lives.

**Myth:** The woman or girl is guilty; she could have stopped the rape if she had really wanted to.

FACT: Most men are stronger than women and rapists use this physical advantage to prevent women from resisting successfully. During a rape a woman sometimes becomes paralysed by fear. In addition, rapists often threaten women with weapons or fists, or with harm to their children and loved ones. Psychological coercion or the exploitation of power imbalances between the rapist and the woman – especially when they know each other – can also overcome a woman's resistance. Regardless of how much physical force the rapist used or didn't use, he is the guilty party, not the woman or girl.

**Myth:** Rape is worse for virgins and girls from 'nice homes' than for non-virgins.

FACT: Any woman can suffer rape. It makes no difference if she has previously had sexual intercourse. Rape is a matter of consent and has no relevance to how a woman has previously spent her life.

Reproduced from the AGM of the Rape and Sexual Abuse Centre for Women in Merseyside, Cambridge Rape Crisis Centre, and the South Essex Rape and Incest Centre.

I'm A Survivor

# SELF INJURY

The following information comes from the Bristol Crisis Service for Women

### What is self-injury?
'Self-injury' is any sort of self-harm that involves inflicting injuries or pain on one's own body. It can take many forms.

The most common form of self-injury is probably cutting — usually superficially, but sometimes deeply. Women may also burn themselves, punch themselves or hit their bodies against something. Some people pick their skin or pull out hair.

### How common is it?
Self-injury is far more widespread than is generally realised. All sorts of people self-injure. Often they carry on successful careers or look after families and there is little outward sign that there is anything wrong. Self-injury seems to be more common among women, partly because men are more likely to express strong feelings such as anger outwardly.

Many women who self-injure believe they are the only person that hurts themselves in this way. Fear and shame can force them to keep it secret for many years. This means that the true extent of the problem is unknown. Our experience shows that where it is acceptable to talk about, many women reveal that they have self-injured at some time.

### Why do women self-injure?
There are always powerful reasons why a woman hurts herself. For most women it is a way of surviving great emotional pain.

Many people cope with difficulties in their lives in ways which are risky and harmful to themselves. Some drink or eat too much, smoke, drive too fast, gamble or make themselves ill through overwork or worry. They might do this to numb or distract themselves from problems or feelings they cannot bear to face (like 'drowning your sorrows').

Self-injury, though more shocking, bears many similarities to these 'ordinary' forms of self-harm. Like drink or drugs, hurting herself may help a woman block out painful feelings. Like taking risks or gambling, it may provide danger and distraction.

Often women say that self-injury helps them to release unbearable tension, which may arise from anxiety, grief or anger. It puts their pain outside, where it feels easier to cope with. For others, it relieves feelings of guilt or shame. Sometimes a woman's self-injury is a 'cry for help'; a way of showing (even to herself) that she has suffered and is in pain. Perhaps hurting herself is a way of feeling 'real' and alive, or having control over something in her life. What lies behind women's distress may be painful experiences in childhood or adulthood. A woman may have suffered neglect or abuse, or may have always been criticised or silenced, rather than supported and allowed to express her needs and feelings. Some women who self-injure, lost parents early, or came from chaotic or violent families. For others, adult experiences of emotional or physical cruelty have led to their desperation.

## What can help?

Self-injury causes great distress, and can seem a difficult problem to overcome. But it is possible for a woman to stop hurting herself if she can understand and resolve the problems behind what she does.

## If you are someone who self-injures

Think about what your self-injury is 'saying' about your feelings and your life. This will give you clues about problems you need to work on. You might find it helpful to talk about your self-injury and what lies behind it with friends or a counsellor. To find out about counselling, you could ask your GP, rape or sexual abuse support service, MIND group, library, Wellwoman clinic, or Citizen's Advice Bureau.

## If you want to help someone who self-injures

Naturally you may feel upset, shocked or angry when someone you care about hurts herself. Try to keep seeing the person in pain behind the injuries. The most precious thing you can offer are acceptance and support. Let your friend know you understand that self-injury is helping her to cope at the moment. She is not 'bad' or 'mad' for doing it. You could invite her to talk about her feelings, or to call you if she is having a difficult time. But only offer as much as you can cope with, and don't try to take responsibility for stopping her from hurting herself.

# SUICIDE

Suicide is the third leading cause of death among people aged 15 to 19 and the second leading cause of death among those aged 19 to 24. I was alarmed at how many women and girls I spoke to had contemplated killing themselves, particularly during their teenage years, including myself.

I tried committing suicide when I was only 11. I had been suspended from school and my mum was furious. I was so unhappy that I assumed that death had to be better. So I overdosed on paracetamol and instead of dying became violently sick. I didn't own up to my parents about what was wrong with me, so they nursed me at home. I'm extremely grateful that I survived because now I know the truth, that even though life at times can be excruciatingly painful it is also incredibly amazing.

We can sometimes be driven to suicide when we break up with someone.

 My boyfriend split up with me and I hurt so much all I could think about was dying. I'd never been in love before and I thought I never could be again. I slit my wrists in the end, but my mum found me and rushed me to hospital where they saved me. It was only recently that it happened, and even though I still find the break up painful I'm thankful to be alive. (Laura, 16)

## THE WARNING SIGNS AND WHAT TO DO

① When someone talks about taking their own life or hurting themselves – listen. It is important to take it seriously. Almost everyone who takes their own life or tries to has given some clue or warning.

② Often, people who have been depressed for some time and then suddenly seem happier are showing the common warning sign of someone who has decided to take their own life and is relieved by their decision.

③ If you feel suicidal, try to talk to someone about your feelings and fears. Having someone who sympathises and listens to share your feelings and anxieties with, and to discuss suicidal ideas with, will help.

④ Talking to someone about their suicidal feelings will not encourage them to take their own life. Having someone to share their feelings with may help deter them. Being judgmental or trying to give advice is unlikely to be helpful – just having someone to listen and who cares could be enough.

⑤ If the crisis is very serious, it may be best to call a doctor, take the suicidal person to casualty, call their psychiatrist, visit a mental health or crisis centre, or dial 999. Don't worry about breaking someone's confidence — their telling you could be a cry for help. It is best to take charge and not leave it up to the suicidal person to get help. Try to make arrangements for them to get professional help and treatment.

If you ever feel there is no other option but suicide, please think again. I've been to that place in myself before, but it did get better and I promise you that your pain will go away as well. You need to find someone you can talk to about what you're feeling, and talk to others who have been through what you're going through now. Life is worth living for.

## YOUNG PEOPLE AND SUICIDE – THE FACTS

There are two suicides every day by young people in the UK and Republic of Ireland.

Suicide is more common in young people than any other age group.

Suicide accounts for over a fifth of all deaths of young people.

29 per cent of young people know someone who has died by suicide.

People who talk about suicide do it. About 80 per cent of the time, people who kill themselves have given out definite signals or talked about it to someone.

An estimated 24,000 adolescents self-harmed in 1998 – 3 every hour*

Young women and girls carry out the most self-harm episodes each year

Alcohol and substance misuse are significant factors in youth suicide

Contributory factors to youth suicide include unemployment, social isolation, recent interpersonal life events and difficulties with parents, peers or partners.

(*data from the Centre for Suicide Research, Department of Psychiatry, Warneford Hospital, Oxford)

I'm A Survivor

# GIVE IT TO ME STRAIGHT

 I started doing Es about six months ago and I thought I'd just try it a few times. But I've now found I'm doing them every weekend and I've stopped being able to have fun without them. My parents have started to get suspicious but I don't want them to find out because they'll stop me from seeing all my mates. I do want to stop taking them though. What should I do? (Sophie, 17)

It's really not good to get into the habit of taking drugs regularly and relying on them to have a good time. I know this might seem difficult, but the best way to stop doing drugs is to hang out with people that don't do them. This might seem impossible because you feel as though these people are your only good friends but your state of mind and health is more important than that. Try talking to them about doing things other than drug taking. Go off to an adventure park for the day or something you haven't done since you were a kid, like going to the zoo. There are other ways of having fun. You just have to remind yourself of what you did before you started taking Es.

 My friend tried to commit suicide recently and at first I really wanted to help her but now I think that she just did it to seek attention and it really annoys me. She tells everyone we meet about it and everyone gives her all this attention and sympathy. Am I just being really mean or am I right to be annoyed with her? (Anna, 16)

You'd be right to be upset with her because you were scared for her and you didn't want her to die. It sounds, though, like you're a little jealous of all the attention she's getting. It can be annoying when you know a friend is being false, but if you look further into it you'll see that she feels as though she needs this attention desperately because otherwise she wouldn't have risked her life. She is obviously deeply unhappy and it sounds like she doesn't get enough attention from the people she needs the most – like her family. It is definitely a cry for help and you need to be extra supportive for her right now and allow her the extra attention she's getting from people because she needs it.

 I think my friend has started self-harming but she won't open up about it. I've seen red marks on her arms but when I asked to check her arms she got really mad and told me to stop interfering. I really care about her and I know stuff hasn't been easy for her recently. Do you think I should approach her again or just leave it. (Vicky, 17)

You obviously care a lot about this friend and it must be painful to think that's she's hurting herself. I don't think you should drop it but I do think you should approach her about it in a different way. Don't talk directly about her self-injuring but about more general things that are going on in her life. Ask her how she is at the moment and if she's spoken to anyone about it. Give her some numbers from this book of helplines she can ring. She will most likely stop self-harming when she is more vocal about what is going on and she's getting help from somewhere. If you're forceful about wanting to see her arms, it's just going to scare her away. Let her tell you about it if she wants to.

 I can't help feeling really down when things don't go how I want them to. I get depressed really easily and I find it hard to come out of my shell and talk to people. I've lost lots of weight recently and I feel uninspired to hang out with people or do my schoolwork. How can I get out of this slump? (Clarissa, 16)

You need to figure out why you're feeling so depressed. Can you locate a specific problem, or is it just a general feeling? Is there anyone you can talk to about it that you think might be able to help? It is common for us to go through really low spells in our lives, especially when we're younger and our hormones are all over the place. You need to remember the essential tool about seeing the glass as half-full (From Girl to Woman, p000). Try and be positive about all the things you do have going for you. When I was depressed I read a lot of books that were about learning to be positive and realising that many other people get down as well. You should try talking to friends about how you feel and you might be surprised at how many of them get down. Coming together and talking to other people about feeling bad can often help us feel less alone and bring us out of a slump.

 I'm getting really badly bullied at school and I've started to do everything I can to not go at all. I either tell my Mum I'm ill or I pretend that I'm going in when I'm not. I really hate myself and I've even thought of committing suicide. What should I do? (Natasha, 16)

Bullying can be one of the hardest things to deal with so I understand why you don't want to go into school and have to deal with it. I think that these kids' parents need to be told what their kids are doing and that they should be the ones who deal with it. Usually children are unhappy themselves if they feel they need to bully others. One thing you might want to think about is changing schools altogether. Are there any other schools near you? Have you been bullied before going to this school? However bad it gets don't commit suicide because even though you might not know it now, life is really an amazing experience full of so many exciting things to come. Be strong.

I'm A Survivor

I'm really worried about a friend who never seems to eat. She has lost loads of weight but whenever I confront her about it she gets really upset and tells me to leave her alone. Should I do what she wants or carry on trying to help her? (Sophie, 14)

What I try and do when I want to help someone is to start by talking about myself. You could mention something to do with your own weight that's quite personal – like, say, you feel that you worry too much about being thin or that you think you're not eating enough. This will give her the opportunity to open up about what's going on for her without feeling defensive. Another thing you could do is to ring a helpline and talk to them. You could then just subtly give her the number and tell her that you spoke to someone there and they were really kind and helpful. If she has the number on a piece of paper she might not ring it straight away, but she might find it at a later date and pluck up the courage to give them a call. If you get really worried and you think she looks dangerously thin, and you know her family, you could maybe talk to them about it. (You could ask them not to say it was you that talked to them about it.) Even if your friend hates you for doing so it will be worth it in the long run if she ends up getting the help she needs.

 Every time I read a magazine I'm shown clothes I can wear to look thinner, food I can eat to lose weight, exercise I can do to be more toned, and it's driving me crazy. I find myself getting sucked into this whole obsession to be skinny and I spend most of my time thinking about food – how much I've eaten and how much I weigh. Does this mean that I have an eating disorder, or are all girls like that? (Karla, 17)

What you've described is definitely a reality for many girls and women out there, but that doesn't mean that it's healthy or the right attitude to have. We are constantly being told to think about our weight and our society as a whole is completely obsessed with it, so it's not surprising that as individuals we are as well. You have to ask yourself the following questions, though, are you:

- Skipping meals or become obsessive about calorie content?
- Sticking to very low-calorie foods?
- Behaving defensively when asked about food consumption?
- Wearing loose clothes to disguise body shape?
- Disappearing from the table straight after meals (to make yourself sick)?

Do you feel guilty every time you eat something? If this is so then you have to be honest about whether it's an unhealthy obsession or an eating disorder. You don't have to be starving yourself or making yourself throw up to have an eating disorder. It is possible to enjoy food and naughty things and still have the figure you want. Just be sensible and maybe think about not buying those magazines any more if they aren't making you happy. If you are really worried about it, ring one of the helplines or see a counsellor, who can explore the extent of your obsession with you further.

Sisters Unlimited

Some of the topics discussed here are extremely serious. It's not meant to scare you, but there are things that can either be done to us or that we can do to ourselves that can deeply scar us, physically, mentally and emotionally. You need to make sure you keep yourself safe from outside harm and get help if you're harming yourself. Life can get tough and adolescence is a particularly difficult time so give yourself a pat on the back for getting this far. Remember, life is worth treasuring and whatever life dishes out to you, you're a survivor!

There is support out there for you and girls and women that have been through what you're going through. Sometimes all you need to do is reach out to others and to know that you're not alone.

I'm A Survivor

# DOING IT!

DEFINITELY NOT THE WAY TO GO!

When people ask me about *Sisters Unlimited* and what it's about, I tell them that it is a book to empower teenage girls in all areas of their lives. Well this chapter is specifically about you – learning to feel good about who you are, having the confidence to speak your truth and the tools to unlock your unlimited potential. I hope it will help you to see your greatness and the limitlessness of your ability (power) more clearly.

Someone once told me he'd heard a saying, 'Women today are the men of the future', and had thought of me. I told him I didn't agree with that statement. Being an empowered female doesn't make you a man. We women are becoming more empowered, but in our own, more feminine way. I'd never think of myself as being like a man, just because I'm driven and confident. I look at myself as an empowered woman (most of the time).

# LIVING WITH FEAR

Fear is an extremely powerful emotion that can creep into all different aspects of our lives. It controls us and stops us from being free. Free in our self-expression, free in our acceptance of ourselves and free in being who we truly are. For example, you might be scared of talking to a new person you've been introduced to, so your fear stops you from meeting new people. Or you might be someone who's scared of singing in front of people, so you miss the chance to be a singer. It wasn't necessarily always like that, though. Think back to when you were a young child and the things you used to do. Did you talk to strangers easily, make new friends all the time and catapult your body around the place without holding back? Most of us start our lives feeling free, but change because of the attitudes of older people and society. Whenever I hear an adult say to a young child, 'My, aren't you becoming so grown-up?' I can't help cringing slightly because being 'grown-up' usually means being more self-conscious and uptight! Next time you see a child, watch them for a moment and see how they interact with others and how they move their bodies. Most of us lose this ability to be so free and instead become controlled by our fear and insecurities.

## HOW MUCH DOES FEAR CONTROL YOU?

Which areas of your life are controlled by fear? Give each issue below a number between 1 and 5. 1 means you're fearless and 5 means that you're scared to death.

Speaking aloud in class or a group

Being around boys

Kissing/being physical

Talking to new people

Performing on stage

Speaking up when someone's upset you

Wearing whatever you want

Fitting in and being liked

Discussing personal issues with family or friends

New and unknown experiences

**Add up your total.**

### A score of 0–20 – You're fearless

Wow! Nothing gets in your way. You're probably admired by everyone for being so courageous and extrovert. You're not ashamed of who you are and in fact you probably quite like being you. Beware of trying to prove yourself as braver than you are.

### A score of 21–30 – You know what it's like to be scared

You know what it feels like to experience fear. There are quite a few things that scare you, but equally there are many that don't. Fear doesn't completely rule your life and you've been known to have a go at things even when you've been really scared.

### A score above 31 – You know fear well

You know exactly what fear feels like and it limits you and the things that you do. It's not a pleasant thing to live with and you often feel really uncomfortable in your body. Don't worry. Just because you feel like this now, doesn't mean you always have to. Read on, and hopefully, by the end of the chapter you'll be freer from fear.

Doing It!

## FACING YOUR FEARS

Being free from fears that stop you from doing what you really want is clearly the best way to live your life. So this section talks about ways you can face them with more confidence.

 I was terrified about performing a song in our yearly school talent contest. I spent the whole year deciding whether I should enter or not. A month before, I finally went ahead and put my name down for it, but I secretly knew I could back out whenever I wanted to. I wanted nothing more than to sing and perform, but I was riddled with fear about actually doing it. The day before the talent contest, I backed out. I told the teacher organising it that my voice had gone. I knew it wasn't what I wanted, though, because I felt so disappointed in myself. I knew that if I couldn't get up and perform in front of my school I'd never be able to perform in front of strangers on a real stage. The next morning, I went into school found the teacher and told her I'd changed my mind. She smiled at me sweetly and told me that she was glad I'd changed my mind and that she couldn't wait to hear me sing. I'd never been so nervous in my life. I must have sweated a bucket load beforehand. But I did it. I pushed myself on stage and gave it everything I had, and guess what, I won. I knew it was only a small school competition but it gave me the confidence to keep on singing, and now it's two years later and I still get a little nervous before getting on stage, but the more I do it the easier it becomes. Who knows? I might even be the next Whitney Houston and you might be buying my records one day. (Tammi, 19) 99

If Tammi had never given it a go she might have given up and never fulfilled her dream of being a singer. She found the courage in herself to try, and that's all she needed to do. Even if she hadn't won the contest, she would have realised that she could stand up and sing in front of people and keep on working her way towards her dream of being a performing singer.

Now, think of the times that you weren't able to do something because you were scared. What did it feel like? When we experience fear we can feel it very strongly in our bodies and notice our behaviour becoming different. Some of the things you might have done or felt are:

- Sweating more than normal
- Becoming quiet because you're too scared to join in
- A quicker heart rate
- Being false so as not to show how you really feel
- A knotted stomach
- Distancing yourself from people around you
- Tensed-up shoulders and neck
- Feelings of panic and quickening breath

Now, notice the times that you've been brave, even if it was about something really small. It might just have been a case of answering a question in class or going somewhere on your own. Remember how you felt after you went ahead and faced your fear. Here are some of the things you might have felt afterwards:

- Physically shaky
- You might have cried
- Really happy and joyful
- Full of love for yourself and everyone
- Lighter and more energetic
- Strong and ready to take on the world

We can clearly see that when we do face up to our fears we always feel a hundred times better than when we didn't. Keep that in mind next time you're faced with doing something you're scared about.

We all use different techniques for dealing with our fears. Sometimes we try and ignore that they exist at all and avoid whatever it is that is making us feel scared. For example, I'm really scared of standing up and speaking in public, so I avoid having to face up to it by declining any offers to give talks. I'm limiting my life by doing this, because it's something that I need to do for my work. So do I keep running from it or do I face it?

What do you do when you feel scared about something? Do you run from it, deny that it's there or do you face it head on? Whichever it is, now is the time to make a decision. Do you want to start being free from these fears, and if so, which fears in particular do you want to be free from? There might be just one or two things in particular that you want to face. Decide that for yourself, NOW.

When you've decided what it is you want to combat, try the following techniques the next time you're faced with it:

❶ Focus on your breathing. Take long deep breaths.
❷ Remind yourself that you don't have to feel like this. Nothing bad is going to happen to you.
❸ Fear is an illusion. When you're feeling fearful, say to it 'You're not going to control me.'
❹ Tell someone you're scared. Just by speaking about it you can let go of it.
❺ Move around, if you can, shake all your body parts or go for a run. Movement will help you release fear from your body.
❻ Just do what you can for now. Don't push yourself too much. If you don't overcome your fear today, come back to it another day and try again.
❼ Keep putting yourself in the position where you have the opportunity to face the fear. Don't hide from it or you'll never be free.

Doing It!

# INSECURITIES

Insecurities are slightly different from fears. Even though they partly stem from fear, they are also due to a lack of love and belief in ourselves – we think we're lacking in some way. We all have insecurities of one kind or another. People who you assume are confident can be just as insecure as everyone else. You can have a really loud talkative person who is just as insecure as a quiet shy person, and you can have a beautiful skinny girl who is as insecure about her weight as an overweight girl. People can be insecure about everything from the size of their bums to how clever they think they are. Most of us feel ashamed of our insecurities so we hide them. The ironic thing is, the more we're open and talk about our insecurities, the more quickly they disappear.

So let's start by having a go now. Write a list of all the insecurities you think you have. If you can't think of any, ask the question, 'If I did have any, what would they be?' Take some time over it. There may be a few that you weren't aware of. ●◁

I asked young women what they had insecurities about. This is what they came up with:

Being stupid

Being ugly

Being boring

Being fat

Being a nerd

Being poor

Being rich

Being different

Being annoying

Being un-cool

## Share your insecurities

Do any of the above sound familiar? If so, you can see that you're not alone; in fact you're in the majority. The more we speak to others about our insecurities, the more we can see that we all have them. But it takes someone brave to bring up their insecurities within a group and to talk about them openly. Try it for yourself. When you're with a few of your close girlfriends (hopefully the ones you're reading the book with), take it in turns to be honest about your insecurities. Each of you take some time to talk about them. You might be surprised to hear their response. You might find out that a friend who you thought was really confident, is actually really shy. Take it in turns to give each other positive feedback about how the insecurities each of you have are unnecessary and you don't need to have them any more.

# Being Shy

There are all types of people – introverted, extroverted and everything in between. If you're shy you're not alone, and it doesn't mean you're going to be shy for ever. Sometimes being shy means that you're lacking self-confidence. So that's what you need to work on, having more self-confidence and self-belief. (Simple, hey?) A lot of the time it's about practice and just giving it a go, by jumping into the deep end. The more you come out of yourself and interact with others, the more you'll realise that nothing bad is going to happen to you. Then you can start to become comfortable with talking to people.

I'm someone who's struggled with shyness for many years. I went from being extremely extroverted as a child to being a shy teenager. I was loud when I was with my friends and in my 'comfort zone', but as soon as I stepped out of it I felt awkward and shy. You might be someone who is happy being quiet and introverted and it's just your nature. I've talked to quiet people before, who have said they're happy being quiet and taking on the role of the listener. If everyone always wanted to be in the spotlight, none of us would ever get listened to.

If you're someone who's shy and not happy about it, here's some tips from one shy person to another (me, that is):

- Even if you're shy now, you don't have to stay that way. Next time you walk into a social situation hold your head high and talk to people whenever you want.
- Your views are just as worthy as everyone else's. I used to think that I had nothing to contribute, everyone was smarter than I was, and that it wasn't true we all have things to contribute. Just trust that what you have to say is valuable.
- You can't go wrong if you remain yourself and stay honest. Don't become someone you think everyone else might want you to be.
- Make yourself connect with others. However hard it is, bring yourself forward in a conversation. The more you start doing, it the easier it'll become.
- Tell people that you're shy. When I had to speak in front of a large group of people, all I could think of was 'I'm so nervous, I really don't want to do this.' Then, when my turn came to speak, I told everyone exactly that. After being honest, I realised that nothing bad had happened to me. I was still alive and no one was judging me, so my nerves disappeared.

Doing It!

# COMPASSION – GOING EASY ON YOURSELF

I keep talking about self-belief and self-confidence, well another SELF that I'm going to throw at you is self-compassion. It's the quickest route to the other two. When you're being compassionate towards yourself, you're able to accept, forgive and turn off the critical part of yourself. If you're someone who has lots of insecurities and fears, you're probably not very kind or loving to yourself. You probably give yourself a hard time about not getting things right or being stupid or ugly. This build up of self-loathing can turn us into insecure people.

We often find it easier to be compassionate towards others, but when it comes to ourselves we don't know where to start. For example, when a friend comes to you and says she's just made a complete fool out of herself, you probably realise she's seeing it out of proportion. So you comfort her by telling her to be easy on herself and that she didn't do anything that silly. We need to be able to do the same when we're feeling insecure or down on ourselves.

## Ways to be easier on yourself

- You'll need to have a certain amount of acceptance for who you are. Know that you're just as great as anyone else and none of us are perfect. You are trying at least – which is more than can be said for some people!
- We do certain things because we don't know any better. You're mostly like you are because of your past experiences and childhood, so you can forgive yourself for not always getting it right.
- Acknowledge that we all mess up now and then – don't spend ages beating yourself up about it. Instead, focus on avoiding repeating the same mistakes in the future.
- Sometimes we give ourselves a hard time for not achieving our goals and we push ourselves too hard. Allow yourself space for not doing it all; don't over-push yourself.

You need self-love and compassion in your life to be properly fulfilled. It's one of the most important qualities a person can have. You might see someone who appears to have it all – a great job, good looks and lots of money – but if they don't really love themselves, I can guarantee that they're never really going to enjoy any of their successes.

So, ladies, start right now. Think about something that you give yourself a hard time about and go through the above list, then apply all of the pointers to it. Note how you felt before you did this exercise and how you feel after. Pretty different, hey? ✎

# SELF-ESTEEM

Another SELF (sorry, girls, but I guess this whole book is about your-self so they can't really be avoided). Anyways, self-esteem is used to describe how we feel about ourselves. How much do you value and respect who you are? When travelling the world and talking to young women, I found a lot of young women were really down on themselves.

> 66 I'm always the quiet shy one at a party. I don't really know how to approach people and I always assume they won't want to talk to me anyway. (Matilda, 15) 99

> 66 I don't have many friends because I don't think people like me. Everyone else in my class seems to be so much prettier and cleverer than me. (Elizabeth, 14) 99

> 66 I feel really low about the way I look and my body. I think I'm really ugly, so I wear loads of make-up and I diet constantly. My friends tell me that I'm obsessive about it, when I really don't need to be, but I'm sure they're just saying that. (Camilla, 17) 99

How good do you feel about yourself? Do you feel confident about speaking your thoughts to others? Do you believe that you're a valuable member of your school/work/family etc? Do you trust your own advice? Do you respect who you are and what you have to offer? Even without directly answering these questions you probably know how you generally feel about yourself. Even though our moods change, it's something that we feel, most of the time.

If you know you have low self-esteem – I can assure you that you're not alone. Most of us feel down on ourselves – it can take years to be able to accept and love yourself (and that's for the lucky ones). All that self-doubt is just a result of the negative messages that have been fired at us throughout our lives – your parents once saying you did something badly, your teachers giving you a low grade, not getting picked for the netball team. The list goes on. We don't need to hold onto these things, though, because none of them are 'true' unless we decide they are. So it's time for you to start seeing the truth – that you, my lovely, are truly wonderful!

Doing It!

## HOW CAN YOU KNOW THAT YOU'RE WONDERFUL?

This might be hard to believe, but believe it, sistah! Just by being yourself you're being wonderful! All of us are wonderful. It's just about accessing that wonderfulness, by knowing that it exists in the first place. When you're only in touch with a small part of who you really are, you're not going to shine as much as when you're in touch with the whole of you. Think of the times you've felt good about yourself. Have you cared less about what others think? Do you feel more comfortable in your body? Are people more drawn to you? Do you feel like the rest of your life, in general, is good? The more we recognise our greatness the more wonderful we become. Obviously, none of us want to seem arrogant, but you don't have to be a fat-headed show-off to feel good about yourself. We British, especially, are experts at being down on ourselves and our lives. (Why do you think we love EastEnders so much?) We feel more comfortable telling people how bad everything is, rather than how wonderful everything is.

When we ask each other how we are, we'd probably prefer someone to say, 'I've failed all of my exams, my boyfriend's been unfaithful to me and I'm skint,' rather than, 'I'm doing brilliantly at school, I've got loads of cash and my boyfriend's just told me he's in love with me.' Some people seem to connect with each other better when things aren't going right. So we're faced with an even bigger challenge in terms of enjoying who we are and being self-confident.

There might be some of you who feel you can't be included in being wonderful because of bad things you've done to others in the past – being mean, lying, stealing and cheating. Just because you're like that now or have been like that, doesn't mean that that's all you are capable of. We all have the capacity to be horrible, but it never gets us far and it's a lonely path. You can stop being an arsehole whenever you want and instead realise your full potential just like everyone else.

### Why you're great

People who are truly confident (not just putting it on) know what they like about themselves. They aren't constantly down on everything they do and they choose to look at their positives. Get a clean sheet of paper and at the top write, 'I am great because'. Then underneath write out a list of all the reasons why you're great. No modesty here chums, reach inside yourself and drag out those qualities if you have to. Then stick this sheet of paper up on your mirror. Every day when you wake up and go to sleep, look at yourself in the mirror and repeat, 'I am great because ...'

Even if you feel down on yourself or it feels a bit silly, read out your list. The more you focus your attention on your greatness, the more you'll become it.

# JUST BE YOURSELF

One of the most common bits of advice I've heard is, 'Just be yourself,' and I know it's probably the best bit of advice that you can be given. It sounds like it should be so easy, but sometimes it's often one of the hardest things we can do. It can seem scary for many of us to stand alone and be true individuals. So we spend our whole lives trying to fit in and following the crowd. When we're younger we often hang out in groups, wearing the same things, listening to the same music and having the same likes and dislikes. Our 'gang' is important to us – an extended part of our identity. We are expressing who we are through our unified clothes, musical tastes and interests. Groups like this feel safe because we don't stand out as individuals. There's nothing wrong with being a part of a group. It's only a problem if you feel you don't fit into any of them but you're scared of standing out on your own. If this is the case, you're holding back from expressing your individuality because you're too busy concentrating on fitting in.

It takes courage to stand out on your own and it's risky. The greatest individuals that have ever lived have been persecuted for standing up, making themselves visible and being honest with who they really were and what they believed in. Nelson Mandela, the Dalai Lama, Gandhi, Martin Luther King and Jesus, to name a few. Think about how much these people have given us, when they've dared to be themselves and stand up for what they believe. Narrow-minded people will always try and knock down individuals who stand up for what they believe. But what do these narrow-minded people ever contribute to the world?

The American chat show hostess and actress Oprah Winfrey was once asked, 'What is the secret to being really successful and making a difference to the world?' Her reply was, 'I have no tricks or advice for you, except to be yourself, find out what it is you really believe and who you really are. Then be that person, don't imitate others, follow your own truth. That is the very thing that really touches people and what contributes to this world being a better place.'

If you're wary about being different from others, then it is time, my dear, you let that go and went for it. Wear that mad hat, dance like a crazy woman and show the world who you really are! It's all there for you and we need you to be you, adding your unique spice and excitement to the world.

# PEER PRESSURE

Have you ever felt pressurised by your peers to do something that you haven't felt 100 per cent okay about? Or have you put pressure on yourself to do something just because everyone else was doing it? Ask yourself how you felt when you were having one of these experiences. Do you remember certain feelings in your body? Can you remember being frustrated at not being able to say no and turn away? Feelings of not following your truth are usually pretty intense. You may be an easy target for others to pick on and pressurise; nevertheless you have to make the right choices for you. You are your own boss. Be clear with people that you don't feel that you have to do something just because they're doing it. If they are real friends, they'll respect you for being honest.

Peer pressure isn't always direct pressure from friends telling you what to do. Sometimes you can put the pressure on yourself – just from being around people you want to fit in with. If, for example, all your friends smoke, you might start smoking just to fit in. Don't spend time worrying about being different. It's far cooler to be your own person and do what you want because YOU want to.

Doing It!

# ♥Doing the Do♥

Here's your chance, girlfriend, to be yourself and express yourself through the most fun way I know. Clothes. Those of you reading this are going to fall into three categories:

1. For you lot, the idea of standing out in a crowd and receiving attention will be buttock-clenchingly cringy.
2. You guys are going to love this exercise, the opportunity to express a part of you that you have been keeping hidden but are dying to show the world.
3. You last lot already wear, say and do what you please. This, for you, should be a walk in the park.

I want you to put on something that you've always wanted to wear but never had the guts to before. It could be anything from a hat to red lipstick to a whole outfit. Most of us have these items already – we bought them in moments of spontaneity and have never had the guts to wear them in public. Well, here's your chance. If that article of clothing doesn't exist yet, it's about to. Go out and buy it, something you've always wanted to wear, but never had the courage (charity shops are a great place to do this). Once you've done that, when you go out you can go the whole hog and wear it at the next big social event or go one step further and organise a day out with your friends. Liberate yourself and take your friends along for the ride. Tell them they all have to do the same thing. I once did it for my birthday and we all had a ball and found it so liberating. I wore a mad hat and funky trousers. The day was filled with laughter and a sense of real freedom. We had been given the opportunity to express ourselves without any judgement and it was a scream.

## Remember what it felt like to feel free and comfortable when you dared to be yourself.

# THE BOTTOM LINE

- Fear is something that most of us come up against at one time or another. Fear can limit us in what we do with our lives and in getting the most from it, so it's essential that you attempt to face your fears. Unless you do they'll never go away.

- Most of us have insecurities of one kind or another. You'll be surprised at what other people are insecure about even if you think they are beautiful and confident. Take some time sharing your insecurities with your friends and know that you're not on your own.

- Lots of us go through a shy awkward stage when we're growing up. Remember that you have just as much to offer to a conversastion as everyone else; butt in sometimes and shut those loud mouths up!

- We all find it very easy to give ourselves a hard time. Try and go easy on yourself and treat yourself how you treat others – probably a lot more forgiving and accepting.

- Lots of teenage girls suffer from low self-esteem. You have to find your good points because everyone has them.

- Easier said than done, but the most important thing you can do is be yourself. It's challenging because we all want to fit in, but the most amazing people in life are the ones who dare to be themselves.

- Don't give in to peer pressure. Dare to be different and stick to what's right for you.

- Get together with your closest friends and all decide to go out wearing something you've never had the guts to before. I promise you, you'll have a great time and never look back once you've done it.

# GET OFF YOUR BUTT

Are you someone who just gets up and does something or are you the kind of person who sits around thinking about doing it, but never actually makes it to the 'doing' part?

One of the biggest things I learnt is that however much you put in to your life, you will get an equal amount back (and it may not be straight away, or in the way you expect).

I'm not suggesting you never do the lazy teenager thing, because once you start working those days will be pretty much over. (Parents are going to hate me for saying that.) What I would be aware of, though, is that one day being lazy and not engaging with the world around you will have to stop if you're serious about your work and building a life for yourself. Our generation, more than any other, is in the difficult predicament of often having too much choice. Other generations before us had a lot less choice and would concentrate on surviving and putting food on the table or going off to fight in war. On one side we're really lucky. With choice comes freedom, and the ability to do more interesting creative things in our lives. With choice we get the chance to explore ourselves and find out what it is we really want to do. The downside is that, with so many choices on offer, it's harder to know what job you want. The careers our grandparents and most parents had to choose between were often not paths they were passionate about, but yet they had to turn up to them every day, for most of their lives. That's why older generations often look upon us as lazy and spoilt – they couldn't afford to spend years deciding what to do; they had to get on with surviving.

## WHAT DO YOU WANT TO DO?

It can be really hard not knowing what you want to do and having pressure put on you by schools and family (and yourself) to make a decision. In most school systems we're prematurely forced into making decisions about the career we want. Most of us need more life experience and self-exploration before we know which career path to take.

> Only a lucky few are clear on what their passion is from a young age.

If you're still at school and these decisions are difficult for you, choose the subjects inspire you the most rather than the career they'll lead to. If nothing captures you and you hate all your subjects, you can look into doing more specific courses like a BTEC or foundation course.

I found school hard because I thought the lessons were boring and the teachers were uninspiring. When I ended up getting kicked out (shocked, aren't you, with me sounding so good and everything?) I had no clue what career I wanted to pursue, so I made the decision to make life my university. I kept on reading books and taking courses in different things. I was privileged in the sense that I had the freedom to explore different paths. If you do need to be completely self-sufficient straight away then consider going travelling and working while you travel. Getting away from your everyday norm can be a great way to discover more about yourself and find the kind of career you do want to pursue.

If you're tempted to leave school early, think about it properly. When I left school I was hit with the realisation of how easy we have it at school. Even though there's lot of hard work, we don't really have to make any decisions for ourselves, it's all laid out for us. It was hard seeing all my friends still at school, messing around when I was having to do a boring 9–5 job and getting paid peanuts for it. There's no rush to get out of the education system; and even though not having qualifications hasn't affected me so far, I'm one of a lucky few, because in lots of jobs they do matter.

I've had the support in exploring different paths and I'm privileged in having my mother as a role model. She left school at 16, too, and she has done brilliantly with her career. She's been great proof to me that we can achieve anything, and indeed she still does. Her book, *The SEED Handbook* is designed to help people start their own businesses. Her name is Lynne Franks and she offered me the following advice for finding out the career you want.

- Think about the things you enjoyed doing as a child and still naturally love doing now? (Not in a work context.)
- Acknowledge your gifts – write a list at everything you're good at: speaking, drawing, communicating, etc.
- Make a list of your weaknesses – rubbish at maths, shy, distracted easily, etc.
- Network – ask around family and friends who have the kind of career you want and find out what it's really like – the good and the bad. Find out if there's anywhere you can do work experience.
- Don't worry about changing careers mid-way – try different things and don't put pressure on yourself.
- Write out the big visions – what you'd like to be doing in five to ten years' time.
- Look for role models and mentors along the way and gather practical experience.

If by the time you've left school you still don't know what you want to do (I didn't have a clue!) then explore. The more you find out about who you are and what you're into the easier it will be to make that decision. You can do that by travelling, studying, trying out different jobs, and doing voluntary work or work experience.

Alternatively, if you're someone who kind of knows the area you want to work in but not exactly what you want to do in it, don't worry. Just do anything in that particular subject. You can keep your options open and explore different avenues. Sometimes we hold out for the PERFECT thing, missing the opportunities that would have led us there had we been less rigid.

Doing It!

# WHY ME?

If you've got big ambitions you might think, 'What makes me good enough and talented enough to do something like that?' Well, why should I have been the one to write this book? Even while I've been writing it I've had patches of self-doubt, believing that I'm rubbish and so is this book (I realise now that it's a work of genius, of course). At these times I've had to reassure myself that it was just my fear speaking and that I'm as good a candidate for writing this book as anyone else. You're allowed to have huge goals for yourself – you don't need to be ashamed of aiming high. For the very simple reason, Why not?

We often view famous, successful people as special in some way. They must have something that we don't possess to have become so famous. It's not true, though. A lot of famous, successful people have a huge amount of ambition and it's often a case of being in the right place at the right time. These 'others' are as normal as the rest of us. All the greatness you believe exists in others also exists in you.

What I want you to understand from this part of the chapter is that you don't have to settle for anything less than what you really want. Success is not something unique to a few special chosen ones. That belief is complete rubbish. All of us have a gift, something that we can offer to everyone else that is special and unique. We just need to delve into ourselves to discover what these gifts are.

You can do anything you want to, but you need some self-belief and, even more importantly, a lot of hard work to accomplish it. Time needs to be put in to achieve your goals. The universe is not biased in who it dishes out success to. It will give results to those who put in the time and effort. You just have to take that first step. Don't sit around assuming that your dream career is going to land on your lap, with no effort. Nowadays there is so much competition, and you've got to be realistic. Likewise, don't see it as an unclimbable mountain. You've got to at least try, so go out there and give it your all!

I want to add here that if you're not someone with huge ambitions and you're actually happier living a simple life, then that's fine, too. A lot of this chapter focuses on fulfilling your ambitions and goals in life and these goals are different for everyone. Even if you don't have huge career ambitions, focus on your life ambitions. If you want to have a family, it's going to take just as much self-belief, confidence and work. There is definitely a lot more to life than a career and these guidelines can be applied to everything we do.

# IT'S USUALLY NOT AS BAD AS IT SEEMS

I remember the first time I realised that many of my worries were pointless. I was sitting in a biology class when I was about 13 and yet again I hadn't done my homework. I was in a real state, thinking I was going to get in trouble and feeling like it was such a huge deal. A thought suddenly popped into my head, 'In a month's time, will I really care? Will it still be such a worry?' and I realised that it wouldn't. What can seem so huge and important in the moment is often an illusion. I'm not saying don't do your homework and that it won't matter further down the line but if you mess up now and then, don't beat yourself up about it. Make the decision that you'll do better next time.

When something disappoints you, remember that the feeling will pass. Sometimes we can place all our energy into getting upset about something that didn't happen the way we wanted, or someone who didn't do something they said they would. It's important you know that what may seem like a disappointment today could easily turn out for the better tomorrow.

Here's a little tale: Once there was a farmer. One night there was a terrible storm which blew off the door to his stable, and his favourite horse escaped. When he discovered this the next morning his neighbour said sympathetically, 'Oh, what terrible luck!' to which the farmer replied with a shrug, 'Well, you never know.'

Later that day, the lost horse returned, leading six beautiful wild horses behind it. When the neighbour saw this he said joyfully, 'What wonderful luck!' to which the farmer replied with a shrug, 'Well, you never know.' The next day, the farmer's son was breaking in the new horses and he fell badly, breaking his leg. 'Oh, what terrible luck!' observed the neighbour, to which our farmer once again replied, 'You never know.'

Some days later the soldiers rode through their village taking all the young men off to war, but with his injury the farmer's son couldn't join them. Once more, the neighbour exclaimed, 'What wonderful luck!', but the farmer just smiled to himself and replied, 'You never know.'

This story tells us that when we hold on too tightly to the idea of something being a certain way we stop ourselves from seeing that alternatives might actually be better. I know it's easier said than done, but just keep it in mind. A wall might come up in front of you just to divert you towards better opportunities in another direction.

---

I think life is humorous in the sense that it always dishes out to us the last thing we're expecting.

---

Keep your attention on the glass being half full rather than half empty. It might be a complete change of attitude for some of you. But even if you've always been a half-empty person, you can change that today. It takes a bit of discipline to remind yourself when you're being negative. Keep bringing your awareness to the positive and remember that you don't have to see it negatively just out of habit. If you keep doing this and catching yourself, in no time you'll have radically changed life's so called negatives to positives.

# PROBLEM SOLVING

We know that everyone has problems; the difference is how we attempt to deal with them. I have listed four types of people and the way they deal with problems. We have all of them in us, but we're usually more prone to favour one of them over another. Which one reminds you of yourself?

## The Blamer – you always believe it's someone else's fault

When we are in The Blamer mode, we always pin our problems on other people. It's always someone else's fault or stupidity that has caused the problem in the first place. If a problem occurs, you act like a victim by avoiding all responsibility for what's happened. If you're The Blamer you often feel resentful and angry.

## The Depressive – you feel lonely and can't see a way out

People who go into a depressive state when faced with a problem will always magnify the problem to an extreme. They feel deeply affected by things and often get trapped into thinking that there's no way out. It seems like the end of the world. If you're The Depressive you can be over-sensitive and overly negative.

## The Denier – you ignore the problem

People like this deny that there is a problem in the first place. They walk away from their problems and do everything to avoid facing them. People of this type are escapists and usually turn to major distractions like drugs or sex. If you're The Denier you can act aloof and hard.

## The Optimist – you always looks on the positive side of things

The Optimist looks for the positive in a situation and, instead of wallowing in problems, looks for ways to improve the situation, or at least learn from it. The Optimist always sees the glass as half full and will encourage others to do the same. The Optimist has to be careful not to pretend everything is okay when it isn't (that's just the Denier masquerading as an Optimist). If you're The Optimist you can be strong and positive.

Can you relate to any of the above? Which one do you feel you are mostly? Apart from The Optimist, the others don't really get anywhere except back where they started. They might feel better in the short-term but long-term they can't avoid their problems, which will always come back.

I learnt this lesson when I'd decided to go and live in Australia. I was in London having an unhealthy relationship, taking too many drugs and not getting passionate about anything. So I decided to move to Australia and start over. My boyfriend at the time pointed out that moving wouldn't change who I was and that eventually my problems would catch up with me, no matter how far away I went. I disagreed with him and thought he was just saying that because he didn't want me to go.

For the first month I lived in Australia I can genuinely say I had a brilliant time. I loved being in Nature, reading books and looking after myself. Then it all went pear-shaped. I soon found myself in another unhealthy relationship, still doing lots of drugs and not being able to find work or get passionate about anything. I realised he had been right. If we don't deal with our problems honestly, they won't go away.

You may feel that your way of dealing with problems already works for you. Good, you're ahead of the game. If, however, you feel that your technique for problem solving doesn't get you anywhere and the problems keep coming back, then maybe it's time to take a different approach.

## How to do this:

- Feel the emotion that arises when you think about a present problem or when one occurs. Don't run away from your emotions, even if it's painful.
- Never take action in the heat of the moment. Before rushing into anything, give yourself some time to let the problem settle. Don't put it off, though. Take action as soon as you're clear on what to do.
- Accept that the problem exists, but don't let it weigh you down to the point of not being able to deal with it. Accept but don't magnify.
- Be realistic. Some problems aren't solvable but that doesn't mean they have to stay problems for ever. If something is out of your hands, there will have to come a point where you learn to accept it.
- Get help if you need to talk to someone about what's going on do. There is always someone that you can talk to and get support from. Helplines, counsellors, teachers, friends etc.
- Follow through, if you attempt at solving something and it doesn't quite work out how you wanted, try another approach.
- Identify how much of the problem is a problem in its own right or just a problem because of the way you're reacting to it.

**When we learn how to conquer and face the challenges that life throws at us, life gets easier and we become stronger people.**

Doing It!

# DEATH

This might sound slightly macabre but I promise you it's not. Have you ever watched a film, or read a book in which someone who has been critically ill or dying, and suddenly do and say things they wouldn't have normally? They start realising that life really is too short to waste by not saying and doing the things they really want to. Maybe you even know someone this happened to. I've often thought about this and asked myself, if I knew I was going to die in a few years' time what would I do differently? For starters, I wouldn't be so shy and I would say anything I wanted to at any time. I would let people know I loved them every day and I'd spend time only with people that I think are great. What would you do differently? Would you have a different set of priorities? Would you do things that you're scared of but want to try and would you be more honest to yourself and others?

If there are things that you'd do differently, what would it be like to start doing these things today? You don't know when it's all going to end so act like today is your last day every day. Don't waste time thinking 'I'll get to that eventually.' Get to it today.

When you're lying on your deathbed contemplating your life, what do you think you're going to wish you'd done more of, or what would you regret the most? Would it be seeing more of the world. Or spending more time with your loved ones or even being kinder to people? Think about what it is that you really want from life and start living it now. Don't have regrets.

# PLAN OF ACTION

We're coming to the end, ladies (I know, you don't have to tell me how sad you are about it). Before you go off back into the wide world I'd like you to choose just one thing that you're going to start doing, or do more of, or stop doing, and keep it up for two weeks. It could be to stop smoking, to do more work, to get on better with your parents, to be less shy, make more friends – whatever. It can be as small or as large as you like, but choose something that you really want to change or do. When you have decided, (you might want to give this one a bit of time to think about), write it down somewhere – IN BIG LETTERS.

Then follow these four steps.

❶ State what it is that you will try and do over the next two weeks that's different from normal.
❷ Explain why you want to do this. What does it mean to you?
❸ Think about how you feel about doing this. What do you think might sabotage it? What are your fears about doing it?
❹ Ask yourself how you will do it. What action will you take?

**Now promise yourself that you will do your best to achieve this over the next two weeks.**

## THE BOTTOM LINE

- At the end of the day you have to get off your butt and go for what you want. Put in hard work and you'll be rewarded.
- Don't think that being successful is something that only other people can be. We all have the ability to do anything we want.
- Sometimes when things don't go exactly how we planned we can get really disheartened. Don't. Instead, trust that what's happened has happened for a reason and pick yourself up and carry on.
- We all have problems – it's how we solve them that's different. Be aware if you're not effectively solving yours and learn how to deal with them efficiently and honestly.
- Decide what it is you want to change most in your life and then make a plan to do it. Once you've achieved one of your goals it'll give you the confidence and self-belief to set yourself another one.

Doing It!

# GIVE IT TO ME STRAIGHT

 **I never used to think about what people thought about me, but now I'm really shy and I am constantly paranoid that people don't like me. How can I go back to being confident like I was when I was younger? (Susie, 16)**

I think most of us go through a patch of being insecure and overly worried about what others think. This is usually from our mid-teens to our late twenties. We begin to become more aware of others' reactions, outside our own little bubbles, and we become more self-conscious. We are also forming our own ideals and shaping into the kind of adults we want to be. Everything is relatively new to us and we are more aware of ourselves. But having said this, we don't need to be obsessed with how we think others see us (and we usually think it's negative when it isn't). One thing that has really helped me is knowing that other people don't necessarily know better than me anyway, we need to trust our own inner wisdom – see From Girl to Woman (pp18-38). Hopefully, the older you get the more you'll accept who you are and maybe even quite like yourself.

 **I really want to be an actress but my parents keep telling me that it's a stupid ambition to have and I should concentrate on my studies. They're worried that I won't make it and this makes me really sad because I'm sure I can. I wish they'd support me and let me start taking acting classes. What can I do without having to get their help? (Caroline, 17)**

Even though it's a lot easier when our parents support us with our ambitions, we can still make it without them. If you have true determination then you can do it on your own. You should find out if your school has any acting groups. If not, suggest to your teachers that they start one. You can look into government-funded courses or any community drama events. Tell your parents that you are going to go for your dream with or without their support so they might as well be behind you. Tell them that you know you can do it and you'd like them to have faith in you as well. I'm sure if you show your parents that you're serious, they'll end up being behind you.

 **I get really nervous when I'm asked to talk in class, like reading out an essay or being involved in a debate. I get so scared that I've even pretended to be ill before. I wish I could speak up more in class and get more involved but I'm worried everyone is going to laugh at me or that I'm going to say something stupid. What can I do? (Catherine, 16)**

It's like anything, the more you practise it the easier it will become. You're not stupid and people could benefit from your contribution to the class. One thing you can do is keep something in your pocket that feels comfortable in your hand to squeeze or rub, like a smooth pebble. Every time you feel yourself getting nervous, hold the pebble in your hand in your pocket and it will help ground you. Try not to think about everyone looking at you but think about what you're trying to say and breathe. Don't feel like you have to say it quickly, take your time and have pauses to gather your thoughts. I promise you the more you have a go at it the easier it will become.

> Recently all my friends have started to smoke cigarettes and they keep trying to get me to try it. I don't think I'd like it as I don't like the smell and I'm worried about looking silly because I might not inhale properly. I do want to fit in though and they do look older and cool when they smoke. What should I do? (Maria, 13)

I want to tell you not to go near them (the cigarettes that is); they are the most pointless disgusting things ever invented, but I'm not going to make that decision for you. What I will say is, don't do it just because your mates are doing it, do it because you want to do it. It's silly that they're trying to get you to do it as well; friends should just let each other do whatever feels right to them. Stick to your guns. It is a horrid and expensive habit and I don't think people look cool or older, I think they look stupid – intelligent people don't smoke!

# WOMEN OF THE FUTURE

That's what you are and you all have a part to play in the future of the world. This isn't a responsibility, but an opportunity to pave the way for our daughters and granddaughters to come. You also have the opportunity to live the most fulfilling, exciting, rewarding life you can imagine. This doesn't mean being happy every minute of the day, but it does mean facing and conquering challenges that come your way instead of living in fear and denial about them. It's easy to want to stay in your comfort zone and avoid anything that makes you feel uneasy – too many people choose this way of living. Just reading this book and making it to the end shows that you are a true modern day warrior-ess. You're going to lead an amazing life and make a significant difference to this messed-up yet beautiful world we live in. It might seem impossible to make a difference on your own but, as Anita Roddick said, 'If you think you're too small to be effective you've never been to bed with a mosquito.' We affect other people's lives the most just by following our hearts and truths. It's the scariest thing you can do, but I promise you IT'S WORTH IT.

Doing It!

# SISTAH

# SUPPORT

# BOD-EASE

**You're in Charge: A Teenage Girl's Guide to Sex and Her Body**
by Neils H. Lauersen and Eileen Stukane
(Ballantine Books, 1993).

**Body Language Secrets**
by Susan Quilliam
(HarperCollins, 1997).

**Breasts: Your 100 Questions Answered**
by Liz Bestic and Claire Gillman
(Newleaf, 2000).

# YOUR HEALTH

## HEALTHY EATING

www.organicfood.co.uk
Ten reasons to buy organic and links to Greenpeace and other environmentally aware organisations. Plus home delivery.

www.freshfood.co.uk
www.organicdelivery.co.uk
www.abel-cole.co.uk
Shopping, cooking, ordering food online.

www.haliborange.com
Fun information about nutrition, games and product news.

**Student's Vegetarian Cookbook**
by Carole Raymond
(Prima Publishing, 1997).

**The Naked Chef**
by Jamie Oliver
(Penguin, 2001).

**Living Organic – Easy Steps to an Organic Family Lifestyle**
by Adrienne Clarke, Helen Porter, Helen Quested and Pat Thomas .
(TimeLife UK, 2001).

**The New Enchanted Brocolli Forest**
by Mallie Katzen
(Ten Speed Press, 1995).

**Body Foods for Women**
by Jane Clarke
(Orion, 1997).

**The Model Plan**
by Maryon Stewart
(Vermilion, 2001).

## VEGETARIAN

www.veg.org/nutshell.htm
Not a fun looking site but factual. What is a vegetarian? Making the change – what vitamins you need, recipes, etc.

www.ayurveda-herbs.com/vegetarianism.htm
Indian looking site surrounded by clouds. Long list about vegetarianism.

www.goveg.com/meatstinks.com
site for youngsters. You can join group of veggies and get starter kits and learn what you can do to promote it.

www.veggieliving.net

**Becoming Vegetarian: The Complete Guide to Adopting a Healthy Vegetarian Diet**
by Vesanto Melina, Brenda Davis, Victoria Harrison
(Book Publishing Co, 1995)

## FITNESS AND EXERCISE

www.exercise-tips.com
Summary of a wide range of exercises, plus you get to talk to a guru and get advice on the best exercises for you.

www.mindbodysoul.gov.uk
A great looking site providing info on everything from sexual health to physical exercise.

www.yogasite.com
A great yoga resource site with masses of useful links.

www.active.org.uk
A government-run website to encourage and give information about getting fit.

www.justwomen.com
A site just for women on exercise.

www.twsnow.com
A snowboarding website.

www.kidshealth.org/kid/stay_healthy/fit/what_time.html
Funky coloured fun site. Talks about 'my body' health problems and growing up.

Astanga Yoga – The Essential Step-By-Step Guide to Dynamic Yoga
by John Scott
(Three Rivers Press, 2001).

The Complete Idiot's Guide to Short Workouts
by Deidre Johnson Cane, Jonathan Cane and Joe Glickman
(Alpha Books, 2000).

The Complete Idiot's Guide to Yoga
by Joan Budilovsky and Eve Adamson
(Alpha Books, 2000).

## PERIODS

www.fwhc.org/moon.htm
Women's health centre. What really happens in those 28 days.

www.kidshealth.org/teen/sexual_health/girls/menstruation.html
Done in questionnaire fun format. Also has info on STD's and birth control.

www.beinggirl.co.uk
Info on tampons and periods.

www.embarrassingproblems.co.uk
Advice on potentially embarrassing health problems.

Growing Up It's A Girl Thing: Straight Talk About First Bras, First Periods, and Your Changing Body (It's a Girl Thing)
by Mavis Jukes, Debbie Tilley
(Alfred A Knopf, 1998).

The Period Book: Everything You Don't Want to Ask (But Need to Know)
by Karen Gravelle
(Piatkus Books, 1997).

Have You Started Yet?
by Ruth Thomson
(Macmillan Children's Books, 1995).

## STDS

www.womenshealth.about.com
Facts about every different disease and how to prevent them.

www.lovelife.uk.com
How to find your nearest GUM clinic and information about sexual health.

Sistah Support

**NHS Direct:** 0845 46 47
Offers advice on what to do if you think you have a STD.

**National AIDS Helpline** – 0800 567 123

**201 Things You Should Know About AIDS and Other Sexually Transmitted Diseases**
by Jeffery S. Nevid and Fern Gotfried
(Allyn and Bacon, 1993).

**The Go Ask Alice Book of Answers: A Guide to Good Physical, Sexual and Emotional Health**
by Columbia Universities Health Education Program
(Henry Holt & Co, 1998).

## CONTRACEPTION

www.fpa.org.uk
Great advice on contraception and where your local family planning or sexual health clinics are.

www.ruthinking.co.uk
Sexwise's website for advice on sex and contraception.

**Sexwise:** 0800 28 29 30: (7 a.m. –midnight every day)
Free advice on sex or contraception

**FPA's contraception helpline:** 0845 310 1334 (9 a.m.–7 p.m. Mon–Fri)

**I'm Pregnant, Now What Do I Do?**
by Robert Buckingham
(Prometheus Books, 1997).

**Tackling Teenage Pregnancy**
by Ruth Chambers, Gill Wakely and Steph Chambers
(Radcliffe Medical Press, 2000).

**Surviving Teen Pregnancy**
by Shirley Arthur
(Morning Glory, 1996).

## GENERAL

www.teenagehealthfreak.org
Great young person's website covering all health issues. Ask Dr Ann any questions online.

www.teenshealth.org
Extensive American website covering all health topics for teens.

www.stressrelease.com
Helpful advice on how to get rid of stress.

**Women's Bodies, Women's Wisdom**
by Christine Northrup
(Piatkus, 1998).

**Teen Health Guide**
by Paul C, Reisser, Vinita Hampton Wright (editor), and Lisa A. Jackson
(Focus on the Family Publishing, 2002).

**Bobbi Brown: Teenage Beauty**
by Bobbi Brown and Annemarie Iverson
(Ebury Press, 2000).

**The Lazy Girl's Guide to Good Health**
by Anita Naik
(Piatkus, 2002).

# LET'S TALK ABOUT SEX

## BEING GAY

www.youth.org
A useful site with advice and general info about lesbianism.

www.gayyouthuk.co.uk
The biggest gay website in the UK.

Lesbian and Gay Switchboard: 0207 837 7324
24-hr telephone service to act as a UK-wide
source of info, support to lesbians, bisexuals or
anyone who needs to consider gender identity
issues.

Free Your Mind: The Book For Gay, Lesbian, and
Bisexual Youth – and Their Allies
by Ellen Bass and Kate Kaufman
(HarperCollins, 1996).

Two Teenagers in Twenty: Writings
by Gay and Lesbian Youth, edited by Ann Heron
(Alyson Publications, 1996).

Annie on My Mind
by Nancy Garden
(Aerial Fiction, 1992).

## VIRGINITY

The First Time: What Parents and Teenage Girls
Should Know About 'Losing Your Virginity'
by Karen Bouris
(Conari Press, 1995).

The First Time: Women Speak About 'Losing
Their Virginity'
by Karen Bouris
(Conari Press, 1993).

## GENERAL

Mermaids: 07020 935 066 (12 p.m. –9 p.m.
every day)
Support group and helpline for teenagers up to
the age of 19. Deals with any gender identity
problems
(www.mermaids.freeuk.com)

Teen Sex: Risks and Consequences (Perspectives
on Healthy Sexuality)
by Julie K. Endersbe
(Capstone Press, 1999).

Handbook for Modern Lovers
by Barefoot Doctor
(Piatkus, 2000).

The Girl's Guide to Getting It On
by Flic Everett
(Thorsons, 2001).

The Big O: How to Have Them, Give Them and
Keep Them Coming
by Lou Paget
(Piatkus, 2001).

Let's Talk About Sex
by Robie H Harris illustrated by Michael Emberly
(Walker Books, 1994).

Sex Ed
by Dr Miriam Stoppard
(Dorling Kindersley, 1997).

# BOYZ

## JEALOUSY

www.queendom.com/tests/fx/jealousy.html
Light-hearted jealousy test (not advice).

Overcoming Jealousy
by Wendy Dryden
(Sheldon Press, 1998).

## BEING DUMPED

www.dumped-online.com
Online advice on how to get over it.

Sistah Support

The Girl's Guide to Guys: Straight Talk on Teens of Flirting, Dating, Breaking Up, Making Up, and Finding True Love
by Julie Taylor
(Three Rivers Press, 2000).

Heartbreak and Roses: Real Life Stories of Troubled Love
by Janet Bode
(Franklin Watts, 2000).

### DATING

Complete Idiot's Guide to Dating for Teens
by Susan Rabens
(Alpha Books, 2001).

### GENERAL

www.adolescentadulthood.com
A site dealing with relationship issues

Teen Love: On Relationships, A Book For Teenagers
by Kimberly Kirberger
(Health Communications, 1999).

The Love and Romance Teen Quiz Book
by Arlene Hamilton Stewart, Annalee Levine, Jana Johnson
(Andrews McMeel Publishing, 2001).

Teen Ink Love and Relationships (Teen Ink Series)
by Stephanie and John Meyer
(Health Communications, 2002).

A Smart Girl's Guide to Boys: Surviving Crushes, Staying True to Yourself And Other Stuff
by Nancy Holyoke, illustrated by Bonnie Timmons
(American Girl, 2001).

# DA SISTAHS!

Best Friends: The Pleasures and Perils of Girls' and Women's Friendships
by Terri Apter and Ruthellen Josselson
(Three Rivers Press, 1999).

Girlfriends For Life: Friendships Worth Keeping Forever
by Carmen Renee Berry and Tamara Traeder
(Wildcat Canyon Press, 1999).

Get Over It: How to Survive Breakups, Back-Stabbing Friends, and Bad Haircuts (Teen Magazine)
by Beth Mayall
(Scholastic, 2000).

Teen Girlfriends: Celebrating the Good Times, Getting Through the Hard Times
by Julia DeVillers
(Wildcat Canyon Press, 2001).

Witch: A Magickal Journey – A Hip Guide to Modern Witchcraft
by Fiona Horne
(Thorsons, 2000).

Or visit her website www.fionahorne.com

# ARE ALL FAMILIES MAD?

### ALCOHOLISM

Al-Anon: 020 74030888 (10 a.m.–10 p.m. Mon–Sun)
Worldwide organisation offering understanding and support for families and friends of problem drinkers, whether the alcoholic is still drinking or not.

www.childrenofdivorce.com
Advice and therapy on divorce for parents and children.

www.kidshealth.org/kid/feeling/home-family/divorce.html
Describes how you feel and what to do about it.

**Why Me? A Teen Guide to Divorce and Your Feelings (Divorce Resource Series)**
by Rachel Aydt
(Rosen Publishing Group, 2000).

**Divorce: Finding a Place**
by Eileen Kuehm
(Capstone Press, 2001).

**Dinosaurs Divorce: A Guide For Changing Families**
by L.K. Brown and M. Brown
(Little Brown & Co, 1988).

**Blue Sky, Butterfly**
by J. Van-Leeuwen (fiction)
(Dial Books, 1996).

## STEP-FAMILIES

childline.org.uk/factsheets/stepfamilies1.htm
A great site dealing with children's worries about step-families. Features extracts of what children have told counsellors.

**Help! A Girl's Guide to Divorce and Stepfamilies**
by Nancy Holyoke, illustrated by Scott Nash
(Pleasant Company Publications, 1999).

**Stepliving for Teens: Getting Along With Stepparents, Parents and Siblings**
by Joel D. Block and Susan S. Bartell
(Price Stern Sloan, 2001).

**Everything You Need to Know About Stepfamilies**
by Bruce Glassman
(Rosen Publishing, 1994).

## GENERAL

**Get connected:** 0800 096 0096 (1 p.m.–11 p.m. every day)
For anyone who has run away or been thrown out of home.

**Talking About Family: Real-Life Advice from Girls Like You**
by Gina Rose Ortiz, Lynn Barker and Karen Willson
(Prima Publishing, 2001).

**Families and How To Survive Them**
by Robert Skynner and John Cleese
(Vermilion, 1983).

## PARENTS

**Confident Teens – How to Raise a Positive, Confident and Happy Teenager**
by Gael Lindenfield
(Thorsons, 2001).
(Great one for your parents).

**Closing the Gap: A Strategy For Bringing Parents And Teens Together**
by Jay McGraw
(Fireside Books, 2001).

## SIBLINGS

**Brothers and Sisters: Born to Bicker?**
By Pamela Shires Sneddon
(Enslow, 1997).

Sistah Support

## ABORTION

www.fpa.org.uk
Advice on contraception and where your local
family planning or sexual health clinics are.

www.gynpages.com
All about abortion with abortion clinics listed
online.

www.plannedparenthood.org/abortion
All information about abortions. 'Should I have
an abortion?' – advice given.

www.brookcentres.org.uk

See also **Contraception**

## ABUSE

www.kidshealth.org/teen/safety/help/family_
abuse.html
Very good site. What is abuse? What you can do?
What it can cause?

www.kidscape.org.uk
Good young persons' section.

**Alateen:** 0207 403 0888
Telephone support for young people aged 12–20
who are affected by someone else's drinking
(usually that of a parent).

**BAC (British Association for Counselling):** 0870
443 5252
Offers information about registered and qualified
counsellors / counselling services all over Great
Britain. www.bac.co.uk

**Childline:** 0800 11 11
24-hour helpline offering free confidential advice
for young people on any subject but especially for
young people that are in danger or trouble.
Listens, comforts and protects.
(www.childline.org.uk)

**Refuge:** 0870 599 5443
24-hour crisis line for women and children
escaping domestic violence.

**A Child Called It: One Child's Courage to
Survive**
by David J. Pelzer
(Orion, 2001).

## BULLYING

www.bullying.co.uk
Young-looking website with problem pages and
tips on how to deal with bullying.

www.nobully.org.nz/advicek.htm
Good all-round site.

www.pleasestop.com/bullying.html
Has a teenager chat board called 'Please Stop
Bullying' where you can talk to other people who
are in the same situation.

www.kidscape.org.uk
Practical tips on preventing bullying.

**Anti-Bullying Campaign:** 0207 378 1446
(9.30 a.m.–4.30 p.m. Mon–Fri)
Advice and support for young people who feel
bullied, and their parents.

**Kidscape:** 0207 730 3300
(10 a.m.–4 p.m. Mon–Fri)

**Wise Guides: Bullying**
by Michele Elliott, illustrated by Harry Venning
(Hodder Children's Books, 1998).

101 Ways to Deal with Bullying
by Michele Elliott
(Hodder Mobius, 1997).

## DIFFICULT MOODS

## Depression

www.depression.about.com
Find out if you're depressed and about the different types of depression. Stipulates the importance of friends.

www.learn-about-depression.com
Facts about depression. What causes it. How to cure it.

**Women and Mental Health Infoline:** 0845 3000 911 (10 a.m.–12 noon Mon and Wed; 2 p.m.–5 p.m. Tues and Thurs. Answer machine outside opening hours)
Information about women's health, plus details of appropriate services for women with mental health issues.

**The Road less Travelled**
by M. Scott Peck
(Rider, 1988).

**The Celestine Prophesy**
by James Redfield
(Bantam, 1994).

**Overcoming Depression**
by Demitri Papolos and Janice Papolos
(HarperCollins, 1997).

**How To Cope With Depression: A Complete Guide For You and Your Family**
by J. Raymond DePaulo and Keith Ablo
(McGraw-Hill, 1989).

## Anxiety and panic attacks

www.panicattacks.com.au
Site contains the largest amount of info on the subject. It's easy to get around and is laid out relatively clearly. I was initially discouraged by the tiny font size on its homepage but the important bits are all clear and easy to understand. Lots of links, support groups and management programs but it is Australian.

www.panicattacks.co.uk
A UK site that is good in terms of its relevant resources. It is, however, not as detailed.

**First Steps to Freedom:** 01926 851 608
(10 a.m.–10 p.m. every day)
Helpline for anyone experiencing general anxiety, phobias, panic attacks.
www.firststeps.demon.co.uk

**The Panic Attack Recovery Book**
by Shirley Swede & Seymour Sheppard Jaffe
(Signet, 2000).

## DRUGS

www.ndh.org.uk
National drugs helpline. Colourful and bright webiste providing information on all drugs and effects.

www.thesite.org/info/drugs
Very easily comprehensible. Information on all drugs.

**National Drugs Helpline:** 0800 77 66 00
Free, 24-hour helpline offering advice and information for drug misusers, their families, friends, carers, and professionals.

Sistah Support

Narcotics Anonymous National Helpline: 0207 730 0009 (10 a.m.–10 p.m. every day)
Helpline and regular self-help meetings for addicts who have a desire to stop using, and who wish to support each other in remaining drug-free.
(www.ukna.org)

Quitline: 0800 00 22 00 (1 p.m.–9 p.m. every day)
Friendly, free, practical advice on how to stop smoking.
(www.quit.org.uk)

Get It While You Can: 01492 533457
24-hour helpline providing information, advice and support for people with alcohol/drug problems. Also has an advice and information centre.
(www.getit.org.uk)

Buzzed: The Straight Facts About the Most Used and Abused Drugs From Alcohol to Ecstasy
by Cynthia Kuhn
(W.W, Norton, 1998).

Drug Crazy: How We Got into This Mess And How We Can Get Out
by Mike Gray
(Routledge, 2000).

Teens Talk About Alcohol and Alcoholism
by Paul Dolmetsch and Gail Mauricette (Editor)
(Dolphin Books, 1987).

## EATING DISORDERS

www.something-fishy.org
Excellent site that has tons of information about eating disorders, links to the Eating Disorder FAQ, poems, chat rooms, and stories from others suffering from bulimia and anorexia.

www.closetoyou.org/eatingdisorders
An eating disorder information source with extensive knowledge about different aspects, from symptoms, causes and side-effects to treatment.

www.eatingdisordersanonymous.org
Fellowship of individuals, giving strength and hope to each other.

www.edap.org
Details of all types of eating disorders and treatments and referrals offline.

www.edauk.com
London-based site especially for young people. Support groups and telephone helpline.

Caraline: 01582 457474
Helpline, counselling and support for sufferers of anorexia, bulimia nervosa and compulsive over-eaters. Weekly self-help group, individual counselling and specialised programmes.

Eating Disorders Association: 01603 765050 (4 p.m.–6 p.m. Mon–Fri)
Telephone helplines for people affected by eating disorders, including anorexia nervosa and bulimia nervosa. Youth helpline for people aged 18 and under. Runs a network of support groups, postal and telephone contacts throughout the UK.

First Steps to Freedom 01926 851608
Helpline for anyone experiencing general anxiety, phobias, panic attacks, obsessive compulsive disorder, tranquilliser withdrawal, anorexia, bulimia. Offers counselling, listening, advice and information. Also provides leaflets, relaxation tapes and videos, telephone self-help groups, individual telephone befriending and newsletters.

**Reachout** 020 8905 4501

Helpline for men and women (16+) who have suffered abuse as children. Also for anyone experiencing domestic violence, eating disorders, obsessive compulsive disorders or emotional distress. Aim to build confidence and improve self-esteem through befriending.

**Over It – A Teen's Guide to Getting Beyond Obsessions with Food and Weight**

by Carol Emery Normandi and Laurelee Roark (New World Library, 2000).

**Anorexia – The Route to Recovery**

by Claire Lindsay

**Anorexia and Bulimia**

by Dee Dawson
(Vermilion, 2001).

**Fat is A Feminist Issue**

by Susie Orbach
(Arrow, 1998).

**My Sister's Bones**

by Cathi Hanouer
(Review, 1996).

**My Body, My Enemy**

by Claire Beekan and Rosanna Greenstreet (HarperCollins, 2000).

## RAPE/ABUSE

www.rainn.org

Website for rape abuse and Incest National Network.

www.rapecrisis.co.uk

Lists range of facilities and centres for counselling.

www.vday.org

great UK-based organisation that aims to help women who have been affected by rape and put a stop to future rapes.

**Rape Crisis:** 0207 837 1600 – (9 a.m.– 5 p.m. Mon-Fri.)

Acts as a referral service to individual women who are seeking advice and/or support around the issues of rape and sexual abuse/assault by putting them in contact with their nearest/local rape and sexual abuse counselling service.

**Rape and Sexual Abuse Support Centre:** 02082 391 122 (12 noon–2.30 p.m., 7 p.m.–9.30 p.m. Mon–Fri; 2.30 p.m.–5 p.m weekends)

Support and information for women and girls who have been raped or sexually abused however long ago.

**Women Against Sexual Harassment:** 0207 405 0430 For advice and support, call 10.30 a.m.– 3.30 p.m. Mon and Tues.

**Street Smarts: A Personal Safety Guide For Women**

by Louise Rafkin
(Mass Market Publications, 1996).

**After Silence: Rape and My Journey Back**

by Nancy Venable Raine
(Three Rivers Press, 2000).

## SELF-HARM

www.palace.net/~llama/psych/injury.html

A very comprehensive site. Also has interactive site details and other relevant links.

www.selfinjury.freeserve.co.uk
This site, while not as detailed as the one above, has a few personal accounts and advice from fellow injurers. There is a list of resources and info to help sufferers in the UK and lots of other good links too.

**Bristol Women's Crisis Service:** 0117 925 1119 (9 p.m.–12.30 a.m. Fri, 9 p.m.–12.30 a.m. Sat; 6 p.m.–12.30 a.m. Sun) on Friday and Saturday nights from 9pm until 12.30am.

**The Language of Injury**
by Gloria Babiker & Lois Arnold
(BPS Blackwell, 1997).

**Bodies Under Siege: Self-Mutilation and Body Modification in Culture and Psychiatry**
by Armando R Favazza
(The Johns Hopkins University Press, 1996).

**Women Who Hurt Themselves: A Book of Hope and Understanding**
by Dusty Miller
(Basic Books, 1995).

**The Luckiest Girl in the World**
by Steven Levenkron (fiction)
(Simon & Schuster, 1997).

**Healing the Hurt Within**
by Jan Sutton
(Pathways, 1999).

**A Bright Red Scream**
by Marilee Strong
(Virago Press, 2000).

## GENERAL

**Young Minds:** 0207 336 8445
A national charity offering services to children and young people. The organisations that make up Young Minds work together to promote young people's mental health and are tied to a lot of school and health projects. (www.youngminds.org.uk)

**Careline:** 0208 514 1177 (10 a.m.– 4 p.m. and 7 a.m.–10 p.m. Mon–Fri)
For counselling and advice on any subject.

**Childline:** 0800 11 11
Call the 24-hour helpline for free confidential advice for young people on any subject.

**Youth Access:** 0208 772 9900 (9 a.m.–1 p.m. and 2 p.m.–5 p.m. Mon–Fri)
Youth access provides contact numbers for young people's counselling and advisory services in the area.

# DOING IT

### SELF ESTEEM/CONFIDENCE

www.kidshealth.org/kid/feeling/emotion/self_esteem.html
Really good site offering questions such as What is self esteem? and Why is it important? Offers good advice on what to do if you have low self esteem.

www.shykids/com/shykidsconfidenceA.htm
Good general site on shyness and making friends, plus you get a chance to talk to people about it.

www.TeenCentral.Net
What it's like being a teen – sharing stories and advice.

**Everything You Need to Know About Peer Pressure**
by Robyn M. Feller
(Rosen Publishing Group, 2001).

104 Activites That Build Self Esteem,
Teamwork, Communication, Anger Management,
Self-Discovery and Coping Skills
by Alanna E.Jones
(Rec Room Publishing, 1998).

Three Black Skirts: All You Need To Survive
by Anna Johnson
(Workman, 2000).

## GENERAL

Reviving Ophelia, Saving the Selves of
Adolescent Girls
by Mary Pipher
(Ballantine Books, 1994).

Ophelia Speaks
by Sara Shandler
(HarperPerennial, 1999).

Chicken Soup for the Teenage Soul – Stories of
Life, Love and Learning
by Jack Canfield, Mark Victor Hansen and
Kimberly Kirberger
(Vermilion, 1997).

Deal With It!
by Esther Drill, Heather McDonald and Rebecca
Odes
(Pocket Books, 2001).

I Know Why The Caged Bird Sings
by Maya Angelou (Any of her books)
(Virago Press, 1984).

The Seed Handbook
by Lynne Franks
(Thorsons, 2000).

Conversations with God For Teens
by Neale Donald Walsh
(Hampton Road, 2001).

Witchin'
by Fiona Horne
(Thorsons, 2002).

## GAP YEAR

www.gapyear.com
Options. Services. Travel. Other people's
experiences – stories.

www.gap.org.uk
What does gap year mean? What do universities
think of it? Should I do one? etc. Where could I
go?

www.travellersworldwide.com
Options like teaching english or work placements
around the world. Site has pictures from all
around the world.

Taking A Gap Year
by Susan Griffith
(Vacation Work Publications, 2001).

## COURSES/UNIVERSITIES

www.ucas.ac.uk
Online course search.

www.sixthform.co.uk

www.education.guardian.co.uk

www.studentuk.com
University information/jobs/housing. Cool, fun
looking site about being a student.

www.dfes.gov.uk/aimhigher
Higher education courses.

The Times Good University guide 2003
by John Leary
(Collins, 2002).

Sistah Support

# INDEX

## A

abortion 154-5
abuse 156
acid (LSD) 167-8
aerosol abuse 170
AIDS 59, 62
alcohol 163-4
ambitions, and self-belief 198, 204
amphetamines 164
anger 140
anorexia 170-2
anxiety 161
appreciation, expressing to your family 148
asking someone out 92-3

## B

balls (testicles) 85
beauty
  different opinions about 46
  feeling beautiful 48-9
being dumped 106-7
being yourself 192-3, 194
best friends 114-15, 116 *see also* friends
birth control pill 65
bisexual women 78-9
bitchiness 115, 118-19
blow job 85
body 38-51 *see also* health
  differences in development 41-2
  eating disorders 170-2
  learning to love it 39-51
  your relationship with 44-5
  what boys think 47
body language 93

  and feeling beautiful 48-9
booze 163-4
boyfriends
  assessing realistically 98
  encouraging potential in 99
  reasons for your choices 97
  turning him on 85-6
boys 90-109
  fighting over 120-1
  what they think about body shape 47
bras 43-4
breast enlargements 42-3
breasts 42-4
brothers and sisters 144
bulimia 170-2
bullying 156-8, 179

## C

career
  deciding what to do 196-7
  going after what you want 198
change, making room for 24-5
childhood, influences of parents 132-3
childlike qualities 23
chlamydia 60, 62
chocolate 56
cigarettes 164-5
clutter, clearing out 24
cocaine (coke) 165-6
communication
  with grandparents 148
  with parents 146-8
compassion, towards yourself 190
condoms 62, 63, 64
confidence 192
contraception methods 64-5 see also sexual
  health
counselling 158-9
crabs 61
cramps 58
crushes 94

# D

Dads, problems with 134-5
dating rituals 94
depo-provera 65
depression 159-60, 179
development, of the body 41-2
diaphragm 64
diary 16
diet awareness 54-7
divorce 142-3
dope 169
drink (alcohol) 163-4
drug addiction 161-2
drugs 151, 162-70, 178

# E

'E' numbers (food additives) 54-5
E's (ecstasy) 166-7
eating disorders 170-2, 179-80
ecstasy 166-7
elders, getting to know 148
emergency contraception pill 65
emotional state, and periods 58
essential tools, for the journey to womanhood 26-33
exercise, benefits of 56-7
expressing yourself 103, 138-9, 192-3, 194

# F

faking orgasms 87
families 130-51
Family Planning Association 63
fat, in the diet 54
fear 184-7, 204-5
feelings

difficulty expressing 103
expressing to parents 138-9, 148
focus 30
food, organic 55
food additives 54-5
forgiveness 25, 140
friends 110-29
  best friends 114-15, 116
  comparing and competitiveness 115, 117
  encouraging 125
  expressing your feelings 122
  giving attention to 125
  letting go of 122
  making up after a row 122
  supporting 124-5
  those who are not good for us 123
  what does friendship mean to you? 112
friendship rules 113
fruit 54
funny side, seeing 30

# G

ganja 169
gay women 78-9
genital herpes 61
genital warts 61
girls
  becoming women 19-37
  competition between 115, 117, 118-19
  differences to women 20-1
giving head 85
glue (solvent abuse) 170
goals
  focus and perseverance 26, 30
  working to achieve them 198
going down 85
gonorrhoea 61
good listeners 124-5
gossip 117
grandparents, getting to know 148
gratitude, appreciating what you have 26, 31

group discussions 14-15
groups
    gathering your own tribe 148
    identifying with 192-3
guardians *see* parents/guardians

hand job 85
health 52-69
healthy eating 54-7
helplines 15
hepatitis B 60
heroin 166-7
herpes, genital 61
HIV 59, 62
humour, seeing the funny side 26, 30-1

individualism 192-3
inner child 23
insecurities 188, 204

jealousy 101-2
    of friends 116, 117
joints (marijuana) 169
jostling 85

knowing yourself 26-8

letter exercise 138-9
letting go 24-5
life, making the most of it now 202
listening, to support a friend 124-5
love *see also* boyfriends; friends; relationships
    expressing to your family 148
    feeling loved 97
    loving yourself 26, 29, 97
LSD (acid) 167-8

magic mushrooms 168
marijuana 169
masturbation 84, 86
MDMA (ecstasy) 166-7
media
    image of women 40, 43
    selling with sex 73
moods, difficult 159-60
moon maiden ritual 126-7
'morning after' pill 65
Mums, problems with 136
mushrooms, magic 168

needs, getting them met 104-5

optimism 30
organic foods 55
orgasms 86-7

panic attacks 161
parents/guardians
  acceptance and forgiveness 140
  as people too 137
  communication with 146-8
  expressing your feelings to 138-9
  feeling responsible for 143, 144
  influence on sexual feelings 72
  influences on us 132-3
  letter exercise 138-9
  letting go of their little girl 144
  pressure from 134
  problems with Dads 134-5
  problems with Mums 136
peer pressure 193, 205
penis
  circumcision 85
  what to do with it 85
periods 58
perseverance 30
PID (pelvic inflammatory disease) 60, 61
plan of action 202
PMT (Pre Menstrual Tension) 58
posture, feeling beautiful 48-9
pot 169
power, of sexuality 77
pregnancy
  and abortion 154-5
  prevention 63 *see also* contraception methods;
  sexual health
problem solving 200-1
processed foods 54-5, 56

rape 172-3
relationships 90-109
  are you getting what you want? 96
  arguing 102-3

balancing with the rest of your life 99-100
  being dumped 106-7
  ending 106-7
  getting your needs met 104-5
  jealousy 101-2
  unfaithfulness 101-2
  what do you want from it? 95
religious pressure 134
resentment 140
respect, between child and parent 147
rituals
  full moon maiden 126-7
  rites of passage 36-7
role models 40
  positive 125
rows, with friends 122
rushing to grow up 32-3

school, deciding to leave 196-7
self-belief 198
self-compassion 190
self-confidence 192
self-esteem 191-2
self-injury (self-harm) 174-5, 178-9
sex
  attitudes of society 73
  bad experiences 74-5
  feeling pressure to have 80-1
  how to pleasure a guy 85-6
  knowing when you are ready 80-1
  protecting yourself 82-3
sexiness 76-7
sexual abuse 172-3
sexual health 59-64
sexual satisfaction 86-7
sexual wants and needs, discovering 84
sexuality 70-91
  awareness of 75-7
  power of 77
shame, ridding yourself of 76

shyness 189

sibling rivalry 144

sisters and brothers 144

smack (heroin) 166-7

smear test 59

smoking 164-5

society, attitudes towards sex 73

solvent abuse 170

speed 164

spermicide 64

spliff 169

STDs (sexually transmitted diseases) 59-63

stepfathers/stepmothers 142-3

stereotypes 40

stress 66-7

success, working to achieve 198

sucking off 85

sugar 55

suicide 176-7, 178, 179

support group, gather your own tribe 148

support network 14-15

syphilis 60

testicles (balls) 85

tossing off 85

transsexual women 78-9

tribe, gathering your own support group 148

truth voice, knowing yourself 26-8

unfaithfulness 101-2

vagina, exploring 84

vegetables 54

virginity, losing 80-1

water, drinking enough 54

website 15

weight

  and eating disorders 170-2

  feelings about 44-5

womanhood

  from girl to 18-31

  essential tools for the journey 26-33

women

  differences to girls 20-1

  encouraging other women 125

  essential qualities 22

  holding onto childlike qualities 23

  of the future 205

worries 66-7

  seeing the positives 198-9

yourself

  being true to 192-3, 194

  getting to know 26-8